Local Online Advertising

FOR

DUMMIES®

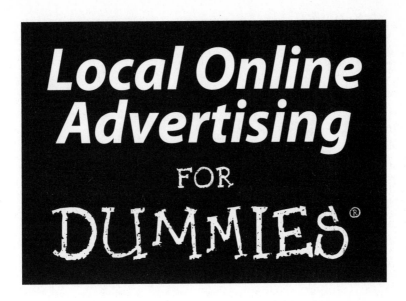

Local Online Advertising

FOR

DUMMIES®

by Court Cunningham and Stephanie Brown

Wiley Publishing, Inc.

Local Online Advertising For Dummies®

Published by
Wiley Publishing, Inc.
111 River Street
Hoboken, NJ 07030-5774

www.wiley.com

WILEY

About the Authors

Court Cunningham is the CEO of Yodle, a leading local online advertising company that works with over 6,000 local businesses across America. At Yodle, Court oversees all aspects of operations and strategy, including technology, product development, sales, and marketing. Prior to joining Yodle, Court held the position of COO at Community Connect, a niche social networking company, where he lead consumer marketing, product management, and development efforts. Before that, as SVP/GM of the Marketing Automation group at DoubleClick, he was instrumental in establishing DARTmail as the industry leading e-mail marketing solution. Court received a BA in English from Princeton University and an MBA from Harvard Business School.

For more information about Court and his company Yodle, go to www.yodle.com.

Stephanie Brown has been evangelizing Internet marketing since 1994. In fact, she specializes in helping clients use many of the tools and techniques contained in this book to grow their businesses. Over the years, she has held management positions at marketing firms and Internet companies, where she has led teams in creating customer-focused online solutions for accounts big and small, local and national. Today she is a partner at Word Communications, an integrated marketing firm in Albany, New York. Her clients are a living laboratory for exploring the latest best practices — in e-mail, social media, search marketing, landing page design, Web analytics and optimization, and offline integration.

Stephanie can be reached at sbrown3@nycap.rr.com or www.wordcommunications.com.

Dedication

Court Cunningham: I want to dedicate this book to all small business owners, the hardest working people I know.

Stephanie Brown: This book is dedicated to the people and the dogs I ignored during the researching and writing of it. (You know who you are.) I also dedicate this book to my mother, Helga Olsson, and my stepmother, Ruth Brown, whose examples have always taught me to persevere.

Authors' Acknowledgments

Court Cunningham: A large number of people on the Yodle team played significant roles in creating this book — not the least of which was Cam Lay — who was instrumental in helping to organize the content of this book, leveraged his own marketing background to give us another set of eyes for each and every chapter, and arduously provided the first round of edits. Additional content contributors from Yodle included Joseph Sievers, Michael Baker, Arpan Jhaveri, Milind Mehere, and the invaluable John Switzer. Finally, I want to thank the Yodle Marketing team members who provided further feedback including Kara Silverman, Herman Mallhi, Allyse Coughlin, and Alisa Adler — as well as our Senior Director of Marketing, Joel Laffer, who encouraged me to do this book in the first place.

Stephanie Brown: It would be a sin not to acknowledge the two people who worked tirelessly (and occasionally feverishly) to bring the best out in this book: Editorial Assistant David Idema, whose wry humor makes this a fun read, and Yodle's Cam Lay, whose steady support and gentle task-mastering got us through. Eat your peas!

Publisher's Acknowledgments

We're proud of this book; please send us your comments at http://dummies.custhelp.com. For other comments, please contact our Customer Care Department within the U.S. at 877-762-2974, outside the U.S. at 317-572-3993, or fax 317-572-4002.

Some of the people who helped bring this book to market include the following:

Acquisitions, Editorial

Project Editor: Jean Nelson

Executive Editor: Steven Hayes

Copy Editor: Jennifer Riggs

Technical Editor: Michelle Oxman

Editorial Manager: Kevin Kirschner

Media Development Project Manager: Laura Moss-Hollister

Media Development Assistant Project Manager: Jenny Swisher

Media Development Associate Producers: Josh Frank, Marilyn Hummel, Douglas Kuhn, and Shawn Patrick

Editorial Assistant: Amanda Graham

Sr. Editorial Assistant: Cherie Case

Cartoons: Rich Tennant (www.the5thwave.com)

Composition Services

Project Coordinator: Katherine Crocker

Layout and Graphics: Christine Williams

Proofreader: Susan Hobbs

Indexer: Potomac Indexing, LLC

Special Help Leah Cameron, Teresa Artman, Becky Whitney

Publishing and Editorial for Technology Dummies

Richard Swadley, Vice President and Executive Group Publisher

Andy Cummings, Vice President and Publisher

Mary Bednarek, Executive Acquisitions Director

Mary C. Corder, Editorial Director

Publishing for Consumer Dummies

Diane Graves Steele, Vice President and Publisher

Composition Services

Debbie Stailey, Director of Composition Services

Contents at a Glance

Table of Contents

Introduction

. . . . .

*N*ot long ago, the Internet came along and changed everything. Or at least it changed the way a lot of things get done, including how consumers look for and find local businesses.

With the rise of the Internet as the primary way consumers connect with local businesses, a huge number of tools and techniques have emerged for local businesses to better capture those consumers and turn them into customers. Not only do these businesses seem to have done so almost overnight, but the smartest companies and Web consultants have already tried them, refined them, and came up with new ones. In other words, the Internet marketing tool kit is big, and getting a whole lot bigger every day.

Understandably, this whole Internet phenomenon can seem pretty complex, even intimidating, to local business owners who've relied for years on traditional advertising channels and methods. In reality, all the Web does is greatly accelerate the speed that traditional marketing concepts can now be applied and responded to by eager customers and prospects.

In *Local Online Advertising For Dummies,* we look at how local businesses can put online marketing to profitable use. We break down the subject into manageable, understandable chunks. By reading this book, you'll become comfortable with the big picture of the online marketing process and with how each of its parts contributes to the whole. Most important, you'll be ready to put many of those elements to work for your own business — and to be happily surprised by the results they bring you.

About This Book

You don't have to read this book from front to back. Rather, think of it as a sort of library from which you can extract and examine only the pieces that interest you. You'll find that (for the most part) the discussions in each chapter — and in each section within each chapter — are self-contained.

Of course, we wouldn't mind at all if you did read everything in order. Local online advertising is one of those subjects that has a natural build to it, so going with the logical flow isn't a bad idea. But, hey — it's your book now, and you can read it however you want.

In any case, this book isn't a textbook; it's a reference, or a guide. This book's purpose is to give you a basic introduction to local online advertising, from which you can then go on to more sophisticated sources, if necessary.

Conventions Used in This Book

We use a few conventions throughout this book to make things easier for you:

✔ We use *italics* for emphasis and to set off a particular term that we define.

✔ We use a computerese font to highlight Web addresses (or URLs), such as www.dummies.com.

Also, 99.99 percent of what we talk about in the book applies to both PC and Mac users. The very few references made to Microsoft applications aren't exclusionary; Mac users can use versions of the same applications.

What You Don't Have to Read

Here and there throughout this book, you see *sidebars* — text boxes that are separate from the regular content and feature a gray background. Sidebars include information that's related to the content in the chapter but is also independent of it. The bottom line is that you don't have to read them, and your understanding of the chapter's subject matter won't suffer if you don't. Then again, if you do read them, you may discover something new. We leave the choice up to you.

Another thing you can safely skip without worrying about it is the occasional paragraphs with a Technical Stuff icon beside them. Big surprise, this is stuff for tech-minded readers. The geekier you are, the more likely you'll value these pieces. The geekier you aren't, the less likely you'll care. And that's just fine.

Foolish Assumptions

In writing a book like this, it's difficult to know how broad and deep each reader's existing knowledge is. We figure it's pretty safe to assume that you know the rudiments of computer use and that you've had some experience with the Internet, which also means you're probably familiar with search engines. Beyond those givens, this book assumes that you're more or less a novice when it comes to local online advertising.

Of far greater importance, however, is our assumption that as the owner of a business, you're nobody's fool. Sure, online marketing may be a new concept, but we're sure you have the fundamentals of business down cold. You know your market. You know your products and services inside and out. You know what kind of customers you sell to and what kinds of prospects you hope to turn into customers. And you understand profit and loss, competition, and the importance of investing your assets wisely. On all those scores, you're an expert. So we don't define universal business terms you already know.

How This Book Is Organized

We organized the chapters in this book into five parts. Each chapter is broken into sections, which are broken into sub-sections, and even into sub-sub-sections.

We compiled this book that way so that you can, with very little effort, get as much (or as little) information you need at any particular moment. Zip, zop, and you're there. If only the rest of life was so easy.

The following sections briefly describe what the five parts in this book cover.

Part I: Getting Started with Local Online Advertising

This part gives you an overall picture of local online advertising: Why it's become such a major tool for local businesses to generate more new and repeat customers, the evolution of search engines as they relate to local businesses, and the kind of pre-planning that the online space requires to be used successfully.

Part II: Setting the Foundation for Local Online Advertising Success

Here you discover the importance of building a quality Web site for your business, including whether you should handle this task or get outside help. We also explore the concept of landing pages, the range of interactive tools available, and the factors that go into analyzing the results of your online marketing efforts.

Part III: Doing the Advertising Part of Local Online Advertising

This is really the nuts and bolts of the book. We look, in some detail, at search engine advertising and the elements of a successful e-mail campaign. You also find out how to employ techniques, such as advertising in banner ads, directories, and sponsorships. We also discuss the uses of social media (such as Facebook) and how public relations can help drive traffic to your Web site.

Part IV: Keeping Your Customers Coming Back

Winning over prospects and turning them into paying customers is no easy task. After you do it, how do you make them repeat customers? We answer that question by examining several ways to keep your business at the top of customers' minds and to reward them for their loyalty. We conclude with a discussion of *database marketing* — that is, how to use the customer data you collect to sharpen your online marketing campaigns.

Part V: The Part of Tens

If you've read through other parts of the book before coming to the Part of Tens, you'll have been exposed to a lot of information. In this part, we provide you with lists of ten do's and don'ts. This part makes for a handy resource that you can refer to quickly whenever the need arises.

Icons Used in This Book

At times in the course of this book, we separate certain points to broaden your understanding of a particular subject by placing an icon next to that paragraph.

Occasionally we give you a little hard-won, real-world insight into how to apply the tool or technique we're discussing. Consider each of these icons as a sort of "If we were you, we'd . . ." piece of advice.

This icon is a friendly reminder of a specific point that we want to make sure you keep in mind as you proceed in your reading.

Take heed of a Warning: This can prevent you from doing something that could get you into trouble (primarily, legal trouble).

For those who like to delve into every technical detail, Technical Stuff icons may be of interest. For the rest, they're eminently skippable.

Where to Go from Here

You're ready to use this book, and the Table of Contents or index is the best place to start. Find the section or topic that interests you and jump right to that page. Or just turn the page and start with Chapter 1. We leave the decision up to you. Either way, we hope you enjoy — and profit by — what you find in this book.

Part I
Getting Started with Local Online Advertising

The 5th Wave   By Rich Tennant

"We have no problem funding your Web site, Frank. Of all the chicken farmers operating Web sites, yours has the most impressive cluck-through rates."

In this part . . .

Call us stuffy old traditionalists, but we think the best place to begin is always at the beginning. To get started, Chapter 1 provides an overview of the online marketing world as it currently exists, including things like search engine marketing, identifying your best prospective customers, planning how best to reach and motivate them, and the importance of measuring your results.

Chapter 2 gets a bit more specific about the tools (and advertising venues) that the Web makes available to you. Chapter 3 talks about the importance of formulating an online advertising plan that makes sense for your business and then dives into choosing the kind of strategies that help you bring that plan to life.

Get ready to cast off, full speed ahead — and get down to business (pun intended).

Chapter 1

Online: It's Where Your Customers Are

*B*ack in the 1920s and '30s, Willie Sutton robbed a lot of banks. When asked why, he responded, "Because that's where the money is." Sutton may have been a criminal, but it's hard to argue with his logic. Which brings us to the 21st century, and you, your customers, and why you should advertise your business online — because that's where the customers are.

In this chapter, we give you some background on the online world and explain some of the general forces that fuel it. In the succeeding chapters, we break down what you as a small business owner need to know about Internet marketing in general and about local online advertising in particular.

Understanding Online Consumer Trends

More and more consumers spend more and more time online, and the numbers of households that are online has steadily increased.

But more important is how much consumers are online and how they've adopted Internet usage as part of their daily routine much faster than anyone could have predicted. For instance:

✔ Ninety-four million American adults use the Internet every day (that's nearly one-third of the total U.S. population).

✔ Sixty-three percent of those folks access search sites every day.

✔ Sixty-four percent of Americans use Internet search as the primary way they search for local businesses.

Given these numbers, the conclusion is fairly obvious: If someone is searching around the 'Net for local goods and services and your business isn't represented there, that customer is going to click with someone else. That customer could have been and should have been yours.

With Internet transactions generating so much business, you probably assume that small business owners (and local businesses) all over America are already all over the 'Net. But guess what? They're not . . . yet.

The U.S. Small Business Administration reports that of the 24 million small companies it keeps tabs on, only 44 percent are currently using Web pages to advertise their goods and services. (And when you remove the top ten or so metropolitan markets, that percentage of current small-business Web advertisers drops like a rock.) Bottom line: A whole lot of room is left for a savvy small business owner like you to make your business's presence felt on the Web.

So what can explain this rather odd situation in which customers are hanging out someplace that small business advertisers aren't? Undoubtedly, one huge reason is that to most people, the idea Internet marketing seems just too complicated. Intimidating, even. Best left to the experts, whoever they may be. We're the first to admit that Internet marketing can be a pretty complex undertaking. The 'Net has its own rules, its own customs and secrets, and above all, its own technology. And the latter changes constantly.

What does local really mean?

Oddly enough, defining *local* as in local business isn't all that easy. For instance, that fast-food franchise just down the road may be affiliated with a multi-national corporation, but at the same time, it's a long-established part of the town's business community, so is it local or not?

We'd say yes. For our purposes, the definition we use throughout this book is that a business is *local* if

✔ It does the lion's share of its business either on its own premises or at a customer's home, office, showroom, plant, and so on.

✔ When it uses online tools and techniques, it uses them to generate *offline* sales.

Some pretty obvious examples are contractors; professional service providers such as accountants, attorneys, architects (plus others that don't begin with an *A*); local retailers; and many more.

But, as with any big and complex subject, the secret to understanding the Internet — and finding out how to put it to work for your business — is a matter of breaking it into smaller, manageable, digestible chunks. And suddenly, Internet marketing isn't all that complicated anymore.

The Rise of the Search Engine

Before any sane businesspeople go to the time, trouble, and expense of establishing a Web site for their companies, the logical question they ask is: Just exactly who's going to find it, and how will they get there?

The answer is largely the *search engine*. Although search engine sounds very mechanical, it's actually just a pathway that customers can follow to find your business's Web site. Essentially, the offline *Yellow Pages* is a search engine. So is the local newspaper's Classifieds section. As opposed to those resources, which help customers sift through a few dozen or so choices, Internet search engines nearly instantly navigate through the millions of businesses that maintain Web sites.

How search engines actually find and index Web sites is pretty complex, and we save the technical details for Chapters 7 and 8. But here's a hint: Search engines use things like spiders and crawlers (and maybe one or two things that go bump in the night).

Google, the big kahuna of search engines

Of the major search engines operating, Google (`www.google.com`) is by far the largest, with Yahoo! (`www.yahoo.com`), and Bing (`www.bing.com`) coming in second and third.

We discuss these and other search engine providers in greater detail throughout this book. All you really need to know right now is that Google didn't grab its enormous share of the market just because it has a funny, catchy name. Over the last decade or so, Google has been the biggest innovator in the search engine space, and today it continues to pretty much define the category by setting the standards and making the rules that the competition then has to adopt in order to stay in the game. Proving, once again, that it's good to be the king.

Customers use search engines to find you

Millions of companies throughout the United States, both large and small, do at least some of their business on the Web. A search engine is what keeps finding any one company from becoming a needle-in-a-haystack proposition. In fact, search engines make successfully finding any one of them pretty darned easy. (Just ask your kids.)

The crucial bottom line is this: According to data for 2008 compiled by the Pew Research Center, 85 percent of Web site visits (or *hits*) originated through one search engine or another. That's how completely indispensable search engines are for any business that wants to have a profitable presence on the Internet.

Local Search: The Latest Search Frontier

Perhaps you're thinking, "I run a small, local business. Search engines are for big companies that get business from all over. I'll never get found stuck somewhere in the middle of all those folks."

Search engines are important to your business because the hottest area on the Web is local search. *Local search* is pretty much exactly what it sounds like: local people looking for local goods and services. Of course, local people have always been looking for local goods and services. What's changed is how they search. That is, on the Web. The defining characteristic of local search is that the people who use it have local intent.

That probably sounds pretty broad, and it is. Local search is broad because customers with local intent can use search engines in various ways to find what they're after:

✔ They can search for, say, *roofer* — and because the more sophisticated engines instantly identify the Internet Protocol (IP) address of the computer the searcher is using, some local roofer listings may well appear on the results list.

Google Maps is a leader in this technique, which you notice when you type a search term and a local map appears with a bunch of local businesses listed beside it.

✔ They can use geographical identifiers, such as *dermatologists davenport IA*, and they'll get (surprise) listings of dermatologists in Davenport, Iowa.

✔ They can shorthand the process by typing the business descriptor followed by a zip code, such as *plumbers 46256*. Local search still works.

In any case, the key development here is that the major search engines, such as Google and Yahoo!, realized very quickly that local search was becoming the Next Big Thing — an enormous untapped market for their services, spread over the 15 million local businesses that operate across America. So these search engines are very busy expanding their capability to render local-market search results and adding to the ways those businesses can quickly and efficiently get themselves listed — and found — online.

The result of all this has been what people with MBAs call a *positive feedback loop* (see Figure 1-1). People go on the Internet and look for local businesses. Early on, they find a few. Then, local business owners and search engine programmers realize that local people are looking for local businesses on the 'Net. So more and more businesses start putting themselves there, and search engines provide more local listings. And so on, and so on.

Another factor that's driving local search is the increasing popularity of smart phones and PDAs that give you Internet access in the palm of your hand. People tend to use these amazing gizmos a lot when they're out and about, so it's only natural that they use their phones to find the nearest restaurant, antique store, or shoe repair shop. With local search, you can easily do just that.

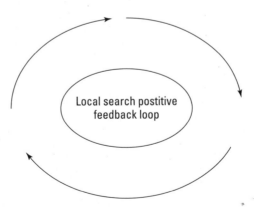

Improved organization and amount of local content online leads consumers to increasingly look for local services online.

Increase in local consumer searches online leads local businesses to see big opportunity.

Local search postitive feedback loop

To better serve both consumers and local advertisers, search engines improve organization of local content and add more local features.

Figure 1-1:
The positive feedback loop created by local search.

Big demand + Tiny supply = Pay dirt

Before diving into local search, the Googles, Yahoo!s, and Bings of the world took a look at the sort of numbers that follow and drew the logical conclusion, that is, that small business is potentially huge business. Consider the following:

- ✔ In 2008, 82 percent of consumers used search engines to find local services (up from 74 percent in 2007). That translates to 1.3 billion local searches every month.

- ✔ Sixty-four percent go to the Internet as their *primary* means of finding a local merchant. But only 26 percent of local small businesses have invested any time or effort in advertising online.

- ✔ Americans consume 35 percent of their media (news, entertainment, and so on) online, but only 7 percent of total national ad dollars are spent online.

What we see here then is the tremendous opportunity gap that exists, though it can hardly be counted on to stay like this forever. That's why thinking about and establishing your online presence now is a very good thing. (And of course, so was picking up this book.) In fact, a number of new search engine options have popped up to cater specifically to local businesses, which only expands the gap between the number of marketing venues and the number marketers who have so far taken the plunge.

Take a site like www.hotels.com. Yes, Hotels.com is a national site, but it depends on local hotel/motel/bed and breakfast/quaint, country-inn owners to provide it with content, which it then showcases on its site. Fandango (www.fandango.com) does roughly the same thing with local movie theaters across the country. Per usual, a bunch of other dot coms use this very effective business model.

Thinking local: It's only natural

People living in Toledo don't look for a plumber in Cleveland. They're looking for a local plumber who can get there in a hurry to fix whatever's leaking, clogged, or making funny noises.

And what local-searching customers everywhere know — and that a whole lot of small businesses don't seem yet to fully grasp — is that the Internet is likely to give them much more information about a local company than any other resource. Even a full-page ad in the local *Yellow Pages* or newspaper would find it difficult to hold all the information about a local business that a Web site can.

Don't let your competition take your customers

If your competition maintains a marketing presence online and you don't, it probably means one of two things:

✔ You don't know they're online.

✔ You know but don't particularly care.

If you don't know whether they're online, that's easy to find out. Use a search engine (just like their customers do — nudge, nudge) and see what your competitors are up to. But if you do know you have competitors on the Internet but haven't done anything about it, we're going to go out on a limb here and guess that that means one of two things:

✔ You think this whole Internet thing is just a passing fad.

✔ You want to get into Web marketing, but don't have the time or expertise.

You can't think the first one because if you've read anything in this chapter so far, you realize that the sheer volume of Web usage is staggering. So we're up against the time and expertise obstacles. As we mention in the Introduction, you can do a number of things on your own to create a Web presence that doesn't cost an arm and a leg or require any particular computer expertise. And as we also mention, many outside consultants and companies create Web sites and online advertising campaigns for businesses large and small, and can do it not only expertly but at surprisingly little expense.

Further, ask yourself this: With traditional print advertising, how can you tell how many people have seen your ad, much less acted on it as a result? Answer: You can't. But with a Web site (or for that matter, an online advertising or e-mail campaign), you can find out exactly how many people have seen it and contacted you because of it. That means you can quantify exactly how much you're spending to get each customer who calls you — and can keep refining your site to make it even more efficient as often as you want (as opposed to a phonebook listing that sits unchangeably frozen for a year).

A third of all search engine queries contain a zip code or a city or state name, such as *taxidermists 43112* or *florists Spokane*. Perhaps more important, however, and regardless of whether a customer tacks on a zip code or a city or state name, 43 percent of search engine users are looking for a local business from whom to buy offline (that is, at the business's physical location).

Lest you think that those numbers don't necessarily add up to much at the end of the day, consider this: In one recent month alone, Google reported 11,345 searches (or as Web savvy folks like to say, *impressions*) for various searches related to veterinarians in San Jose. So either Northern California is in the grip of a major hairball epidemic, or local people in general are searching for small businesses in a big, big way.

We've made a number of distinctions so far between local search and the conventional *Yellow Pages*. But there is one important respect in which they are very similar: Customers use them at the *moment of relevance*. For example, you don't look through the *Yellow Pages* for lawn care companies until you actually need a lawn care company. The same goes for local online search. Simply put, the moment of relevance comes about when need meets needfulfillment. And at that critical, highly sales-message-receptive moment, a potential customer can use all the information about you she can get to make you her source or supplier of choice. This is precisely the kind of persuasive, in-depth information that only a Web site can give.

Methods You Can Use to Advertise Online and Their Benefits

In this chapter, we take a look only at the proverbial tip of the local-online-advertising iceberg. Even so, you probably already realize that success requires the use of a variety of tools and tactics used in combination.

Here are a few of them:

- **Pay-per-click (PPC) online advertising,** which is a way to enhance how your business appears in search engine listings and to give you an instantaneous read on your listing's effectiveness.

- **Search engine optimization (SEO),** which involves adjusting and designing your Web site to make it more search engine friendly and increase your position in the organic section of the search engines.

- **Company landing pages** — pages that people come to directly when they do a search using particular keywords and then click the link posted from the search engine. The landing page takes them straight to the information specified by the keywords they've used to find you, without making them navigate to that information through your home page, which they might find too complicated to pursue.

- **E-mail blasts** that let recipients download, say, a coupon and thereby helps you start a relationship with them.

- **Social networking sites** like Facebook that can be used to generate interest in your business.

This may all sound a little intimidating at this early stage, but take heart. None of the tools and tactics are all that complicated by themselves. The real trick — or art, if you want to get fancy about it — is deciding how to combine them to create the most effective (and cost-effective) advertising campaign for your business.

Despite what may at the moment seem like a lot of work on your end, try always to keep this in mind: Unlike many forms of traditional advertising methods, online advertising is completely measurable in real (or near-real) time. That means you can find out almost instantly how well your efforts work, which parts perform better than others, what kind of customers you attract, and what specifically about your advertising catches their attention. Best of all, because your online advertising is something you can alter on virtually a moment's notice, you can change, refine, or otherwise tinker with it as soon as your measurements tell you what to do more of and what to leave behind.

Going beyond search engines

Earlier in this chapter, we mention the three biggest and best-known search engines operating: Google, Yahoo!, and Bing. Any (or all) of them can be a really cost-effective way to advertise locally and bring customers to your business who are looking actively for the kind of products and services you offer.

Although your online efforts may well begin with the big three search engines, the marketing opportunities provided by the Internet certainly don't end there. In fact, those other opportunities are vast. For instance, a lot of smaller, more localized search engines operate on the same principles as the three biggies but can offer greater efficiencies for your business. And you can use non-search ways to reach potential customers, too. We touch on e-mail (Chapter 10) and social-media marketing (Chapter 13), but you may also want to explore the use of banner advertising (Chapter 12), online PR opportunities (Chapter 14), industry-specific directories (Chapter 11), and so on.

Each of these possible tactics has its own nuances and strengths, and you're probably best off trying a variety of them to see which ones generate the best results for your company.

Targeting the right prospects

Any business worth its salt has a lot of potential customers, but those potential customers aren't all created equal. What you want to find are those prospects who are the most motivated and ready to act, the most financially able to buy what you're selling, and the most likely to become long-term customers. And one of the great things about having lots of online options is that they let you directly zero in on the cream of the crop.

With search engines, you can narrow your advertising efforts to specific zip codes, towns, or cities or to location-specific key phrases (such as people living near the strip mine). Banner advertising lets you put your name and message on other people's sites, sites that tend to attract the same kinds of customers you want to reach, demographically, by topic of interest, or by some other criterion important to you. And those are just a couple options. If you read on, match the profiles of your target prospects to the marketing tactics we discuss and see which promises to provide the best fit for your needs.

Turning clicks into new customers

Regardless of how you attract prospects to your Web site — via search, e-mail, banner ads, and so on — the real trick is getting them to take action when they're there. As the tacky expression goes, you're after engagement, not just eyeballs!

For a local business, turning clicks into customers means using the online medium to close an offline sale. Maybe your site lets them schedule a massage with an online form, request a construction quote via a Live Chat feature, or contact your limo service right from the Web page with a special tracking phone number. The possibilities are pretty much endless.

You discover everything you need to know to qualify prospects and convert them into customers in the chapters that follow.

Taking an active role in optimizing results

In the days before online advertising, you had basically two ways to measure the effectiveness of the medium you were using: anecdotally or by pure hunch. Hardly scientific, to say the least. But online advertising lets you optimize your results. You can measure how many people are coming from where, and what it is that's tickling their fancy or leaving it woefully untickled. And then you can do something about it, now!

Maybe you want to change a keyword or phrase, use different colors, put the elements on your site in a different order, or replace the picture of grandma with your dog Buster looking playful. Whatever. The point is that you can fine-tune your message (and your medium) until the cows come home — and see exactly which changes most benefit your return on investment (ROI).

Whether you do this or have outside professional help, optimizing results means taking a much more active role in your advertising than ever before. And being better and more quickly rewarded for it, too.

Chapter 2

Engaging Your Advertising Arsenal

Many years ago, a wise, old marketer lamented, "I know that half my advertising dollars are wasted — I just don't know which half."

And that was true enough then because major advertising media, such as newspaper, TV, and radio, were very hard to track. You just couldn't know who was reading, watching, or listening, or what sort of immediate effect your ads had. You had to wait for sales figures to roll in, and even those usually didn't tell much about what in your ads moved the sales needle.

Although technology has made tracking mass-media advertising somewhat easier and more precise — and although those media are still essential for many national brands — they remain something of a gray area as far as assessing their actual, immediate effects.

Enter online advertising, which offers local businesses — and an increasing number of national ones — an extremely cost-efficient, trackable, and tweakable way to reach customers. The variety of communication techniques (or *tactics*) available to an online advertiser means a local business can try several tactical combinations and quickly determine which one works best.

This chapter gives you an overview of the pros, cons, and unique characteristics of each of these online tactics so that you can put together an online advertising plan that will generate the biggest bang for your buck. We explore many of the subjects here in greater detail later in this book, but this chapter is a great starting point.

As you read over the options, think about which ones are most likely to reach and persuade your current customers as well as help you to recruit a growing bunch of new ones.

Getting Your Business Found Where People Are Looking

Advertising makes sense only in media outlets in which your customers are both present and engaged. That may sound obvious, but often, this truism is forgotten in the whirl of doing business.

A classic example is the *Yellow Pages.* People who break out the phone book and thumb to the Yellow Pages category they're interested in are certainly present and engaged. They're on a specific mission, such as looking for the nearest bowling alley. Today's *Internet Yellow Pages* (IYP) play the same role that their paper counterparts always have — and, not surprisingly, they're doing so somewhat at the expense of the paper version, as shown in Figure 2-1.

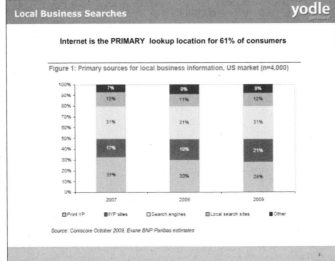

Figure 2-1:
The use of paper *Yellow Pages* has declined in proportion to the increased use of IYP.

Search engines represent another place where people go to find exactly what they're after. (They search for *bowling alleys* as opposed to *stuff to do.*) This is exactly why pay-per-click (PPC) advertising is so widely used today. And search engine optimization (SEO) efforts accomplish much of the same thing.

However, online advertising also contains an important exception to the Be Exactly Where They're Looking for You rule. You can think of that rule as the Be Exactly Where They Don't Think They're Looking for You, But Actually Kind of Are. To explain, we have to back up a step.

The online world is packed with market niches. Blogs deal with just about any subject or issue you can imagine. And with other social media, such as Facebook, MySpace, YouTube, and Twitter, people hang out with folks who are just like them in terms of their interests.

People who frequent social media aren't consciously looking for business advertising. In fact, one of the joys of social media for many individuals is probably the expectation that they *won't* be exposed to advertising there.

But more and more, they're mistaken because savvy marketers have found subtle ways to sell themselves and their wares where people socialize online. Doing this right is tricky, but it's very possible and online advertisers are getting pretty darned good at it.

In a rather lumpy nutshell is where things stand: Online advertising is good at reaching audiences that are specifically interested in finding what you have to sell (via search engines, IYP, and the like) and audiences that simply stumble across you (via Facebook and YouTube, for instance) where they're not expecting to find advertising but are nevertheless susceptible to learning about businesses like yours.

In other words, online advertising presents an extremely broad variety of venues, tactics, and tools that marketers can use to build business.

That said, we look more closely at the direct channel that leveraging search engines represents.

Leveraging search engines for success

As we emphasize in Chapter 1, people use search engines now more than ever before to find local businesses. So, as a local business, your first — and most important — step is to make sure you can be found there.

The Big Three in the search engine world are Google, Yahoo!, and most recently, Bing (formerly MSN Search). Because they've all recognized the huge potential that local searches hold, they've poured a lot of resources into local search features and capabilities. On such goal is to integrate local search results into their regular search engine pages, which is excellent news for you.

Here are three basic ways to market your business through a search engine:

✔ Organically

✔ With local listings

✔ Via pay-per-click

Figure 2-2 shows a typical search results page. (Note that the organic listings would appear below the local listings, and so aren't shown in the figure.)

Keywords (the word or phrase you enter in a search engine) play a major role in all three search engine options. Quite simply, no search occurs until someone enters something into the engine's Search field — and that "something" is the keywords or phrases that people use to find you, no matter which approach you use to make your site appear on the results pages.

Each method of promoting your business with search engines has advantages and disadvantages — and you discover a lot more about them throughout this book. For the moment, suffice it to say that there isn't just one answer, so using multiple approaches is usually the best option; that includes two — or even all three — of these online tools.

Figure 2-2:
A Google results page showing different kinds of search engine marketing.

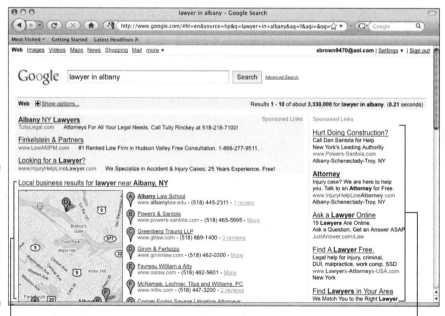

Local listings; organic results below   Pay-per click ads

Getting found organically

Organic listings (as in unpaid search engine results) are the most common kind of search engine results that people encounter online. Why the most common? Because each Web site that shows up in organic listings is found automatically by the search engine based on the keywords that appear on the site.

Search engines, such as Google, create their organic listings automatically by using programs — dubbed *crawlers* or *spiders* (which we refer to as simply *spiders* throughout this book for clarity) — to search the Web. (Spider? Web? How clever those search engine people are, eh?) Then you search through what the spiders have found.

Spider-based search engines consist of three primary elements:

✔ **Spider:** The spider visits a Web page, reads it, and then follows links to other pages within the site, which is why people refer to the site as *spidered* or *crawled.* The spider then returns to the site on a regular basis, such as every month or two, to look for further changes.

✔ **Index:** Everything the spider finds goes into the second part of the *index* (or *catalog*), which is like an unbelievably huge book that contains a copy of every Web page the spider finds. If a Web page changes, the index updates with new information.

Time is a factor: It can sometimes take a while before new pages or changes that the spider finds are added to the index. Thus, a Web page may have been spidered, but not yet indexed. And until the Web page is added, people can't find it on that the search engine.

✔ **Search engine software:** The program sifts through the millions of pages recorded in the index to find matches to a search and then ranks them in order of what it believes to be the most relevant.

How do spider-based search engines determine relevance when confronted with hundreds of millions of Web pages to sort through? They follow a set of rules built into a computer program, which computer geeks would call an *algorithm.* This is sort of the black-box part of the search because exactly how a particular search engine's algorithm works is a closely kept trade secret. However, all the major search engines' algorithms focus on two basic criteria: *location* and *frequency* — particularly the location and frequency of keywords on a given Web page:

✔ **Location:** Web pages that have a search term(s) at or near the top of the page, such as in the headline or in the first few paragraphs of body text, are assumed as highly relevant to the topic at hand and give the Web site an advantage in how it's ultimately listed relative to competing sites. Search engines assume that any truly relevant page will mention keywords right at the beginning, which is usually a pretty safe assumption.

> ✔ **Frequency:** A search engine analyzes how often keywords appear in relation to other words on a Web page. Those with a higher frequency of keywords are usually deemed more relevant than Web pages with a lower frequency of those keywords, and they're thus treated more kindly in the listing hierarchy.

What if you change your Web site in some way? The search engines will eventually find these changes, but what you've changed — your page titles, body copy, or other elements — can affect how your site is then listed.

Using local search listings

To better capture local search traffic, the large search engines have created special areas to cater to the local searcher. Two examples are Google Maps (`http://maps.google.com`) and Yahoo! Local (`http://local.yahoo.com`). And the best thing is that with most of these sites, at least some level of local listings are free. All you need to do is upload basic information about your business to the search engine's computers and then your site appears within organic search results. Simply go to Google's Local Business Center (`http://google.com/localbusinesscenter`) or the Basic Listing section of Yahoo! (`http://listings.local.yahoo.com/basic.php`).

Google, Yahoo!, and Bing feature these local listings next to a handy local map that has pins or flags sticking out of it. The letter or number on the pin that represents *your* site corresponds to the letter or number attached to your Web site address in the results list. In the case of Google, click that map and you're served up even more local listings, as shown in Figure 2-3.

Getting listed locally isn't always as easy as you might think; it can actually get downright frustrating. Why? Because the number of local businesses that want to be found via local search is expanding like crazy, and search engine providers are overwhelmed by the demand. So getting where you want to be often takes longer than you want. And there simply isn't much you can do about it but be patient.

Although always subject to change, the local search arms of the major search engines are

> ✔ **Google Maps:** `http://maps.google.com`
>
> ✔ **Yahoo! Local:** `http://local.yahoo.com`
>
> ✔ **Bing Maps:** `http://www.bing.com/maps`
>
> ✔ **AOL Local Search:** `http://localsearch.aol.com`
>
> ✔ **Ask: City Search:** `http://city.ask.com`

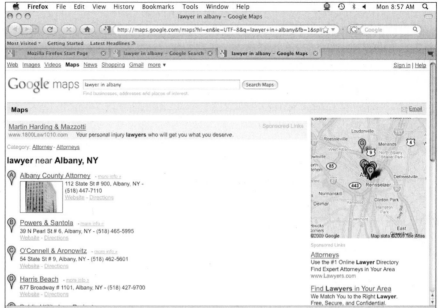

Figure 2-3:
Most search engines generate a local map that displays your location and Web site address.

Running pay-per-click ads

Pay-per-click (PPC) is simply search engine advertising, and it requires that you pay to get your ad into a high-visibility position. With most search engines, that ad position is at the top of the first page of search results and/or alongside them. You've almost certainly seen PPC ads when you've searched, and maybe you've wondered: How come those folks get such a prominent, almost impossible-to-miss spot? Answer: Because they pay for it.

Putting the pay-to-play aspect aside, however, here are two good reasons to use PPC ads:

✔ **They're upfront and personal.** Because people using search engines are primed and ready to find a business like yours, you can't do better than to put yourself (or really, your Web address) right in front of them. Buying PPC space means your ad has a better chance of not getting buried on some later page where only the most curious searcher will see your listing.

When weighing the option of using a PPC ad, keep in mind that several studies show just how impatient search engine users really are. As a general rule, searchers don't go deeper into the listings than the first half of the first page! So if your listing appears on a page much deeper than that, you're in search engine Siberia.

As a result of showing up in a highly visible spot in the listing results, PPC ads (unsurprisingly) are extremely effective at generating qualified clicks — which, of course, is the whole idea.

✔ **You get what you pay for.** Before you run away shrieking at the thought of laying out money for a search engine ad, consider one very important fact: Done correctly, PPC ads can be extremely cost-effective because you pay only when someone actually clicks your ad and thus becomes a legitimate prospect. And producing legitimate prospects is exactly your goal.

Another PPC benefit is that it tells you on a nearly real-time basis how many clicks you're getting, and that, in turn, lets you do a little seat-of-the-pants market research. Does one version of your PPC ad generate more clicks in a day (or week or month) than another version? Will yet another version do even better? You can find out easily and then take that lesson to the proverbial bank.

Unlike organic searches (which leave you at the mercy of spiders and your keyword strategy), PPC is eminently controllable and even kind of scientific. If you want to be the first rank for a certain keyword, you usually can (if even just for one day) so that you can test it, but you have to pay top dollar for the privilege. Then you can take the ad down the very next day and use whatever knowledge that experiment gave you.

We explore all the PPC nooks and crannies in Chapter 9. But for now, we describe the basic concepts so you can start thinking about whether PPC is something your business might find beneficial.

First, with all major search engines, the actual cost-per-click (CPC) is based on an *auction market.* This simply means that the more a business is willing to pay for a click, the higher its ad will appear in the search engine's paid listings section — and consequently, it's likely to get more clicks.

The net result of all this is that the CPC for a local business can run from a few cents to several dollars. And how fast and to what extent those individual expenditures add up is largely the result of decisions you make.

That said, you need to be aware of the basic PPC mechanics:

✔ **Develop a keyword portfolio:** Decide which search terms you want to use to trigger the appearance of your ad in the search results. (***Note:*** The capitalization of search terms doesn't matter.) If you're a dentist in New York City, you might settle on terms like *dentist in manhattan, teeth cleaning in midtown,* and *dental office nyc open saturdays* (assuming, of course, that you *are* open on Saturdays).

✔ **Write ad copy:** When people type one of your keywords, your PPC ad shows up, but it needs to contain more than just your Web address if PPC is going to be a worthwhile investment. Use this ad copy space to say something of interest about your business. The available space here is limited, so your copy can't be very long — and therein lies the challenge.

✔ **Decide whether to use campaign options:** Most search engines offer all sorts of nifty add-ons to help you target the right people. For instance, you may want to target people who search for *dental office nyc* (potential patients) but not those who search for *dental office jobs nyc* (potential employees). (Again, the capitalization of search terms doesn't matter.) You can also target a certain radius around a particular zip code, and that's just for starters. The search engine you want to use can give you a full list of the campaign options it offers.

✔ **Bid and budget:** As we mention earlier, PPC ads are usually auction-based, so you have to bid the amount you're potentially willing to pay for each click, which is your *max bid*. **Note:** The max bid isn't how much you necessarily will pay (your final, accepted cost-per-click will often be much lower), it just represents your personal ceiling — and it gets the process started. For example, say the most that a competitor is willing to pay for a click on a particular keyword is $1 whereas your max bid is $2. You get the top spot for $1.01 per click (not $2 per click). In essence, your max bid simply gets you into the game. When you have your CPC nailed down, search engines also usually let you determine the maximum amount you want to spend per day — which is really handy if you're on a strict budget.

✔ **Get it live:** This is the most exciting — and commonly the scariest — part of PPC. After you get your ad together and your CPC nailed down, it only takes a mouse click to make your ad go live. That's right: One teensy little click, and you're out there for the whole world to see. The immediacy that's baked into today's technology may give you a split second's worth of *yikes* just before you go public. But then you're done. For now.

✔ **Measure, learn, optimize, repeat:** This book has one recurring theme: Always test what you've done to figure out the best way to market and advertise your business. All the preconceptions, opinions, and intentions you might have are liable to get blown to pieces when they come up against real, hard data. You have to prepare for that — and to be willing to accept what the data tells you. Maybe a keyword you thought would be a surefire traffic-builder turns out to be a total dud. Maybe you're getting a fair number of clicks, but not getting any business. Don't worry, this happens to even the savviest marketers. Even if your campaign's working great and bringing in leads hand-over-fist, you always have room for improvement. And one of the best, most immediate ways on the whole wide Internet to sharpen your marketing skills is to step into the PPC advertising arena.

Understanding the Quality Score

Although the way the search engines order their PPC ads is technically the result of an auction system, it isn't just a simple Top Spot Goes to the Top Bidder system. For instance, if you're a plumber in St. Paul and (for some strange reason) want to show up when people search for *tattoo parlors in Los Angeles,* you probably aren't going to show up on top — or anywhere else, for that matter — regardless of how much money you're willing to shell out.

Why? Because the ad doesn't agree with the search terms. Google calls this the *Quality Score.* The Quality Score gets thrown into the mix with an advertiser's PPC bid, and out comes that person's ad position. Don't even try to figure it out. But do know the following two things:

✔ Search engines want to make (lots and lots) of money.

✔ Search engines want to give their searchers meaningful, relevant results (which will wind up making them even more money).

Those two things being the case, pretend you're the hypothetical plumber and your search engine listing popped up in front of people looking to get a little ink on their arms in L.A. Nobody's going to click your ad because, well, you're a plumber. And if you don't get clicks, the search engines aren't going to make money — and as far as they're concerned, *that's* a low Quality Score.

In case you're worried that those CPCs could soon start adding up to serious money, keep the following in mind: You decide how many keywords you bid on, what your maximum bid is for each keyword, and how much you spend per day. Additionally, whatever money you do spend may replace what you may already be spending on far less efficient and effective advertising vehicles (like say, newspaper ads) because the cost of each click by a motivated potential customer represents a possible sale. And the size of that sale will often dwarf the few pennies (or even dollars) you've spent to attract that customer.

Similar to the rules that apply to choosing what sites to serve up to searchers for particular keywords and phrases for an organic search, search engines running PPC ads insist that those keywords and phrases are legitimately and thoroughly relevant to your landing page or Web site content. If they're not, search engine employees won't come to your house and flog you — they'll just refuse for all eternity to run your ad.

And that, dear reader, is pay-per-click (at least for the moment). We know it may sound terrifyingly complicated just now, but you can console yourself with the fact that hundreds of thousands of local businesses use PPC every day without anyone's head (or budget) exploding.

Seeing how you look in Yellow

That trusty old standby, the printed *Yellow Pages,* has been around for over 100 years, but time marches on. And the recent advent of the Internet has convinced the good people who publish the *Yellow Pages* that their business model has a lot to gain by embracing the Web.

Enter the *Internet Yellow Pages (IYP).* Today's IYP include `www.yellow.com`, `www.yellowpages.com`, `www.superpages.com`, `www.dexknows.com`, and many other online counterparts to the printed phone books. Figure 2-4 shows a typical IYP listing, and Figure 2-5 correlates the IYP with its paper counterparts.

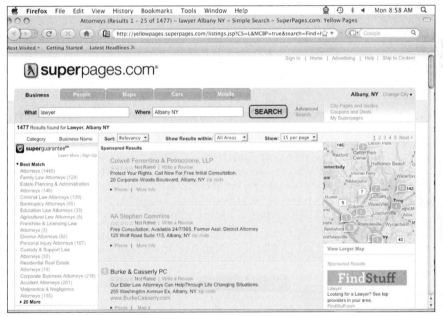

Figure 2-4: Listings from Superpages.com.

IYP enjoy reasonably high user volumes (though individually they still lag far behind Google from a market-share perspective). And it's worth noting that a good deal of IYP's traffic actually comes from organic searches on Google and other search engines, not just from customers navigating directly to the IYP Web address.

The good news about IYP is that the most basic listings are usually free. That being said, larger, premium listings are definitely not free and vary dramatically in cost, depending on the market you're in. Moreover, the usability side of IYP has some pretty heavy-duty bad news too . . .

The price is right — where to claim free IYP and directory listings

Many IYP and Internet directories provide at least some basic listing free of charge. Here are some links where you can claim those free listings:

✔ **Local.com:** `https://advertise.local.com/Default.aspx`

✔ **MerchantCircle:** `www.merchantcircle.com/signup`

✔ **Superpages:** `www.supermedia.com/business-listings`

✔ **Yellowbook.com:** `http://corporate.yellowbook.com/products/internet-free-listing`

✔ **Yellowpages.com:** `http://listings.yellowpages.com`

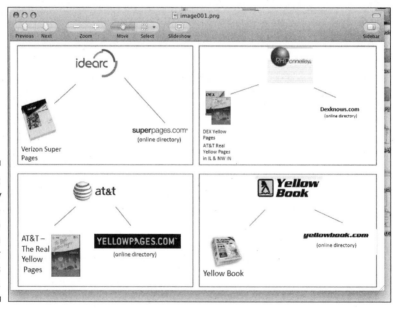

Figure 2-5:
A *Yellow Pages* family tree, so you can keep your Yellows straight.

Many IYPs are flat and static, which makes them seem kind of dusty compared to the vibrant search engine world they compete with. IYP are organized by category and return results in alphabetical listing and based on whether you've purchased a premium listing. Some IYP, such as Yellowpages.com, are moving toward an auction-based system that returns results based on relevance and price, which makes them stronger competitors to the search engines over time.

So should you advertise on the IYP? Absolutely. As we said, basic listings are often free, and you can potentially get equally qualified traffic, usually for a lower price than you get on the search engines. The hassle is that with so many of them, organizing a media buy across four or five IYPs and setting up your listings is time-consuming. If you do decide to go the IYP route, it may make sense to find out which IYPs serve your geographic area and have the most traffic for your type of business. The general rule is that the top IYP for a given area is almost always the one associated with the local phone company's printed book.

Getting listed on directories

Although roughly similar to IYPs, *local directories* are indigenous to the online environment and are often richer in content than IYPs. The content of local directories usually consists of a local business's name, phone number, hours of operation, ongoing promotions, and so on. Yelp, Citysearch, and other local online directories are particularly powerful for lifestyle-type businesses, such as salons, restaurants, and spas (see Figure 2-6). They may often include value-added information as well, such as user ratings and reviews. In a sense, directories can be considered mini-search engines, but without the same algorithm and screening process that search engines apply.

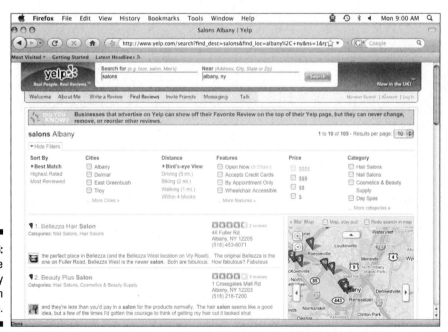

Figure 2-6:
A sample directory page from Yelp.

Directory advertising can, should, and often will be a superb lead generator. The only fly in the ointment is that you'll find yourself going head to head with dozens of your local competitors.

This isn't necessarily a big drawback because the really nifty thing about directories is that you can choose from so many different kinds, representing virtually all the different ways that people look for local businesses. Still, you obviously have to put your best foot (and face) forward, competitively speaking, if you're going to attract the best prospective customers.

Here are some of the best-known names in directory advertising:

- **Online lifestyle guides:** Augment their localized listings with things like maps and customer reviews; many also offer a share feature to add value to their sites. Some examples are:

   - *Citysearch:* `http://citysearch.com`

   - *Yelp:* `www.yelp.com`

   - *MerchantCircle:* `www.merchantcircle.com`

   - *Insider Pages:* `www.insiderpages.com`

   - *Business.com:* `www.business.com`

   - *Local.com:* `www.local.com`

- **Online classified ads:** For products and services ranging from electronics to pet sitting to plumbing to legal services. Check out the following, which is a busy, busy place:

   - *Craiglist:* `www.craigslist.org`

- **Local listings by area:** One such example is Oodle, which pulls together and organizes millions of local listings from all over the Web and then presents them by area:

   - *Oodle:* `www.oodle.com`

- **Vertical directories:** Feature information about a specific type of product, service, or business keyed to local markets. Check out the following examples:

   - *Hotels.com:* `www.hotels.com`

   - *BookFinder.com:* `www.bookfinder.com`

   - *Florists.com:* `www.florists.com`

- **Local media online:** Local newspaper, radio, and TV sites typically host directories offering free listings to local businesses.

   - *The local NBC affiliate in (Dallas/Fort Worth):* `www.nbcdfw.com`

   - *Wild 94.9, a radio station in San Francisco:* `www.wild949.com`

In short, directories are loaded with potential for driving people to your Web site, and thus to your local business. They really do deserve some serious checking out.

Lead aggregators

Lead aggregators generate qualified leads — either by phone or via the Web — for local businesses by grouping those businesses into user-friendly categories that consumers use to find the products and services they're after. In a sense, they create one-site shopping. One popular example is *ServiceMagic,* which is a lead aggregator focused on providing homeowners with listings of contractors — from plumbers and painters to cabinet makers and cleaning services, as shown in Figure 2-7. After finding out about the consumer's need, the lead are then sent to multiple contractors.

Figure 2-7: Part of a form through which Service Magic aggregates leads.

As with just about everything else having to do with online advertising, lead aggregators have pros and cons that you need to consider before deciding to list your business with them:

✔ **Pros:** Because a local business pays only when it actually gets a lead, you don't risk paying for non-results. Aggregators can work really well for some categories but not so wonderfully for others; their strength is in finding companies that do simple, home-based jobs, such as a locksmith or an electrician.

> ✔ **Cons:** A given lead can be passed to multiple merchants at the same time, creating a race among merchants to get to that consumer before anyone else does *(survival of the fastest).* Consequently, a consumer may get overwhelmed with calls from lead-receiving merchants and get annoyed with the whole process.

Driving Direct Navigation Traffic

Direct navigation comes about in three ways:

> ✔ A customer types your business Web site URL directly into the address bar in the browser.
>
> ✔ A customer clicks a link on a listing, profile, or another business site and is taken to your site.
>
> ✔ A customer clicks a link in a promotional e-mail.

Look for affinity Web sites to share links — an *affinity site* has a logical connection to your site due to a common interest. So, if you own a plumbing business, you might want to look for a site maintained by a local building contractor and ask to have your Web address included in that Web site content. People do this all the time.

Other sites to consider partnering up with include

> ✔ Trade associations
>
> ✔ The Better Business Bureau (BBB)
>
> ✔ Your local Chamber of Commerce and Visitors Bureau
>
> ✔ Local newspapers that run local business directories

You can use each of these options to help create visibility for your business by joining them, getting listed on them, advertising on them, supplying key content to them, or creating some other sort of natural connection. Properly selected, the sites you partner with will provide a good way to steer targeted traffic to your Web site and build your brand awareness in the community.

You can also put a link to your Web site in promotional e-mails that you send to existing and potential customers. Using e-mail is a pretty broad subject, which we cover in Chapter 10. For now, just be aware that e-mail campaigns can generate a lot of Web site traffic at very little (if any) cost.

Going viral with blogs

Viral advertising — word of mouth that spreads through the Internet — is cheap, easy to implement, and can be highly effective.

Those blogs that you hear so much about are the key viral vehicle for local businesses. (A *blog,* short for Web log, is a Web page made up of posts, shown in chronological order. Readers of the blog can post comments, which the original poster or other can reply to.) As an advertiser, you can use blogs in one of two ways:

- ✔ Add a business blog to your Web site to share your company's expertise, build additional Web traffic, and connect with potential customers. A business blog can also improve your search engine rankings (more on that later).

- ✔ Start posting to blogs or even ask a particular blog administrator to occasionally mention you in his blog. In either case, present yourself as an expert in your field — and don't forget to include a link to your site.

Use blogs only if your target audience uses them and then use only those blogs that are relevant to you *both.* Don't get carried away and promote yourself on a blog that focuses on nothing to do with your business. You won't just come off looking silly, you'll likely be branded a shameless marketer, or worse, an *Internot* (or *leper*) — and find yourself ostracized.

Using social networks

Another mode of viral advertising is social networking. Ever hear of Facebook, MySpace, or Twitter? Of course you have.

A decade or so ago, the big thing in business was to participate in networking events. A bunch of professionals would get together someplace to make small talk, eat shrimp, and forge connections with each other — connections they'd presumably capitalize on down the road. Well, social networking on the Internet is based on the same idea, except it isn't just about business, and you can do it in front of a computer while wearing your pajamas.

Despite the overall social nature of social networks, more and more businesses are discovering that these networks are great places to find out what people think and thereby capture the mood of the market, so to speak. And a lot of these networkers like to give their personal reviews and ratings of what other people are selling or otherwise making available — a few good reviews can be worth a few dozen ads.

Small wonder then that businesses are increasingly looking at social networks as a good place to demonstrate their expertise, engage existing customers on a personal level, and drive qualified leads to their Web sites.

The big social networks are Facebook, MySpace, YouTube, Twitter, Flickr, LinkedIn, and Friendster. Figure 2-8 shows an example of the Yodle business's Facebook page. You can reach customers through Facebook in the following ways:

✔ You can advertise on Facebook and target your audience by demographics, interests, and lifestyles.

✔ You can create your own Facebook page where you offer and share business information. Or you can advertise an event and then invite your fellow Facebookers to attend.

✔ You can put a link on your Web site that takes visitors to your Facebook page to read more about the nice, down-to-earth person behind the business.

Figure 2-8: The Yodle Facebook page.

Twitter — home of the tweets

Twitter currently occupies a social network niche all its own. (Though probably not for long with copycats out there.) Twitter is essentially an online message site that covers a million topics, based on the simple question: "What are you doing now?" Twitter is also a bit of a word game because each message (or *tweet*) can be no more than 140 characters long (including spaces!). An example might be: *Doing pastel drawing of a lighthouse on rocky coast. May get framed, give to Dad, born Maine, turning sixty. A good idea? Just tacky? Opine.* It's both harder than it looks and lots of fun.

Local businesses are finding a comfortable spot among *tweeters* (those posting messages). To read about how one local business successfully used Twitter to increase sales, check out the article at `http://pistachio consulting.com/twitter-to-go`.

Using other free media vehicles

Free media sites like YouTube and Flickr make viral marketing campaigns extremely easy to implement for any business, including local ones. For example, you can:

- Participate in chat rooms and on message boards, both of which are good ways to spread the word subtly that you and your business are worth knowing. Prime spots for this sort of thing are:
  - *Google Groups:* `http://groups.google.com`
  - *About.com:* `www.about.com`
  - *Yahoo! Groups:* `http://groups.yahoo.com`
  - *Open Directory Project (dmoz):* `www.dmoz.org`
- Put your TV commercial on YouTube (`www.youtube.com`) — and maybe *only* on YouTube and not on TV at all — and prominently feature your Web address somewhere in it.
- Host a photo gallery of your latest work. A stone masonry company, for example, could post pictures of its latest patio or decorative stonewall installation on Flickr (`www.flickr.com`), maybe accompanied by a How To discussion board.
- Add a Forward to a Friend feature in your e-mail promotions.

These all create opportunities to position yourself (and your business) as the local expert, and at the very least, begin to increase online awareness.

Using Facebook in the real world

Check out the "Social Media Marketing Case Study: Using Facebook to Promote a Professional Photography Business" article at *The Caffeinated Blog* for a good example of how one business harnessed the energy of Facebook to boost his local business. You can find the article here:

```
http://thecaffeinatedblog.typepad.com/
        the_caffeinated_blog/2008/11/
        social-media-marketing-case-
        study-using-facebook-to-promote-
        a-professional-photography-
        business.html
```

What makes this particular example so interesting is that the business owner became socially entwined with his potential customers by using Facebook, and his repeated exchanges with them gave him a serious leg up on his local competitors. And that's just smart marketing.

Going from Offline to Online: A Lesson in Cross-Pollination

Although your overall marketing effort may lean heavily on online advertising to create momentum and growth for your business, don't do so at the expense of a fully rounded effort. The fact is that offline advertising tactics can be integrated quite smoothly with online tactics to extend your advertising investment. Here are some examples of how this kind of cross-pollination can work:

✔ Direct mail can be enhanced with online offer fulfillment. In other words, the mail that shows up at a consumer's home provides your Web address as where to go to receive a special discount (or whatever it is you're offering). This can be an extremely powerful marketing combination for use with existing customers.

✔ The knowledge you gain from using pay-per-click advertising — ads that generate the most interest in your products or services — can be applied to your offline marketing and make it less a case of hit-or-miss than one of hit-and-hit.

✔ Networking offline can help you move people into an online network that you have a continuing presence on.

The number of ways you can get offline efforts to stimulate online activity is pretty much unlimited. And it's a strategy that no clever local business should ignore.

Getting Seen with Banner Advertising

A *Web banner,* or *banner ad,* is simply a form of display advertising that you place on someone else's Web page. This type of ad is meant to attract traffic to the advertiser's Web site and offers a link to take people there.

Banner ads are usually either wide and short, or tall and narrow. That's why they're called *banners.* And they're usually placed on pages that have interesting content, whether informational or editorial.

Because they're traditionally more about establishing a brand than about generating a direct response, banner ads can be a particularly powerful tool for attracting new customers to local businesses that offer high-value products or services. Car dealerships, law firms, and medical offices looking to build awareness and/or relationships (rather than just constructing a sales funnel) are prime examples. The theory is that if you spend enough time creating a very positive image for a brand, the mega-sale will follow sooner or later.

On a local level, consider placing banner ads on the local newspaper's Web site (in the Entertainment or Business section, for instance) and on other affinity sites. One example: A bicycle shop places a banner ad on the local cycling clubs' Web sites and on the sports pages of the local community sites.

Moving Out with Mobile Advertising

Mobile ads are messages formatted to appear on company Web sites that provide mobile services, such as cellphones and PDAs (Personal Digital Assistants), or ads that can show up directly on someone's iPhone or smartphone as either text or image ads. As a local business, you're interested primarily in the direct-to-device option.

Mobile search — and consequently, mobile advertising — came to be because search engine providers and mobile network service providers (Verizon, T-Mobile, and so on) realized that people running around with their cellphones and PDAs wanted to do local searches. (Say your car went phlooey on the road; you want to use your cellphone to find a local tow truck.) Mobile searches were a no-brainer.

In the industry, *mobile search* is more formally referred to as *searching with local intent* — and it's become obvious that mobile device users are just bristling with that intent.

Say a cellphone or PDA user launches a local search on Google (or one of the other search engines). Among the things that will pop up are ads, such as the ones we discuss earlier in this chapter in the "Running pay-per-click ads" section. But here, the super-important key fact is that the searchers are out and about, right now. Odds are, at this very moment, they're searching for something with immediate local relevance to them (like the aforementioned tow truck). Otherwise, they wouldn't be searching at all.

This means that the sales trigger is just waiting to be pulled — and smart local business find a way to capitalize on that immediacy. Some offer ads that, when clicked, notify the mobile user of a special, limited-time sale, a free giveaway, or the option of being connected directly to your business phone — which can all happen immediately.

Movie reviews, maps, menus, store locations, and hours of operation are perfect items to put just one simple click away on millions of mobile phones. A great case in point: Someone searching for Thai restaurants sees your mobile ad, clicks to find out your location and read your menu, and then gets connected directly to your take-out number. How cool (not to mention, profitable) is that?

Earlier in this chapter, we discuss how traditional pay-per-click advertising can be a relatively cost-effective sort of expense, and mobile PPC is largely the same in those regards. And if you decide to go the click-to-call-your-business-right-now route, you use something known as pay-per-*call*. You don't bid against anyone; you just pay a few dollars for each call that someone makes to your location through your mobile ad.

Here's a biggie, though: Most major search engines let you do the same sort of geo-targeted mobile ads that you can do with your primary online search engine ads. Plus Google Mobile, Yahoo! Mobile, and Bing Mobile can help you seamlessly extend your desktop-targeted campaign to local mobile users.

As you might expect, lots of new and simple resources have sprung up in the mobile marketplace to help put your business front and center with consumers on the go. These include

- ✔ **Bango:** http://bango.com
- ✔ **mobileStorm:** www.mobilestorm.com
- ✔ **Mobile Visions:** www.mobilemarketing.net

Local businesses that can benefit most from mobile search include restaurants, laundromats, movie theaters, florists, taxicab companies, salons, locksmiths, and similar businesses.

Mixing and Matching Your Methods

Unless you have scads of time on your hands — and what local business owner does? — you're going to have to pick and choose among the possible online advertising techniques available. But nowhere is it written that you can use only one. You may be best served to slip two, three, or more arrows into your online quiver — the better to leave no prospective customer unreached. Test them and see. If two of the three methods are producing reasonable results and the third is a flop, swap it out and try a fourth.

Before you make any decisions about which online advertising routes to follow, you have to get the current, competitive lay of the land. And that's best done by conducting your own research.

Your starting point is to determine who your online competitors are. To do this, get online and punch in the keywords and phrases that reflect the goods and/or services that your business offers. You may be surprised to see what comes up. You may be even more surprised to see what *doesn't.* (You'll be very happy to discover that one of your major competitors hasn't put her business online.)

Also try to identify which sites of any (respectable) kind target the same sort of buyers that you want to reach. Then, backtrack to see just what *their* online efforts consist of. This not only gives you some insights into the kinds of things that your target consumers respond to, but it also gives you a list of sites where they congregate — and with whom you might be able to link up to promote your business.

In a similar vein, check out your competitors' sites to see whose links they provide on their sites. Is one of your fellow local florists including a link to *Flowerworld Magazine* on his site? (There's really no such magazine.) Then contact *FM* to see whether you can get a link on its site if you put its link on yours. The lesson here is that everyone is looking for ways to cross-sell, and the number of possible, tactical ways to do that is almost unlimited.

Finally . . . surf's up! Go online and surf local sites, directories, and social networks. Find out what advertisers in all categories are doing — and even take note of which tactics make *you* want to act. You might just be surprised.

After you determine that you want to use online advertising tools A, B, and C, don't forget to track the results of each to the extent you can. Does changing A make it a little more effective? Why do you suppose B is outperforming C? You'd considered putting tool D to work, and maybe now's the time, and so on. One of the great things about online advertising is that it makes this kind of mixing, matching, and adjusting so easy. And ultimately, you *will* find the right marketing mix . . . the happy one that you can ride all the way to the bank.

Chapter 3

Planning Your Online Advertising Campaign

*W*hat does effective local advertising take, first and foremost? One word: Planning.

And why could that pose a problem for you? Because local business owners tend to be doers, not methodical analysts and strategists. Analyzing and strategizing tend to not be in the average independent go-getter's genes. But you can become those things — at least in the advertising arena — and, as we demonstrate in this chapter, you'll find it isn't all that hard to do.

At bottom, planning requires asking the right questions before you start running any kind of advertising, whether online or offline. And planning will save you a lot of headaches, false starts, and wasted effort and resources down the line. Plus, planning will reward you with what you're ultimately after — more customers and more sales.

Planning also requires banishment of one all-too-common impulse, namely, bouncing from one marketing idea of the week to another in hopes that the law of averages will eventually produce a silver bullet. That approach just doesn't work. Worse, that approach promises nothing but confusion for you and your customers while wearing you down (and out) in a hurry. This chapter helps you resist the temptation to resort to that kind of reflexive spur-of-the-momentness and instead to start applying some good old, tried-and-true strategic discipline.

The payoff is that you will come up with a solid advertising plan. And that plan will be more than smart and effective enough to last you a long time.

Making a Pact to Plan

Your first step toward building an effective advertising effort is to figure out exactly who the audience for your product or service really is. Decide what sort of customers your product or service appeals to, what benefits of the product or service will move those people to act, and what's the best way to communicate those benefits to those same folks.

The answers to those questions lead to your company's *unique selling proposition (USP):* The factor or consideration presented by a seller as the reason that one product or service is different from and better than that of the competition. When you have that, you're well on your way.

After you have your USP, you need to understand just how your customers buy your product or service. That may sound like an odd step, but it really isn't — and your answer will help you determine how best to *reach* them (that is, which online tactics to use) and to *move* them (that is, what actions you want them to take as a result of your advertising).

The fact is how people buy varies by the kind of business you're in. For example:

- ✔ If you own a local pizzeria, you probably aren't too concerned with the quality of the leads you generate; you just want as many people as possible to come in for a slice. Recognizing that, you may want to consider an online advertising mix that includes listings on Yelp and Citysearch. Here customers can post reviews and ratings, and you can post directions to your location and a mobile ad campaign that promotes, say, a 10 percent discount to customers who are looking for a place to have lunch.

- ✔ If you're a local dentist, you don't want a lot of walk-ins; you want people to make an appointment before they show up at your office. In a case like that, you might consider a pay-per-click (PPC) campaign that drives people to your Web site where they can get your phone number or fill out a form to schedule an appointment, or you can list on an Internet Yellow Pages (IYP) site.

The moral of the story is that no matter what kind of business you own, your advertising mix is going to be dictated largely by your customers' routine behavior with regard to your business. Your advertising mix is the old hand-in-glove thing — and it's important.

Positioning Your Business for Success

Before you can establish a local online advertising plan, you need a few key marketing basics in place. After you have that, you'll know that you know what you need to know (follow that?), and your plan will be grounded firmly in reality and primed for success.

Although most of these basics hold true for traditional media advertising, the beauty of online advertising is that you can test it quickly and affordably — and make adjustments to your mix or your message in almost real time.

Here are the six building-block tasks that any serious marketer has to tackle:

1. Define your target market.

   Look at who you're currently doing most of your business with and then figure out why they do business with you and what it is about them and their needs that are unique.

2. Write a paragraph that defines your target market.

   This helps you keep your customers' unique characteristics in the front of your mind. Write what you think they want out of life and how your offering fits into their plans.

3. Identify your value proposition.

   Determine what your business does best — and why customers should choose your business over any of your competitors. This is where your USP comes in.

   If you honestly don't know what it is about your business in particular that appeals to your customers, call a few and ask. You're likely to get good, actionable answers. Your customers might even come away from your call feeling flattered that you sought their valuable opinions.

4. Create your key messages.

   Create a list of several compelling benefits that give people a reason to deal with you rather than with that guy across town and then look for ways to incorporate those benefits into your online advertising — whether via a PPC ad, an e-newsletter, or a blog entry.

5. Analyze your competition.

   Make sure you know who (and what) you're competing against. How and where do your competitors advertise? What are their strengths and weaknesses? How can your business be competitive with theirs?

A great way to do this is by searching for one of the services you offer. Do your competitors appear in the paid listings? If so, do their ads contain an offer? Are they listed with the local IYP or do they maintain a Facebook page? In the same vein, search one of the major engines for your competitor's name. The results show you where they have an advertising presence. Pay particular attention to any places you hadn't yet thought of but that also make good sense for you.

6. Research your market online.

   Research can consume valuable time, but it's time well spent because the better you understand your customers' online behaviors, the more effective an online advertiser you are.

   Start by searching the major and the local search engines with keywords that best represent your business. That simple act produces a lot of search results, but that's the goal. Now, follow up those results and see where they take you.

   Chances are the keywords will bring up a big, messy mix of IYP listings, local sites, blogs, social networks, local search results, and more. As you chase down each, make your own assessment of their potential to drive business. Does the content reflect what your business is about? Do the keywords take you to places where businesses like yours are discussed and where you might participate in the discussion? Would your customers search the way you just did, or would they not dig as deep? Are some of your best customers on Facebook or LinkedIn?

After you do these six steps, you're definitely closing in on what your ad mix should be. You're also about to figure out (if you haven't already) precisely how to position your local business to attract qualified local customers. And when you've done that, you can start establishing some informed, realistic, attainable, and maintainable marketing goals for your company, which is half the battle.

Setting Your Goals and Expectations

Imagine that you're on an airplane. Your advertising planning starts with a view from 30,000 feet of what you want your advertising to achieve. You have to clearly identify your goals, assess honestly how many of those goals you can realistically afford to accomplish and in what time frame, and then set your expectations accordingly.

You can easily get carried away and decide that you want to accomplish eight things in two months for $38. You're far better off starting with limited goals, an ample time horizon, and a good deal of budgetary padding built in to your estimate of just how much reaching those goals will cost. If you get where you intend to with this plan, you then have a base of success from which to launch your next phase. And odds are you'll learn some helpful lessons along the way that you can use to make that next phase even more effective.

Begin with a clear accounting of your objectives, such as:

- ✔ Generate new customers
- ✔ Expand into new geographic markets
- ✔ Announce a new product or service
- ✔ Drive more repeat business
- ✔ Support your current customers more effectively
- ✔ Become the area's premier provider of whatever it is you provide
- ✔ Create more local visibility and improve your company's image

You don't have to pick only one objective — as long as you don't ask your advertising to do too many things simultaneously. That will only muddy your message.

To keep up the airplane analogy, you descend quickly to 10,000 feet. (The air sickness bags are in the seat pocket in front of you.) Take a look at your goals from an operational point of view, and understand what it will take to support and accomplish them.

Say your goal is to generate new customers. If you're a plumber, getting new customers might involve getting your phone to ring as often as possible. Because you spend most of your day under somebody's sink and you may not have a retail location to handle walk-ins, your phone (or answering system) is probably your best way to capture new customer leads.

If you own a salon, on the other hand, with a reception staff always on duty, getting new customers might involve a combination of incoming phone calls, walk-ins, and online advertisements, such as fliers or booking appointments.

Whatever kind of business you run, knowing how your customers consume is the key to achieving the goals you've set — and the key to getting the maximum results every day, from the online advertising you run.

Knowing what will happen

After you establish your goals and figure out how your operation best meshes with them, be aware of what online advertising does for you. Because online advertising is different than traditional advertising, going online means changing the way you think.

Does that sound a little scary? It isn't. Just keep the following in mind:

- ✔ **Online advertising can automate a lot of what you've traditionally been personally responsible for.** For example, using online forms means you no longer have to be physically present to help a customer schedule an appointment.

- ✔ **Online advertising is fluid.** Unlike print advertising, you can start and stop your online campaigns almost at will, and you can test, measure, and refine them on an ongoing (and almost immediate) basis until you find your most effective marketing mix.

- ✔ **Online advertising requires that you stay involved and take an active role in the details of your advertising campaign.** This isn't set-it-and-forget-it stuff; this is getting in up to your waist, elbow, or some other upper body part . . . and staying there.

- ✔ **Online advertising can typically generates some pretty healthy response rates and return on investments (ROIs).** These often far exceed those that conventional print ads, direct mail pieces, and trade shows can give you. Be ready to handle that new bump in the number of prospective customers.

- ✔ **Online advertising usually costs less to develop and *place* (or view) than conventional advertising.** As a result, you may find that you suddenly have more money to work with than you used to.

Setting reasonable expectations of success

The other kind of expectation is the dollars-and-cents kind. That means figuring out just what sort of increase in business you can realistically anticipate enjoying. *Realistically* is the keyword here. It's far better (at least psychologically) to have modest expectations and be proved wrong than to have super-ambitious ones and come up short.

Far be it for us to tell you what these expectations should be. (After all, we hardly know you, much less your business situation.) For argument's sake, say that you're looking for online advertising to increase your customer traffic by 10 percent over the first three months. That's probably not a crazy number, generally speaking. If that's what happens, congratulations. Ten percent might not be enough to fund that Ferrari you've had your eye on, but you're onto something. That percentage tells you to keep going — maybe invest a little more effort and expense in your efforts and see how far that level of online activity generates.

On the other hand, if you come up short on that hypothetical 10 percent, your expectations were too high, or your online methods were too few or too weak, or both. And that's also valuable because those can be adjusted easily.

In short, let the market — and the results it brings you — guide you in answering the time-honored question: What do I do now?

Identifying Strategies for Success

We realize this may sound elementary, but it's also hard-as-titanium true: In advertising, everyone's goal is sales related, whether you aim to bring new people in the door or to get existing customers to buy more of what you're selling. The question then becomes, how will your online advertising deliver the results you're after?

If you just opened a pet grooming shop, your immediate priority will probably be to generate leads that can then drive sales. In other words, *lead generation*. But if you're a kitchen and bath remodeler who's been in business for years, you may simply want to grow more business from the customer base you already have. In other words, *lead nurturing*. Finally, you may want to obtain the contact information (name and e-mail address, at least) of the people who respond to your online advertising. In other words, *lead capture*.

Lead generation

Lead generation, referred to in the hallowed halls of marketing as *lead gen,* is pretty much what it sounds like: The creation (or generation) of interest or inquiries into a business' products or services by prospective new customers. In less formal terms, lead generation means walking into your office one morning and finding ten new e-mails from people you don't know who want information about or from your company.

Online lead generation has great appeal for local businesses like yours because it lets you

✔ Determine your pricing on a per-lead basis.

✔ Choose the product or service you want to tell prospects about.

✔ Select the geographical area(s) that your business is interested in farming.

✔ Control the number of leads that come in each month, which assists in budgeting your time and resources.

✔ Pay only for the traffic and leads received (which is particularly true with PPC search engine ads).

If your calendar currently has a lot of holes in it and you need to drum up business fast, lead gen is a good way to grow your business rather quickly. That can, in turn, increase your ROI and put more business on the books.

How do you actually generate the leads you want? Employ one or more of the highly cool online tactics that you can read about in Chapters 7–13. Ultimately, all online advertising has some form of lead generation as its goal. And if the tactics you decided to use at first aren't doing the job, you're not necessarily doing something wrong; you may just not be doing something sufficiently right yet.

Your approach to lead generation needs to be the same as with any advertising endeavor. Set aside a reasonable budget to test a given technique — and then see if it works. If that technique works, great. If not, change or refine the technique. This is hardly rocket science, although it might seem like it at times.

Lead gen becomes a truly successful effort when your *conversion skills* (which is a fancy way of saying your ability to sell) are polished enough to "convert" those leads into actual buyers at a high rate. If you're underequipped in some way to follow through on the leads you get, throttle back on the incoming leads, sift those leads down to the super-best ones — or, we suggest respectfully, polish your skills.

Lead capture

Lead capture usually happens at the same time as — or right after — lead generation and before lead nurturing. You're using online advertising that prospects respond to. If their responses don't already give you contact information, find a way to get it. That's the capture phase and then you can go on to nurture (or yeah, okay, *schmooze*) them.

Leads can be captured via phone, or increasingly via Web site. So you don't necessarily need to put up a site for lead capture, but you're almost certain to increase leads, traffic, and sales, if you do. In Chapters 4 and 5, we discuss a lead capture page on your Web site, or a *landing page*. This page appears when a potential customer clicks your online ad or the link to your business that they find on a search engine. This page usually displays content that's a logical extension of the ad or link, but more important, it can (and should) offer a variety of calls to action that will get people to respond and give you their contact information in the process.

So now you've captured a prospect's contact information. Great. Time to follow up. You can safely assume that people who just gave you their info expect to hear from you. Don't leave them hanging — make contact.

People who have willingly given you their names and contact information constitute leads that are about as high-quality as leads can get. They're your birds in the hand.

Asking for the opt-in

You've undoubtedly seen *call, click,* or *visit* on a lot of Web sites. The invitation to click is often displayed on or near a button that you're expected to click. When people click that button, they generally get whooshed to a page asking them to fill in their contact information. In return for doing that, they get something from the site sponsor (a discount, a case history, a bobble-head doll — something). And the sponsor, of course, now knows how to contact them and start revving them up for a sale.

Most contact info pages also ask the visitor to opt-in to your e-mail program. This just means that the visitor is giving you permission to send him e-mails. Without that permission, you can potentially be in a whole stewpot of trouble. (Chapter 10 goes into the gory details of the penalties that can be imposed on you for e-mailing without permission.)

So there's no reason not to ask for a visitor's opt-in permission at the same time you get her name, e-mail address, and any other reasonable identifying information you need. (Hint: Asking for blood type generally sends the wrong message.)

Lead nurturing

Lead nurturing is the process of building relationships with qualified prospects to grow them into buyers at some point. As you know, a lot of leads just aren't sales-ready yet. Those leads need some gentle prodding, persuading, and a little TLC. It's either that or just throwing them away, which doesn't feed the proverbial bulldog.

When does lead nurturing make sense?

- ✔ **When you're selling a big-ticket item.** Almost always, the bigger the price tag, the longer it takes a prospective buyer to hand over the cash.

- ✔ **When repeat business is a strong driver of your sales.** In other words, when you have actual buyers in hand, you want to keep nurturing that relationship so they'll come back and buy again.

- ✔ **When your opt-in e-mail list grows.** Figuring out a way to do lead nurturing on a broad scale increases your chances of expanding your sales.

Here's a pretty basic example of a lead nurturing program that's designed to instill trust in your business and position it as the best, most expert place for your nurturees to do business:

Day 1: Prospects opt-in on your Web site for you to contact them.

Day 2: You e-mail a welcome to these prospects.

Day 28: You e-mail them a recent customer success story.

Day 42: You e-mail them a recent article of interest you found on the Internet; it's an article that puts a product or service like yours in a good light.

Day 63: You e-mail them a touching-base note, a "Hi, how are things with you" kind of message.

Day 80: You e-mail them a discount offer on something you sell.

Day 85: The prospect calls you: *Voilà!* You have a qualified lead.

"Wow," you say, "That's a long stretch of nurturing." But think about it: None of the steps are difficult to do, and over time, you may get to the point where you already have everything (except the customer success story and Internet article) in the can, ready to be sent off almost automatically. And the time frame for the nurturing stage can shrink (or expand) depending on how much a sale is worth. If you're selling a bicycle, the nurturing stage will be shorter. If you're selling an RV, this stage could easily run a lot longer.

Is lead nurturing really worth it? Yep. One study reports that lead nurturing programs can increase a business's sales opportunities by an average of 20 percent. (Don't take our word for it? Read the Marketo article at `http://pages2.marketo.com/real-roi-wp.html`.) Plus, this stage can improve your closing ratios, strengthen your sales pipeline, shorten your overall sales cycle, and enhance the overall image of your business in the marketplace. So, like we said, the answer is yep.

Creating a Time and Action Plan

Okay, now comes the creative part because now is when you take all that useful stuff we cover earlier in this chapter and put it to work in a time and action plan. You decide what time frame you want to work with and what you want to accomplish at different points along that timeline. And then you write that plan.

The nearby sidebar, "A sample time and action plan," shows an example plan for the fictional landscaping service owner Leo.

A sample time and action plan

We created a sample plan that can be used as a guide in creating a plan for your own business. Of course, the actual objectives and tactics for your own plan will vary based on your specific needs. Moreover, your own plan will likely be significantly more detailed.

Leo's Landscaping — Your bushes are our business!

Primary goal: To become the preferred landscaping service in the Tri-City area.

Objective One: Increase new customers and sales for the residential side of the business.

1. *PPC advertising:* Use Google AdWords to promote key residential landscaping services and our statues and fountains specialty.

   Measure results by the number of people who click each ad, the number of people who convert on the Web site (call or fill out a form to schedule an appointment), the number of people who hire us, where the best leads come from, and the new customer cost.

2. *Lead aggregators:* Sign up with a lead aggregator such as ServiceMagic to buy leads they generate online.

   Measure results by looking at the number of new customers gained through these leads and dividing by the cost for leads (customer acquisition cost).

Objective Two: Develop programs that increase repeat sales and word-of-mouth referrals.

1. *Current customers:* Start creating a customer opt-in database (names and e-mail addresses) by offering discounts to customers who provide their contact information. E-mail a coupon as a thank you. Do maintenance with new sign-ons every month.

Begin a "Gardening Tips" newsletter for customers who provide e-mail addresses.

Measure results by getting 100 new names.

2. *Prospects:* Create a Facebook page for Leo's Landscaping. Use a Facebook event to invite fans to participate in an online drawing for a free plant.

   Measure results by the number of new names and e-mail addresses gathered on the Web site.

3. *Brainstorm further ideas:* Survey current customers online for feedback on quality and variety of Leo's services, customer relations skill, employees' knowledge and so on.

Objective Three: Develop a commercial client base.

1. *PPC advertising:* Add keywords and campaigns to Google AdWords account to promote key commercial landscaping services including our special on year-long maintenance contracts.

   Measure results by the number of people who click each ad, the number of people who convert on the Web site (call or fill out a form to schedule an appointment), the number of people who hire us, where the best leads come from, and the new customer cost.

2. *LinkedIn presence:* Solicit recommendations, participate in relevant Q&A forums, and lead discussion groups on relevant topics to establish professional credibility.

   Measure results by the number of contacts established and the number of recommendations received.

When you write a time and action plan to achieve a particular goal or outcome, stick to a few disciplines:

- ✔ **Clarify your goal:** Can you conjure up a visual picture of the expected outcome? How will you know if and when you've reached your goal? What about your goal makes it measurable? What constraints are you working under: time, money, and other resources?

- ✔ **Write a list of actions:** Focus on generating and writing as many ideas and options as possible. Have paper with you so you can jot ideas as they come to you; when doing this, don't edit yourself — no one ever has to see this list but you, and you never know what amazingly great idea might just pop up if you let it.

- ✔ **Analyze, prioritize, and (now) edit:** Looking at the list of actions you put together, ask: Which are absolutely necessary? Are these necessary steps also likely to be the most effective ones? If not, do these steps at least set the stage for some truly effective steps down the line? (They can be valuable in either case.) Which, if any, action items can be dropped from your plan without significantly affecting the outcome? Be honest and then cross them off.

- ✔ **Organize your action list into a plan:** Decide which order to take your action steps. Recognize whether some action will require some preliminary steps before it can be put into place; this could affect the overall order of your actions. Then rearrange actions that make for a better flow.

  Look at the plan one last time: Can it be simplified even further? If so, do it; you'll end up saving some time and effort down the road.

- ✔ **Live by a calendar:** Figure out what you need to do to accomplish each action and then plot them on a calendar. Don't give yourself more (or less) time than you'll realistically need; too much time can make you complacent whereas too little time can make you crazy. Pledge that you'll meet those calendar dates; if you've planned properly (and realistically), this is all manageable.

- ✔ **Review your plan regularly and monitor your progress:** How far have you actually progressed toward you goal to date? Has new knowledge or situation change intervened that might require adjusting the plan? Make any necessary adjustments to your plan to take that new information or change in circumstances into account, or to simply speed your progress. Scrapping the whole plan isn't an adjustment (just in case you were wondering).

Establishing a Realistic Budget

Back in the olden days — before Al Gore invented the Internet and a menu was something you found only in restaurants — most businesses operated with an advertising budget of 2–5 percent of the previous year's gross sales. Determining budgets were easy that way, even though it was very hard to measure results.

Now the Internet is nearly taken for granted. Businesses have a lot more flexibility to set their budgets at whatever level they believe necessary to be successful — and to measure the results of each of their advertising expenditures against their spending. If the world isn't a brave new one, it's at least more efficient.

Determining the right amount to spend

Your first budget is probably the hardest to come up with, but it's worth the effort. This budget gives you something to analyze the results of your online advertising against and lets you see easily where your advertising campaigns will need to be refined. By the next business year, you'll have actual results on which to base your budget that you didn't the first time — and your time and action plan will be that much more effective.

For your first budget, your best initial step is to do a breakdown of the costs you can reasonably associate with each of the tactics you want to use. For instance, if you plan to send a monthly e-newsletter, factor in the cost of your time. And don't forget to also factor in the cost of creating and distributing it (all while knowing that as your list of customers grows during the year, those costs will grow, too).

Even with a tight budget, you can generate, capture, and nurture leads because of online advertising's built-in cost-effectiveness. If you can afford to spend more, you can choose among high-ticket items (like a really first-class Web site) and other tactics that are (almost) free. That gives you a lot of flexibility to customize your plan — and your expenditures. Remember, too, that multiple expenditures to your message through the various online vehicles you use will have a cumulative effect: The more prospects see of you (within reason), the better they'll remember you and the better your chances of closing sales. And keep in mind that the efficiencies of online advertising make this kind of message repetition possible at just about any budget level.

Determining your potential return on investment (ROI)

At this point in the planning process, keep a close eye on three *metrics* (which is just fancy talk for numbers):

- Cost per lead = Cost from marketing effort ÷ Number of qualified leads generated

  For example, if Bob's banner ads cost $500 and generated 50 leads, his CPL is $10 (500 ÷ 50 = 10)

- Cost per acquisition = Revenue from marketing effort ÷ Cost from marketing effort

  For example, if the 50 leads Bob gets turn into 10 sales, his CPA is $50 (500 ÷ 10 = 50)

- Return on investment = Revenue from marketing effort – Cost from marketing effort ÷ Cost from marketing effort

  For example, if the 10 sales Bob earns result in $1,000 in revenue, his ROI is 100 percent (1,000 – 500 ÷ 500 = 1 or 100 percent)

CPL

Cost per lead (CPL) expresses the cost of bringing a lead in your door. This usually requires some action on the part of the lead-to-be: opting-in on your Web site, phoning you, filling out an online form, and so on. Now, generating that lead costs you something. The cost of maintaining your site, the cost of getting your phone number in front of the person, or the time it takes to harvest the information from the online form and turn it into data for later use.

Measuring your CPL is important. Otherwise, you're giving without receiving, which may be a nice, virtuous thing to do, but it doesn't help your bottom line.

CPA

Cost per acquisition (CPA) expresses the cost of actually acquiring a new customer. Measure your CPA because spending money on advertising that isn't converting leads into new customers for your business is simply a waste of time.

ROI

Return on investment (ROI) typically expresses the rate at which you recover your investment in online advertising. Why is this important? Simple (and critical): Your ROI tells you whether your online advertising plan is working. If you spend $1,000 on advertising, you want at least $1,001 coming back to you — otherwise, what's the point?

Sure, that's oversimplified. But even at such an elementary level, you have to think about your cost of goods and the dollars-and-cents value of your time in view of the margins you're hoping to realize. You need either lower costs or higher profits — and generally both — to produce a hefty margin. Figure out realistically what your costs and your profits are likely to be, and your ROI won't hand you any nasty surprises.

How the numbers all come together

You might reasonably conclude that CPA could potentially be so important to your planning that there's really no reason to use CPL. To which we say, unequivocally: yes — and no. Customer acquisition can take an ungodly amount of time, so you may have to wait quite a while before you can calculate your CPA. In the meantime, CPL — measuring the more immediate collection of leads — can be extremely helpful in its own right.

Here's how all three of these factors intertwine. Say you're a dermatologist. You may find you can generate a much lower CPL by using PPC ads than by using banner ads. However, you may also find that banner advertising generates a lower CPA overall (meaning that you're getting more leads from your PPC ads, but your banner ads are pulling in more leads that actually turn into patients). Does that mean you go lighter on the PPC front? Or heavier on the banner ads? Probably both. However, the last metric, ROI, is really the most important metric because not all customers (or patients) are equal, and some may end up providing you a lot more revenue and profit.

Pretty simple, eh? All these acronyms look like alphabet soup, but it's really just good old-fashioned, outlay-versus-intake business practice. And we assume that's something you already have nailed down. For some more handy examples on how to handle some of this marketing math, check out Chapter 6.

Part II
Setting the Foundation for Local Online Advertising Success

The 5th Wave   By Rich Tennant

"Come on Walt – time to freshen the company Web page."

In this part . . .

When people get interested, even excited, about what they've seen in your online advertising, where should they go? Your Web site, where prospective customers can learn all about the products and/or services you sell as well as get a firm sense of your company's personality. Without a Web site, even the best online advertising plan leads nowhere.

Chapter 4 delves into the questions you need to ask before your site takes shape, including the pivotal question of whether to build the site. If you break out in hives at the thought of seeing HTML, no problem. Scores of resources are available to take some or all the phases of Web site construction off your shoulders.

Chapter 5 discusses the specialized landing pages on a Web site as well as some of the fancier features that today's best Web sites offer.

Chapter 6 talks about collecting and measuring the results from your online advertising efforts and then refining those efforts to get even better results.

Chapter 4

Building a Great Web Site: The Key to Online Advertising Success

*Y*ou know the old saying, "The eyes are the windows to the soul"? Well, your Web site is the window to your business. For many people, your Web site is the first thing they see when they connect with you — and first impressions count.

Your site is the primary fulfillment vehicle for all your online advertising because it's where people come to find out more about you, take advantage of an offer you've made, or sign up for a newsletter. Most important, the site is where you begin — then continue — to convert prospects into customers. If your Web site is effective, you're golden. If it's not, you'll waste money on your entire online advertising program.

Think of your site as the halfway point between your advertising and your front door. And that site has to be good enough to get prospects to pick up the phone and call you. (Or maybe even to rouse themselves out of their chairs and into their cars to come to your place of business.) Done properly, your Web site establishes your business's credibility and allows your prospects to gather information about you. And that information should be the same as your best salesperson would give them in a face-to-face encounter — except it's available on your site 24/7.

In this chapter, you discover exactly what it takes to get an effective Web site built and to keep it current, relevant, and compelling.

Asking the Right Questions before Building Begins

Virtually all your online advertising tactics — your pay-per-click (PPC) and banner ads, your local listings, your Facebook pages, and whatever else — either link directly to or at least feature a link to your site. Savvy Internet users expect this. They expect to be whisked to your URL to read more about your business, to find contact information, and to take advantage of special offers — something that both entices and enables them to take some action or in some other way, engage with your business.

But before we talk about how to create an effective marketing Web site, you need to resolve one pivotal question: Is it better to build your Web site or to get professional help?

Unlike, say, putting together a bicycle for your child, building a Web site involves enough moving parts and pieces that completely doing it yourself is only one of three options — plus a fourth approach that isn't DIY (do-it-yourself) at all. Before we list them, though, here we explain what a few of those parts and pieces are:

✔ **The template:** The template is the basis, or foundation, that your Web site is built on. (Some business owner decide, mistakenly we think, to try building their sites without one. Although technically possible, we definitely don't recommend this unless you happen to have some serious Web-design chops.) Most of these templates are predesigned, but you can customize them however you like. All you need to do is add your own content — and you're on your way.

Practically speaking, a template is really just a kind of frame. The elements of a Web site, such as logos, copy, graphics, and so on, are placed in the different inner frames as desired. These internal spaces can usually be expanded and contracted to fit the stuff that goes in them.

Maybe the designer — who could well be you — wants a big central area for the body copy. Done. Then three smaller spaces where pictures or illustrations will go. Got it. Then narrower, horizontal spaces at the top and bottom of the page for the logo, contact information, and legal disclaimers. Okay. And so on, until the page is (tastefully) filled. An example of a basic template is shown in Figure 4-1, and how that template might then be filled is shown in Figure 4-2.

Figure 4-1:
A template
provides a
framework
into which
the text
and visual
elements of
each Web
page are
placed.

✔ **Hosting:** Obviously, after a site is designed fully, it's somehow has to
be put up on the Web for any and all to access it. Hosting is the process
of getting the site online. Through hosting, you get the site placed on a
third party's computer server (where the site then resides) from which
it can then be called up by users who enter the Web site's URL or click
a link from an ad or an e-mail. This can get a little tricky and is usually
given to someone well-versed in computer skills to get it done (for a fee,
of course — usually $10–$50 a month).

✔ **Maintenance and updating:** No matter how wonderfully designed and
executed a Web site may be, it isn't completely immune from mystery
gremlins that occasionally make it start acting funny, or even stop acting
at all. Making the necessary fix isn't usually all that hard, but finding the
problem — often buried somewhere deep in the site's code — can be a
real challenge. Consequently, a site owner is nearly always best advised
to put a real expert on the case.

Figure 4-2:
By adjusting
the size of
the spaces
in the
template,
you can
customize it
to accom-
modate the
elements
you want
the page to
include.

Updating the material on a site is generally a lot easier than holding the aforementioned gremlins at bay — which is a good thing because updating a Web site is something that is done periodically, no matter how solidly the site is running. A business's product line changes as do its prices and policies. On the technical side, sites have to be able to respond to improvements that search engines make in their own mechanics; plus, new engines may appear on the scene to which a site has to be made compatible. Sometimes you just need to freshen the site with new graphics to keep it looking as current as your competitors' sites. If you choose to update the site, pick a vendor that has easy-to-use editing tools so that you can update your site as quickly and easily as you can update your Facebook page. We list vendors, later in this chapter, that have strong tools to help the novice create and maintain attractive sites.

A local business owner often can do these maintenance and updating jobs (if they've selected the right Web site management tool), but making even a simple update incorrectly (say, by accidentally changing or erasing code) might break the whole site. Here again, the best advice may be to put an expert at the helm.

Reviewing your Web site building options

If you've followed along so far, you're armed with an understanding of all that needs to be accomplished to get a Web site up and running (and to keep it that way). Here we look at the available options:

✔ **Doing it 100 percent DIY, without even so much as a template:** Unless you're a Web site programming and design wizard, we don't recommend the 100 percent DIY approach. For most business owners, the time, hassle, and learning curve are too steep.

✔ **Creating a DIY Web site with a template:** A local business owner can find a good number of free or low-cost, good and thoroughly workable templates (many of which you'll find listed in the section, "Finding a template that best fits your Web site"). This is a credible option for folks who have a tight budget, little spare time, or both. However, this option still leaves you with a lot of things to do on your own (like hosting and maintenance) that you may simply lack the skills for.

✔ **Having a Web site built for you based on a template:** You can hire an outside Web site company (or an independent consultant) to do your site design based on a template you like; after the site is done, this same outside resource takes care of the hosting. You're still often left holding the reins as far as maintenance and updating are concerned, but you have an expertly designed Web site that works properly and reliably. For a lot of local businesses, this approach represents the best balance between cost, time, and results.

✔ **Having a fully custom Web site built for you:** This is pretty much the soup-to-nuts approach. This option is almost always pain-free for a business owner, and consequently, it's the most costly of the options. Actually, here are three sub-methods of getting a custom site built. Each may entail a different level of expense (research to find the one that best fits your budget). These sub-methods are

- *Use an agency or an experienced independent professional.* Of these two, the independent pro will probably be the more costly. But either way, you'll wind up with a high-quality, high-performance site. Be aware, however, that not all custom builders are as competent at building in the right lead capture and conversion methodologies for small businesses as they are at designing, and you may find that you need still other experts to handle these deeper functions.

- *Use a Web design firm that specializes in providing turnkey Web site solutions for local businesses.* These firms can do absolutely everything, including building your site, registering your URL, hosting, providing ongoing maintenance, updating, and sending you a nice card for the holidays. Yes, this is the Rolls-Royce approach, and it's a terrific option for those local businesses that can afford it. You can, however, usually buy somewhat smaller packages of services from these folks if you're willing to, say, handle all future updating — and that can save you some marginal expense.

> • *Use a local online advertising firm that specializes in providing exten-sive Web site services to small business clients.* Note the word *clients.* That's because although these firms can be very good at what they do, most of them won't build and maintain a site unless you also engage them to do your online advertising. (We delve deeper into local online advertising agencies in Chapter 9.) For now, just be aware that where your costs shake out in this kind of combined arrangement can fall almost anywhere on the price spectrum.

Finding a template that best fits your Web site

The possible templates available for your Web site design range from the fairly simple to the fairly complex, and their price points ride the same curve.

Basic templates

Basic Web site templates are ready-made designs that can accommodate pretty much any Web site design. Most of the companies that offer them have large portfolios of templates for you to choose from based on your profes-sion. And nearly all the templates allow for not-too-difficult customization with regard to your text, graphics, and logo. These companies can also help you choose your own domain (your URL), get it registered, and bonus, they may even do so at no cost. What's more, they can generally take care of your site's hosting for a monthly cost of about $10–$50.

The cost of basic templates will likely run from free (yes!) up to around $500. Not surprisingly, the more you pay, the higher template quality you get and the more customizable it will be.

Some of the companies that offer basic Web site templates are

- ✔ **Template Monster:** These folks have one of the largest portfolios of small business templates for you to choose from. Their templates are reasonably priced, from $50–$100. (www.templatemonster.com)

- ✔ **Dreamweaver Graphics:** These inexpensive and easy-to-use Web site templates are based on Adobe Dreamweaver software and range from $20–$75 each. These templates make it pretty simple to house your graphics, text, and logo as well as to change them, if the need arises. Helpfully, business owners who are new to this whole template thing can dive in with a Starter Series. (www.dreamweavergraphics.net)

- ✔ **Homestead:** This company has a portfolio of over 2,000 templates and offers three tiers of Web site packages, ranging from a Starter Package for $4.99 per month to a Platinum Package for $49.99 per month. (www.homestead.com)

✔ **Weebly:** Offers an easy-to-use tool in which you can create your own site for free and include a variety of multimedia elements, such as photo galleries and video. (www.weebly.com)

High-end designs — template and otherwise

Today's high-end designs are a good deal more sophisticated than basic ones and are typically done on a case-by-case custom basis by a professional Web site designer or design team (whether they start from a template or from scratch). These specialists base the design of your site on your personal objectives, and they're in frequent contact to make sure the site design is in line with your expectations. You can include elements, such as video, extensive photo galleries, e-commerce capabilities, appointment request forms, and so on. And the sites produced by these companies may also incorporate coding that can improve your search engine optimization (SEO) efforts (which we cover in Chapter 8). Finally, your design people remain available to you to handle any changes to the site that you want or need to make down the road.

Some of these high-end template providers are

✔ **dzine it:** This company builds customized Web sites for businesses of all types and sizes, and it offers various packages that range from what Budget 1 to specialized sites that are super-sophisticated and priced accordingly. (www.dzineit.net)

✔ **Web.com:** Builds Web sites for individuals and businesses of all industries and automatically optimizes the site for search engines. You can contact them for a free consultation to get a quote based on your specific needs. (www.web.com)

✔ **Officite:** This Web site design firm specializes in producing custom Web sites for medical practices. The Web sites it creates typically allow patients to make appointments through appointment request forms and to view educational videos. Officite also includes *Site Editor,* a standby utility that lets business owners easily make changes to the site, any time they like. These custom sites run from a few hundred dollars to a few thousand, depending on the number of features that are involved. (www.officite.com)

✔ **GNC Web Creations:** Another excellent custom Web site design company, GNC tailors its services to small businesses. GNC even has an Internet marketing consultant on board to ensure that its small business clients generate maximum traffic. GNC can also give you a well-practiced hand in creating your business's brand identity, which usually includes logo design, typeface guidelines, and other proprietary elements. (www.gnc-web-creations.com)

Local online advertising companies

We include local online adverting companies because even though they typically specialize in developing advertising plans for small and mid-sized local businesses, they usually also do Web site development. The primary focus in all cases though is increasing the visibility of a client's site, including making sure that the site shows up prominently in search engine results.

Here are some local online advertising companies (we delve a little more into these in Chapter 9):

- ✔ **Yodle:** www.yodle.com
- ✔ **ReachLocal:** www.reachlocal.com
- ✔ **OrangeSoda:** www.orangesoda.com
- ✔ **WebVisible:** www.webvisible.com

Thinking it through

The fact of the matter is unless you're really eager to create the Web site, don't. A big range of alternative options are available — and odds are that more than one of them will suit your budget.

Assuming (safely, we think) that you aren't already a professional Web designer, your decision as to which approach to take depends on three things:

- ✔ The time you can put into the project
- ✔ The budget you have to work with
- ✔ Your understanding of just how high-end your site really needs to be

For example, if you just opened a locksmith business, a simple DIY-with-template site may be more than adequate to get you started. But if you're a plastic surgeon in Beverly Hills with a reputation to uphold, consider having a site built for you. In either case, make a realistic assessment of the end-product you need.

Before sitting down with a Web consultant, bounce around the Internet and finding other business' Web pages that appeal to you. Print them, take them with you, and say, "Kind of like this, with a little bit of that." You can also find some glossy magazine ads that you like the look of to take with you. (Print ads are often a close cousin to Web pages, design-wise.) Either approach is miles better than showing up empty-handed and telling the consultant something like, "I want it to be symphonic, yet tubular," and expecting the poor designer to figure out what on earth you're talking about.

Finding a professional Web designer

Finding the professional Web site help you need really isn't all that difficult. Ad agencies are usually listed in the phone book as are Web development companies. But being the enlightened soul that you are, you're best off using a search engine.

You can also see who designed your competitors' Web sites, which is becoming increasingly easy as more and more developers are signing their work somewhere on the site (most commonly in the footer at the bottom of one or more pages). You can also get recommendations as to Web professionals from people in your local trade associations who may be using those professionals. Today, you can even find regional associations of Web professionals, and they're often listed on search engines and/or in Web provider directories.

After you find a few potential designers and/or developers, ask to see the sites they've designed or built for others. And by all means, ask for references and then contact those references before you hire them.

Web provider directories

Here are a few Web provider directories to get you started, whether you're looking for a full-service company or individual specialists, such as designers:

✔ Web designer directories:

- *Web Design Directory:* www.designdir.net
- *WebDesign Finders:* http://webdesignfinders.net
- *Web Site Design Directory:* www.web-designers-directory.org

✔ Design firm directories:

- *DesignFirms:* www.designfirms.org
- *Xemion Designer Directory:* www.xemion.com
- *TopDesignFirms:* www.topdesignfirms.com

Understanding Your Site's Role in Your Overall Strategy

Imagine it's spring, things are blooming, everything smells nice, and most important, it's prom time. If you own a limousine service, prom is pretty much to you what taxes are to accountants: Big and competitive.

Say a high school senior wants to hire a limo to chauffeur him and his date to the prom. He immediately goes to the Internet, fires up a search engine, and — lo and behold — your business comes up first in the local listings. Perfect! This young hero clicks through to your site. And then . . . well, just what happens is the reason you need to understand the role of your site in your overall strategy.

Your Web site is integral to your online advertising success. If the advertising tactics we discuss in Chapter 2 are the spokes of a wheel, your Web site is the hub — the central point where everything comes together and your crucial *lead capture* (a concept we discuss in Chapter 3) takes place. This state of affairs in which all the components of your online advertising work together — enmeshed and in sync — is *integrated marketing,* and that's what makes the whole of your efforts greater than the sum of its parts.

Even in a small local business, your Web site has to succeed on a number of levels if the online advertising dollars you spend are going to bear fruit. Why? Because what's the point of working (and spending) hard-to-drive, well-qualified prospects to a site that then disappoints them or fails to instill confidence in your company? Lose those folks at this pivotal point, and they'll likely never come back — and your entire advertising effort will have been reduced to sound and fury, signifying nothing.

That being the case, here are three things your Web site needs to accomplish if your online advertising is going to be successful:

- ✔ **Catch and hold attention:** From the headline, to the photos, to the fonts, to the design and the copy, everything about your site has to be made appealing to the audience you're after. If you're that limo company owner, show a picture of your white, 47-foot-long Hummer. If you're a landscaper, show a photograph of your latest work when the grass is green and the flowers are in bloom. This is the same with all the other elements of your site; they have to tell visitors, "Wow, you've come to the right place!"

- ✔ **Instill confidence:** Engage your customers with what you have to offer, and give them great confidence in your abilities. Some of the things that nearly always instill confidence are before-and-after photos, testimonials from satisfied customers, favorable reviews, and the logos of trade association you're affiliated with. (You can find more on this in Chapter 5.) Make it immediately clear what you can do for them — in short, sell them on the benefits of doing business with you. (After all, no one's really going to care why you went into the awning business; they just want to know that your products are great at keeping them out of the sun.) Provide useful information that's easy for visitors to find — and make it as interesting as you possibly can.

✔ **Get visitors to take action:** Here's where the proverbial rubber meets the hypothetical road because you want your prospects to take some concrete action — whether it's calling you, signing up for an e-newsletter, or booking an appointment online. Whatever the action is that you've convinced them to take, you've moved them one step closer to becoming real, dollars-and-cents-spending customers.

Having a conversion strategy

A *conversion strategy* is — prepare to be shocked — the strategy you use to convert your site visitors into leads and your leads into sales. Determining what conversion strategy you want to use starts with identifying your Web site's primary goal. What's the one overriding action you want people to take upon visiting your site? To call you? Fill out an online form? Subscribe to a newsletter? Come to your location? Answer that question, and everything else starts to fall into place because your answer will direct you straight to

✔ **Using a clear call-to-action (CTA) strategy:** A CTA is simply a prompt for prospects to take a specific action, and you need to put CTAs throughout your site. Say you want your site's visitors to fill out a form; put that form (or at least links to it) on most or all your pages. Doing so is like dropping baited fishhooks off the side of a boat: The more of them you put in the water, the better your chances are of a catching what you're after.

✔ **Making it easy for people to take the desired action:** Don't make visitors to your site jump through hoops to take the action you want them to take. Asking for too much information or placing too many demands on their patience (like making them go from one page to another to another to complete a form) will turn them off and send them away.

Say you're an electrician and you want your site to generate sales leads, which in turn requires visitors to fill in a form with their contact information. Put that form on every page of your site (rather than making your prospects have to navigate to it) and keep the information you ask for both simple and brief (pretty much just their name, phone number, and e-mail address).

✔ **Providing an offer to reward their action:** Offer visitors something of value as an enticement to act. This could be a free consultation, a special discount on a product or service, or even a zippy, free T-shirt. Whatever the prize is, the bigger and better your offer, the greater the likelihood that your prospects will act and that you'll boost your conversion rate.

One tried-and-true method of enhancing the perceived value of an offer is to tag it with an actual value. For example, if you own a day spa that offers Swedish massages and you want to offer prospects a free 20-minute session, express it as Sign Up Now for Your Free Massage — a $40 Value! rather than just Sign Up for Your Free Massage. Forget about trying to fathom the psychology of it all — doing this just works.

Knowing what to measure and why

Knowledge is power, and you'd be amazed how much knowledge about your customers and your market you can gather from your Web site. You can, for instance, figure out where your prospects are coming from, how they're finding you, and even what they do while they're actually on your site. When you know these important things, you can use what you find out to make your site — and your ad spending — even more effective.

We discuss tracking, measuring, and reporting in Chapter 6, but for now, you need a broad sense of just what — and how much — your Web site can tell you. Namely, your site can help you

- **Identify what your users like (and dislike) about your site:** Web analytics tells you which pages on your site get the most traffic as well as the site's most common entry and exit pages. You can then use this data to refine and optimize your site. Knowing the most common exit page is especially useful because it poses the simple question: Why? How can that page be made more interesting, more compelling, and a better gateway to other pages on your site? Solving just the exit page problem alone can do wonders for your site's effectiveness.

- **Find out where your traffic comes from and why:** Are search engines your site's biggest source of traffic? Or are you benefiting from unsuspected on-ramps from other, complementary Web sites? Or maybe you're getting a bunch of folks from one of the local industry blogs. Whatever you discover will help you make your primary source of traffic one to exploit even further and spur you to make your secondary sources more productive.

- **Determine whether your lead generation efforts are working:** Did your last e-mail blast produce the number of form completions you were hoping for? Is the new online form you're using to get people to sign up for a free estimate converting prospects into leads? Or are more people contacting you by phone after visiting your site? Answer questions like these, and you'll know what to fix and what to leave as is.

- **Evaluate the effectiveness of your online advertising:** If, for instance, you're spending a lot on search engine ads and keyword buys, you want to know which ones are performing for you and which aren't. Here again, Web analytics ride to the rescue and point you toward better ads or keywords, or at least a smarter allocation of your advertising dollars.

Having even a rough idea of the sort of measurements you want to take before your site is built makes taking those measurements easier down the line. For example, you can design and arrange your site's content into independent chunks, or *modules,* each of which are relatively simple to measure to find out whether it's working hard or sleeping on the job. In the latter case, swap in better, more productive modules without doing a major site overhaul.

Creating a Framework for Success

Creating a strong and effective local business Web site is often a lot like designing and writing a sales brochure. In either case, start by figuring out what you want to say and how to portray your product or service offering in the best light. Then, group these thoughts and ideas into logical categories of information and arrange them within the space you have. Finally, add color and graphical elements like your logo, prominently display your address and phone number somewhere, and you're pretty much done.

One difference between a brochure and a Web site though, is that the latter is subject to certain conventions that users expect from any site they visit and will automatically expect from yours. For example:

- ✔ **Clicking the company's logo will (almost always) take you back to the home page.** That doesn't mean you don't also include a Home link on the pages of your site, just that you better make sure visitors can go home via the logo route as well.

- ✔ **Business Web sites almost always have an About page that allows users to read about the company whose site they're visiting.**

- ✔ **Sites generally have a Contact Us page, and those that don't, need one.** You want to give prospects as many access routes to your business as possible, so consider some sort of Contact Us page a must.

Of course, certain attributes are unique to the online medium, and interactivity is one of the most important. By letting users interact directly with the business behind the site — and/or with other users via a live chat — they become significantly more involved in the site, and that can only be good for business.

The following sections take a closer look at the elements that comprise an effective local business Web site and show how each of them needs to function.

Selecting, registering, and hosting a URL

Domain names, or *URLs (Web addresses),* provide the identity of a Web site. Each one is unique, and at this point, a lot of the best names have already been taken — which means that choosing your URL might be harder than you'd think.

Ideally, you want to pick a URL that's the same as your business's name, or a shortened version of it. Failing that, a URL that's extremely representative of your business is okay, though not great. (Dora's Pets, for example, would love to use www.doraspets.com, but could probably make do with www.doraspetstore.com.) Go too far beyond that, and no one will associate your site with your business and then, what's the point?

Make your URL easy to say, spell, type, read, and above all, remember. For example, www.socks.com is good (though probably not available), but www.fuzzythingsinsideyourshoes.com is silly.

You also have to decide what you want your *top-level domain name* to be. This is the name extension or suffix that each site has attached to it. Everyone wants the old standby .com as their extension, but it may not be available for your URL. That's why you see more and more sites that end in .net, .org, .us, or even .biz. The suffix really isn't that big a deal as long as you can somehow impress on the public consciousness that your site has a different extension than .com.

After you settle on the domain name you want to use, you need to find out whether it's available. When you have an available URL in hand, you're almost home free. All you need to do is register it and get it hosted, neither of which is particularly tough. *Register* simply means taking ownership of the URL, which generally costs from $10–$30 a year. *Hosting,* meanwhile, is the process of retaining space on a server that provides connectivity to the Internet.

And the really great news is that a lot of domain-name registrar companies can handle the name-checking, registration, and hosting jobs for you, and they don't charge you very much for the service (figure around $13 a month for the whole package). Some of the better registrar/hosts are

- ✔ **Register.com:** www.register.com
- ✔ **GoDaddy.com:** www.godaddy.com
- ✔ **Network Solutions:** www.networksolutions.com
- ✔ **Active-Domain:** www.active-domain.com
- ✔ **Domainmonster.com:** www.domainmonster.com
- ✔ **FatCow Web Hosting:** www.fatcow.com
- ✔ **FastDomain.com:** http://hosting.fastdomain.com
- ✔ **Lunarpages:** www.lunarpages.com

Finding the perfect URL

Here are some things to know and keep in mind when you set out on the Great URL Hunt:

✔ Keep your URL short and sweet.

✔ Make it memorable; don't use hyphens or numbers unless you're being held at gunpoint.

✔ Although it's important to pick a URL (if possible) that's built on or around your company name, it's okay to think beyond your name and if possible, to snap up additional URLs that may drive business your way. For example, if you're Joe's Pizza, you're going to want `joespizza.com` (or `.net` or `.biz`). But if calzones are a specialty you're known for, you might also want to register `joescalzones.com`. Even if you don't use this alternative right away, it may come in handy for a special promotion at a later date.

✔ Don't forget the social sites. For instance, you could also register on Facebook (maybe with something like `www.facebook.com/joespizza`). Be aware though that Facebook requires a business to have 1,000 fans before it'll give you a URL, and some other social sites have similar restrictions.

✔ If someone improperly — repeat, *improperly* — owns the URL you want and that URL is logically connected to your business, you can initiate legal action, preferably with an attorney who's familiar with Internet-related law. (When the Web first started exploding, several dastardly squatters bought thousands of domain names that other companies would naturally want, hoping to extort huge amounts of money from them to get the URLs back. Laws were passed quickly saying that individuals couldn't legitimately register a trademarked company or product name.)

✔ Because registering domains is pretty inexpensive to do, consider protecting yourself against competition by owning as many top-level variations as you can; for instance, not just `luckyplumbing.com`, but also `luckyplumbing.org`, `luckyplumbing.net`, and `luckyplumbing.biz`.

✔ Consider buying disparaging variations of your domain name. A really disgruntled customer might register `joespizzasucks.com` — or some other painful and embarrassing URL twist. But you can beat them to it, provided you can imagine yourself in their place and just for a moment, think like a Neanderthal. Then register what you come up with.

✔ Including your service, city, or other relevant keywords in your domain name (such as `joespizzadenver.com`) can help boost your *search engine optimization* (SEO), a subject we dive into in Chapter 8.

Mapping out your information

When you have a URL, you're ready to start conceiving your Web site. Start by developing an outline that's an overview of the pages within a Web site, or a *site map*. This may sound like a pain, but it keeps you organized and on track, both of which you can't afford not to be.

The site map includes a list of each section you want on the site (more on this in a bit), along with a description of the content that will appear on each page. This map also describes, in as much detail as you can muster, what features — such as video or a sign-up form — will go on the site and where.

It's important that your site map is accessible from somewhere on the site, acting as a sort of Table of Contents. Most folks put their site map in the form of an outline, with the pages arranged by topic and include a link to the site map in the footer of the home page. This gives visitors a good overall picture of how the site is organized and clearly defines what resources the Web site has to offer. Figure 4-3 shows an example of a site map.

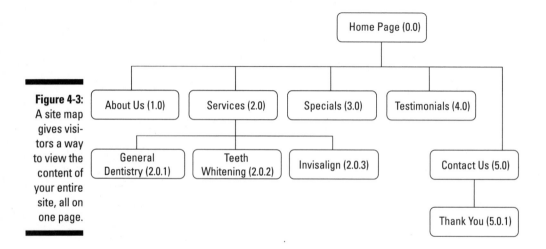

Figure 4-3: A site map gives visitors a way to view the content of your entire site, all on one page.

The home page

Your home page is your Web site's front door; it's where people will arrive when they enter your URL into their browser. The home page's primary purpose is to present a strong sense of what your business is all about. Need we add that, consequently, it's very important to get the execution of your home page 100 percent right?

Typically, visitors to your home page find

- ✔ Your company logo
- ✔ A brief description of what your business does (which is sometimes also referred to as your *elevator pitch*)
- ✔ A menu-type section that lays out the major content areas of your site (such as Products, News and Events, Contact Us, and so on)
- ✔ Plenty of links to content within your site so visitors can get easily to where they want to go

In essence, you can think of your home page as the crossroads of your site, the central point from which all roads lead to somewhere interesting and informative that makes visitors want to be customers. Figure 4-4 shows an example of a well-designed home page.

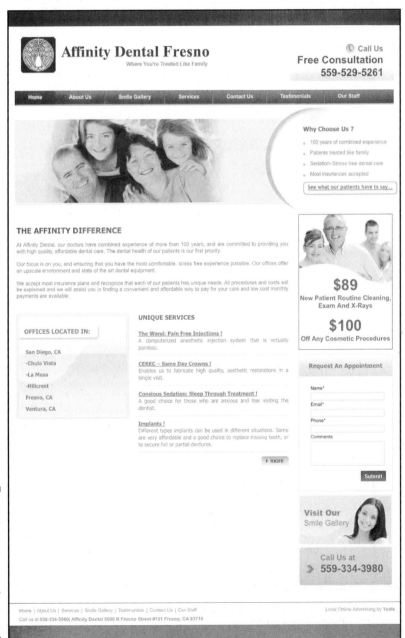

Figure 4-4:
The home page is where visitors can access all the other pages on your site.

Landing pages

Because local business Web sites focus primarily on generating leads, set up pages for people who clicked through to your site from your (stunningly effective) online advertising. These are the pages that visitors coming to you from online advertising will land on, hence the term *landing pages.* You can consider them the side doors into your site, and like the side doors in most houses, they get a lot of traffic passing through them. An example of a landing page is shown in Figure 4-5.

Figure 4-5:
A typical landing page.

What makes landing pages distinct from your home page is that they're the logical extension of the ad that your prospects rode in on. So although your home page gives a good overview of your business's many attributes and abilities, a landing page gets right to a specific point. Landing pages also typically provide visitors with an opportunity — usually via some kind of sign-up form through which they can take you up on some kind of offer — to convert themselves into leads.

Here's an example: You're a dentist who specializes in teeth whitening, and one of your PPC keywords is *teeth whitening*. When someone clicks your PPC ad, it only makes sense to bring her directly to the page on your site that gives specific information about teeth whitening rather than make her navigate to that information from your home page. Your landing page might even include a first-visit offer of some kind to motivate these prospects to take action.

Nine times out of ten, a landing page is about one product or service that you provide, and in that sense, it's the real meat-and-potatoes of your business. So, if you're a local hardware store, one landing page might be about the array of tools you have for sale, one about the equipment you rent out, and one about the lawnmower tune-up service you provide.

Because landing pages are so important — not only for lead capture but also from an organic search standpoint — we talk a lot more about them in Chapter 5.

The About page

The About (or sometimes About Us) page is a fixture on most business Web sites, and for good reason. Remember that you want your Web site to create and solidify a relationship with a customer. Therefore, spend some time establishing your credibility and creating rapport with your prospect — and the About page is where to do it.

This is particularly true when you're focused on selling a service because that usually entails a long-term relationship with a customer than the simple (and often quicker) product sale. In either case, relationship-building is important, which is why you use your About page to tell folks who the owners of your business are, how long you've been doing what you do, and how you view the value of the product or service you provide. You can also use this space to show pictures of you and your staff. Here you become an actual person for visitors to feel good about dealing with.

The Product or Services page

The Products or Services page presents specific descriptions of what you offer. If you're a dentist, your Services page (which you might choose to call Dental Procedures) would most likely include details about cleanings, composite fillings, veneers, bonding, crowns, and so on. If you're a power-tool dealer, on the other hand, your Products page would probably include a roster of the Black and Decker, Skil, and DeWalt tools you carry. You might also use your Product or Services page to tell prospects about your delivery procedures and any guarantees or warranties you provide.

The Testimonials page

Having a Testimonials page is optional, but it can be highly effective in establishing your business's credibility. Ask your satisfied customers (of whom you no doubt have legions) to scribble down some nice things they have to say about your company that you can then post (with permission, of course) on your site to convince new prospects that folks just like them have found you a great source of whatever it is you're a great source of. The more testimonial you can put on your site, the better. They just work.

A Gallery or Portfolio page

A Gallery or Portfolio page is a near-must for service businesses whose work has a highly visual aspect to it. Are you a bathroom and kitchen remodeler? Put up before and after photos of some of your jobs. Ditto for landscapers, house painters, and even dentists. Before and after images can make an extremely powerful and memorable point — and also do wonders for your credibility.

The Contact page

A Contact (or Contact Us) page is essential, no matter what you're selling. Include your phone number, your physical and e-mail addresses, and a short contact form where the prospect can provide his name, phone number, and e-mail address. The Contact page gives people a variety of ways to reach you, and that makes it a rock-solid must. Figure 4-6 shows how a Contact page might appear.

The footer

The *footer* is the content that appears at the bottom of each page of your Web site (refer to the earlier figures in this chapter — each sample page includes a footer at the bottom). Here most users expect the fine print, such as legal information about terms and conditions, privacy policies, and so on. Most footers provide immediate links or shortcuts to other areas of the site.

Inclusion of these links or shortcuts can be a big help to prospects who want to burrow into your site without scrolling up the page to the standard menus. Commonly, the links/shortcuts provided in the footer are

- Customer Service
- Satisfaction Guarantee
- Terms and Conditions
- Privacy Policy
- Site Map

The footer is also where a lot of Web designers and developers leave their signatures as a link that connects to their own Web sites, just in case visitors want to, you know, hire them or something.

Figure 4-6: A Contact page typically displays your e-mail, physical address, and your business phone number.

Do your customers have your number?

For many local businesses — especially one- or two-person operations — you may be tempted not to put a contact phone number on the Web site and just provide an e-mail address instead. Posting a phone number means that someone has to be available to take incoming calls, which can be a bit labor-intensive.

Resist this temptation. For every good reason you may have to omit a phone number, you have a whole bunch of prospective customers who'd rather talk to you than use e-mail. And they have their reasons:

✔ A phone call that someone makes is relatively anonymous. She doesn't have to give you her name, so you can't bother her in the future.

✔ Businesses that are exceptionally slow in responding to e-mail inquiries have given

e-mail use a bad name. People are on your site now, they're interested now, they have a question now, and they may even be ready to buy now. Respond a week or even a day later, and that train may have already left the station.

✔ People like using the phone because sometimes their questions are too complicated to state properly in written form, and it's going to take a conversation with you to get them answered fully. (Plus, a conversation is a great way to start building a prospect's trust and confidence in you.)

In a nutshell, the phone is your friend, and you may just be shafting yourself if you take it out of the mix. The moral: Make sure your phone number is *prominently* displayed on your site.

The privacy policy

Most businesses put their privacy policy in the footer, although some feel it's important enough to have its own page. In either case, having a privacy policy has become increasingly important as more and more disreputable people have figured out how to use a company's Web site to grab the addresses of innocent folks whom they can then harass.

Your privacy policy discloses how you plan to use any customer data that you collect from prospects while converting them into leads. This includes information you get from e-mail sign-ups or any other online forms that you use. For example, if you collect someone's e-mail address, let that person know you won't share it willy-nilly with other parties. Helpfully, several privacy policy generators can supply you with a free policy language that's been well-established as sound and effective. A couple of these are

✔ **Direct Marketing Association:** www.dmaresponsibility.org/PPG

✔ **FreePrivacyPolicy.com:** www.freeprivacypolicy.com

Setting the Mood: The Right Look and Feel

Your business competes for every potential customer in your market — and so does your Web site. That means your site had better look like a prime contender — no sloppy graphics, shabby layouts, typos (especially typos!), or poor color choices. Any of those just look, frankly, awful — and makes you look unprofessional at best.

Your site has also to feel right, which means welcoming, yet highly efficient. The average consumer is savvy and short on time. So you have to make it easy for her to learn more about your business and your specific products and services. The Golden Rule is to design your Web site from your customer's perspective, not from yours — and that means making it extremely clear, logical, and easy to use.

Look and feel basics

The following points can help you decide how your site needs to look and work:

- ✔ **Think of your logo as a jumping-off point.** What does your logo say about your business? What colors does it use? What personality does it convey? If your business is a person, would that person be friendly? Aggressive? Sophisticated? Down to earth? Does your logo reflect that? If not, get help — fast.

- ✔ **Use color wisely.** If you already have a great logo, chances are it has some colors in it, and if so, you're probably well on your way to figuring out what colors to use throughout your Web site. Follow that impulse because the right colors can help tie together your site nicely. If your logo is black and white, pick some other suitable colors; it makes a world of difference. Imagine what sort of colors your customers want. A law firm might go for grays and dark blues to suggest solidity and trustworthiness, whereas a florist might opt for bright, vibrant colors to suggest beauty, health, and growth. And so on. Oh — and people have used black type on a white (or very, very light) background for eons because it's eminently legible. Don't force your customers to read, blue type on a purple background, or you run the risk of making your customers, quite literally, sick.

- ✔ **A picture says a thousand words.** Imagery has long been known to communicate with great power, so use photos or illustrations to enrich and enliven the information you present. Not only are pictures often more involving than language, they also allow would-be customers to visualize how well a particular product or service will serve them in reality.

✔ **Keep it easy on the eyes!** Like the black-text-on-white-background rule, some things just work and other things just don't. *Serif* fonts (the ones with little hooks and swirls hanging off the characters) read very well only if they're large, whereas *sans-serif* fonts (the letters without any doodads) are easy to read in any size. Don't use too many different fonts or font sizes on your site pages. Establish a simple hierarchy of sizes, depending on the importance of the words, and use two different fonts at most. For instance, decide that your *headline* (the copy at the top of the page that announces what the page is about) will always be the largest size, the subheads that set off sections will be the next largest, and the body text will be the smallest font size.

✔ **Make contact information clearly visible.** Make sure your site's visitors can contact you easily. Give them your e-mail address, your business phone and fax numbers, your physical address (and mailing address if it's different), and any other relevant information (like your store or phone-answering hours). And make sure this information is highly visible on — and easily accessible from — *every* page of your site.

✔ **Add a personal touch.** Include photos of your office, your staff, and your company mascot. (*Hint:* Weasels make lousy company mascots.) On the other hand, don't go overboard. The point is to put a face behind the name, without getting too chummy. This is one of those subjective areas where you recognize the right balance when you've struck it.

Common Web site design mistakes

Make sure you avoid the following mistakes when you're planning and designing your site's look and feel:

✔ **Don't get addicted to glitz.** In a nutshell, don't put in anything that gets in the way of the sale or otherwise causes confusion, especially if it's gratuitous. Graphically speaking, the best advice we can offer is when in doubt, leave it out.

✔ **Don't be too formal.** Use every day, conversational language. The more relaxed prospects feel on your site, the greater the chance they'll buy from you. Remember that the Internet is a two-way medium. Hold up your end of the conversation by writing the same way that you speak — and don't, as grandmothers everywhere used to say, put on airs.

✔ **Don't be too folksy.** Adopting an aw-shucks tone may help you sell a jackknife, but not orthodontia. Write as you speak, but also as your *customers* speak.

✔ **Don't be long-winded.** Make your sentences short, punchy, and to-the-point. Use bullets whenever possible. Try to make the reader's eye flow down the page rather than across it. People's eyes are naturally drawn to text that's set apart from the rest.

✔ **Don't be disorganized.** Place important information at the top of the page, such as calls to action, promotions, or other key information. Put the good stuff too far down and you may as well leave it out altogether.

✔ **Don't jam in too much information on any one page.** You can add as many pages as you want to your Web site. Spread out the information you present into readable, comprehensible chunks.

✔ **Don't be indirect.** This is no place to get cagey. Make sure that customers can easily find the information they're after by using clear menus, site maps, and section/page titles. Don't hide your offer — or hide the vehicle that people can use to respond to it — in some easy-to-overlook place.

✔ **Don't be unbalanced.** Too many graphics can frustrate a reader's thirst for information. Too much text can put him into a stupor. As in all things, so the ancient Greeks told us, the Golden Mean is what you should strive for — a nice, workable, attractive *balance.*

✔ **Don't let your Web site content get old.** You'll often run across a business site in which it's obvious that no one's refreshed the content since it was first put up. Talk about looking irrelevant. Revisit your own site regularly and see what needs updating. (Then, of course, actually update it.) That gives your customers a reason to keep checking to see what's new.

Striking the Perfect Balance between Information and Promotion

To be truly good, a Web site has to be both informational and promotional. Where do you draw the line between the two? Well, it isn't an exact science, but some ways of looking at are

✔ **The information you present must be useful and actionable:**

- *Useful means that information is useful to the customer.* Useful really amounts to saying that something has a benefit.

  You can easily get benefits confused with features. Say you sell home theatre equipment. One of the things your Web site talks about is that all the audio and video cables you sell have gold-plated connectors. That's a feature. But what sort of benefit does gold plating provide? The answer is that gold is an extraordinarily good conductor of electricity — so it gives superior clarity to audio and video signals. See? Gold plating is the feature. Better clarity is the benefit.

Some sellers of products or services think that just stating the features of what they offer is enough. However, until you carry this a step further by stating what benefit that feature creates, your information isn't really useful.

- *Actionable means that the information must be something that creates interest on the prospect's part to do something — and therefore, to get involved with your local business.* Touting gold-plated cables that make for clearer signals is just academic unless you carry them, sell them, and have them in stock for immediate delivery (or can get them in quickly). If you do, your customers now have something they can act on: They can stop in and pick up some of those great cables or maybe even have you install them.

✔ **The promotion you use to induce action must be relevant.**

Promotion is simply what sellers of goods or services use to inspire potential customers to act. Promotion is usually an offer of some kind that customers can take advantage of if they act — and act soon. But that offer must be relevant to the consumer. Buy a Set of Gold-Plated Cables and Receive a Free Squirrel Pelt won't induce much activity. On the other hand, Buy a Set of Gold-Plated Cables Online Today and Get 20% Off is a winner because it's highly relevant.

When in doubt, keep the obvious in mind: Getting something for nothing or at a substantial savings is always relevant — so much so that any other kind of offer doesn't even come close. People like money. Give them some of yours (or something that has monetary value) and they'll give you some of theirs. If you want people to take a specific action, put a relevant offer — usually a monetary one — on your site to induce exactly that action.

Maybe you think that much of what's in this section is too elementary to need saying, much less explaining. Remember what we warn about earlier in this chapter: When you step into online marketing, your Web site can easily end up as an endless empty canvas that you fill with any and all kinds of self-serving ego food. That's absolutely the wrong approach, but it happens far too often. (One telltale sign that you've gone over the edge is if your About page runs longer than your Products page.)

The key is to stay disciplined. What's the benefit of what you sell and how can you induce people to buy it? If virtually every page of your Web site isn't answering one of those two questions, look at that page again. Odds are you'll find it's just cluttering the canvas.

Chapter 5

When You've Hooked Your Customers, Reel 'Em In!

*I*n Chapter 4, we describe how to create an effective Web site for your business. But just having a site doesn't get you very far. What you actually put on the site has to work hard if you're going to succeed at converting visitors into customers.

Among the hardest working Web site elements are landing pages. We talk a bit about these little gems in Chapter 4, but here, we look at exactly what makes them tick and succeed. And why are they that important? Because although not a lot has officially been published on the matter, in our experience working with thousands of small businesses, landing pages can increase conversion rates by 8–10 percent over the rates generated by home pages alone. (In case you're keeping score, that increase represents nearly double the normal home page rate.) And who can overlook the potential to land up to twice as much business with relatively little effort?

But that's just the start. Several other, commonly used site elements can play a big part, too. These range from the lowly-but-ever-potent coupon, to chats, to online video. Getting these site elements up and working doesn't take all that much time or expense, but their combined effect can be amazing. In fact, you could actually double your conversion rate (again!) after you get your site running on all its various and hyper-effective cylinders.

The key is that every site element you use has to go toward engaging your prospects. Engage them, and you can convert them. Convert them, and you can get them to buy whatever you're selling. Before you can cross that particular goal line, you need to capture some specific information from them. We discuss just what that information is and then describe the ways you can use it to (hurrah, hurrah) close the deal.

Implementing Proven Landing Page Techniques

When any technology has been around long enough, it becomes apparent through use that some ways of working with that technology are effective and others aren't. Bundle together the things that work, and you have what stuffy folks refer to as *best practices*.

Defining landing page and home page

A *landing page* is a type of Web page that someone automatically goes to when they click an online ad or type in a URL they discovered elsewhere. Landing pages are designed to be highly relevant to whatever messaging got the consumer to the site in the first place. (See Figure 5-1 for an example.)

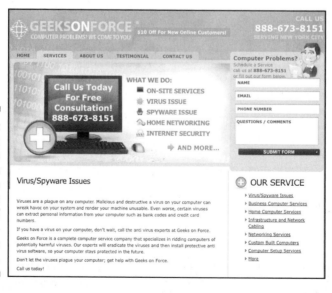

Figure 5-1: A landing page gives your Web site visitors immediate access to the information they're after.

The logic behind landing pages is pretty unassailable. Something about your ad — some language, some offer, and so on — motivated consumers to visit your site, and the landing page they come to picks up right where the ad left off. The subject is the same but is explained in greater detail. The page seamlessly continues the train of thought that the ad sparked, and that in turn, keeps customers right on track to where you want to take them.

A *home page* is usually the main page — or, as the techies would say, the highest level — of a Web site. The home page offers a global view of the entire site, which makes it a sort of visual table of contents. Visitors to your home page use the links they find there to get to more specific sub-pages of the site. The home page, therefore, is the central point from which all paths lead to somewhere else, as shown in Figure 5-2.

Simple. The home page is about familiarizing visitors with your business as a whole. A landing page is about converting customers who want to know about a single facet of your business that attracted their attention when they saw it in one of your ads. The former is general. The latter is specific.

Figure 5-2: A home page is the hub of a Web site.

Using the power of landing pages

Landing pages are consistently effective at increasing conversions for several reasons:

- **Specificity and relevance:** A visitor who follows a link in (or from) an ad — be it a traditional media ad, search ad, banner ad, or some other kind — immediately hits the landing page and finds exactly what she's looking for right off the bat. Because that page gives specific information about whatever initially spurred the visit, it's highly relevant to the visitor. She gets the info in an instant — no muss, no fuss — and that leads to increased conversions.

- **Simplicity:** Because landing pages are so specific, they can also be very concise, which tends to keep a visitor's eyes on the prize (the prize in this case is the call to action). The page aims a visitor straight at the conversion method — the call or click — you want him to use. A home page has lots of stuff on it, and that equals a lot of potential for distraction. But a landing page has but one thought in its head, a thought that can't be mistaken or easily veered from. All that's left is for the visitor to take the action you've specified on the page, and many visitors do.

- **Easy to test and optimize:** The elements of a good landing page are so specific and so few, it's a simple matter to test them and then to swap out what isn't working particularly well for something more effective. Analytical tools, which we discuss in Chapter 6, can tell you exactly which elements on the page are pulling their weight in generating conversions. You can even track the number of phone calls the page inspires. And as you find out more, you can consistently improve your page — and, of course, your return on investment (ROI). Among the elements you can test are

  - Different headlines

  - Different graphics, including photos

  - Different offers; for example, Buy One, Get One Free; Free Shipping; or 40% Off

Understanding the elements of the landing page experience

The elements that make a truly effective landing page are

- ✔ **The call to action:** Every landing page needs to tell the visitor how he can act now. A good call to action

  - Uses verbs that suggest the action you want the reader to take, such as *call, buy, visit, read, sign up,* and the like.

  - Adds the subject of the offer and a benefit of that offer. Call Now for Our Time-Saving Widgets, for instance, touches all the bases: *Widgets* is the subject, *Time-Saving* is the benefit, *Call Now* is the action the reader's being asked to take.

  - Imparts a sense of urgency that makes readers want to act now instead of tomorrow or next week, such as Offer Expires Tomorrow (assuming the offer actually does expire tomorrow) often works well.

- ✔ **Value messaging:** Every landing page needs to explain clearly, even bluntly, the value of your business and/or your offer. (See the discussion of your unique selling proposition [USP] in Chapter 3.) State what makes you unique, or at least special enough to make readers want to act on your offer and start engaging with your company. For example:

  - Are you the fastest or cheapest?

  - Is the quality of your products or services superior to your competitors' quality?

  - Have you been in business longer than your competitors, and as a result, are you smarter, more experienced, more professional than they are?

  - Do you provide some sort of added value (say, a free rosebush with the purchase of six 50-pound bags of mulch)?

  - Are you #1 in your market in terms of sales, customer satisfaction, and repeat business?

- ✔ **The reason to buy:** Every landing page should tell visitors what's in it for them, namely, the features and benefits of what you sell. We provide a feature versus benefit distinction in Chapter 4, but Table 5-1 offers a quick refresher.

Table 5-1	How Features Differ from Benefits
Features	**Benefits**
Your plumbers are always on time.	Customers don't have to wait for you to show up.
Your product is guaranteed for life.	Even if it breaks, customers won't have to pay for another one.
You service your customers 24/7.	Customers can get their problem solved at any hour, on any day.

✔ **Trust and credibility incidentals:** Every landing page is an opportunity to overcome buyer skepticism and build trust. A common way to accomplish this is by including quick (but glowing) customer testimonials, relevant awards, or professional accreditations, such as:

- If you're a member of the Better Business Bureau, add their logo to your pages.

- If you won the Best in Town award from your local newspaper, say so on your landing pages.

- If you've been around for 10, 20, 30, 50 years, or more, say so.

Please note that we call these things *incidentals* because they result from your being in business while not actually being a part of your business. But that doesn't mean they aren't important.

Engaging Customers with Two-Way Communication

Most traditional advertising media provide one-way communication. The TV or radio talks, you listen, end of story. Print ads are equally one-sided. The result is that consumers can't really participate in the conversation and engage with the brand.

That's one key reason why online advertising can be so effective: It really is a two-way street, and your customers can participate in whatever you have going on. Maybe they take part in a poll or a survey you run, use your special calculator to figure out something complicated, post to a bulletin or a blog, or engage in real-time chat.

Understanding and implementing chat

Chat allows two or more Web users to communicate with each other in real time with text. Chat usually takes one of two forms: Live chat and proactive chat.

Live chat

Live chat is often used for sales and customer support. A customer types a question into a space on the Web site and gets an answer back right away. (The reason for the speedy response is that companies usually have a knowledgeable person or two ready to field chat inquiries.) Among the benefits of live chat is that the customer doesn't have to leave the Web site to ask his questions. He doesn't have to pick up the phone or physically visit the company's location. Three other nice benefits are

✔ **Quicker answers than with e-mail:** E-mails (and voicemails) pile up quickly on the company's side of things, and the traffic jams that result can mean that forward progress becomes very slooooowww. But chat gets answered much faster. Type in a one-sentence question, and the answer returns at the speed of typing.

✔ **A paper trail:** The conversations a customer has with a business's representative compile on the screen. At any point, the customer (or the representative) can save or print the entire conversation and have a record in writing.

✔ **Personalizes the business:** Chat goes a long way in letting customers know you care about them and their interests in what you sell. They ask, you answer. They ask more, you answer more. And so it goes. Conversation — even if it's just in the form of text — puts a personality on the business, and what better way to engage a prospect and start building that all-important relationship with them?

Figure 5-3 shows what a typical chat window looks like.

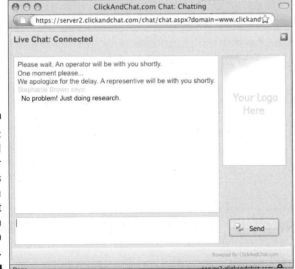

Figure 5-3:
You and your customers chat using a window that appears on your Web site.

Proactive chat

Here's how proactive chat works. A prospect dabbles on your Web site when a pop-up appears that invites him to chat. He doesn't have to perform any action; the opportunity to converse is just presented to him, all ready to go. (Think of it like the old Operators Are Standing By . . . message you used to hear on commercials except in this case, the operator initiates the interaction.) The pop-up is usually accompanied by a small chat window that floats within the browser window and lets the customer decide whether to accept or reject the chat.

The wonders of chat

Making use of two-way conversation has some big benefits. Forrester Research, a company that conducts technology and market research for major corporations, created a sample company with an instant two-way communication chat system to respond to Web site customers who wanted product information. Approximately 75 percent of the chat interactions that occurred represented contact with the company that wouldn't have otherwise happened via phone or e-mail.

Companies with Web sites that include only a phone number and an e-mail address often discover that their Internet customers are impatient with those communication methods. According to another Forrester report, 25 percent of those intending to complete an application for an insurance quote abandoned the idea because they didn't feel that a call or an e-mail to the company would give them enough information to justify applying. Fast as it can be, e-mail is apparently considered by many consumers to be too slow, whereas phone contact is seen as too hit or miss when it comes to reaching the person with the right information.

Put together these two views, and you can see why chat can be a particularly effective way to go — though that doesn't mean that every business can benefit from it. A two-person locksmith shop, for instance, is likely to have people out on calls a good deal of the time, so they aren't available to chat. On the other hand, a large beauty salon probably has a reception staff, any of whom could be the business's designated chatter.

Proactive chat might seem a little too pushy, but it's no more intrusive than what a salesperson does in a typical brick-and-mortar store. In that case, a customer wanders through the store, the salesperson approaches and asks, "Can I help you?" The customer either says, "Yes, I have a question about . . ." or, "No thanks, just looking." Just like in the brick-and-mortar world, after the salesperson talks with the customer online, good things can easily happen.

Raising your conversion rate with chat

When you get customers involved in either kind of chat, your conversion rates can rise significantly. Here's why:

- **The captive audience factor:** The longer visitors engage in a helpful dialogue, the less likely they are to abruptly leave your Web site — and the greater the opportunity for you to initiate or close a sale.

- **Generation of sales leads:** A chatting customer is a lead, pure and simple. In the course of the conversation, you discover the nature and intensity of his interest. From there, it's a small step to asking that customer if you can get back to him later with more information he might find interesting. If he says "Sure," *voila!* You have a live one.

✔ **Plucking customers from the depths of confusion:** Getting a prospective customer straight on the benefit of your product or service does you both a favor. The prospective customer comes away a lot more informed and, probably, a little grateful. In the course of your conversation, not only can you potentially do some real business, but the prospect can also alert you as to any problems she's having with your Web site — problems that you can then promptly fix to make future, site-based interactions with other customers more productive.

Letting the pros set up a chat feature

Chatting may be simple, but setting up the mechanics (such as the computer coding) isn't. The good news is that it isn't expensive to get a chat feature up and running. In some cases, doing so is even free.

Some chat providers worth checking out are

✔ **BlastChat:** www.blastchat.com

✔ **Olark:** www.olark.com

✔ **ClickAndChat.com:** www.clickandchat.com

✔ **WebsiteAlive:** www.websitealive.com

✔ **Activa Live Chat:** www.activalive.com

Helpful and productive as chat can be, here's the downside: Someone has to man it. If your organization doesn't have a designated chatter — an office manager maybe, or someone who's nearly always on a computer — the whole immediacy thing disappears, and your chat feature becomes just another bottleneck. If you're planning to use chat, make sure you have a plan in place to support it.

Using proper chat etiquette

Like just about everything else in life, chat has its own rules of the road. Which is to say, chat demands the proper behavior (although it can be done with your mouth open and your elbows on the desk, so there's two thing you don't have to worry about).

The tips that follow can help you communicate via chat more effectively and by doing so, convert more prospects into paying customers:

✔ **Use a businesslike screen name and avatar:** Funky, funny screen names are fine for casual conversations with your friends, but a business environment requires seriousness. Don't use Zoltan the Crusher of Worlds, just use Phil (assuming your name is Phil). The same goes for any *avatars* (a photo or other graphic that shows next to your screen name) you use. Sorry, exploding ninjas are out. Something related to your business is the way to go. Figure 5-4 shows several business-appropriate avatars, assuming you have a photography business, fruit stand, or landscaping business.

Figure 5-4: Some appropriate avatars.

✔ **Introduce yourself:** At the start of any chat, introduce yourself by name. Giving your title — if you have one — is always a good idea, too. This is really no different than what you do when you initiate a phone call. For example, "Hi, this is Larry Levine from Levine Limousine Service" is good, whereas just saying, "Hi there" doesn't cut it.

✔ **Don't SHOUT:** Some people think that WRITING EVERYTHING IN UPPERCASE is a surefire way to get attention, and it is — if you want people to think you're an idiot. Writing in uppercase is considered shouting, hyper-aggressive, and rude. Unless you're warning of an imminent missile attack, keep your messages in sentence case.

✔ **Avoid jargon, slang, and abbreviations:** Here again, what flies in your personal correspondence doesn't necessarily work in business chats. Jargon, slang, and abbreviations may just make you seem unprofessional or worse, if the customer isn't in on the lingo — and can make the whole conversation way too confusing. On the other hand, if the customer starts slinging the slang, feel free to indulge in it. In that case, you'll come across as seriously cool. But let the customer lead; otherwise, dare to be (a little) dull.

✔ **Don't use custom fonts, text sizes, and colors:** We don't want to burst your balloon on this, but message text in 22-point hot-pink italic doesn't look good and it isn't easily readable. This is no place to get overly creative or make your customer put on shades to cut the glare coming off your fonts. Just stick to standard type/size/color messaging fonts.

✔ **Don't end the conversation without asking for business:** Don't assume that just because you think the chat is over, your customer does. At some point in the conversation, you customer may need a few minutes to compose her next response, so don't go bowling. Stay at your computer until you're absolutely sure the chat has ended. The best way to do that is to summarize the discussion that's gone before, identify any action items that have come up, ask the other person whether she has any more questions, and then ask for business! That doesn't mean asking the prospect whether you can deliver the truckload of wet concrete tomorrow at noon, but it does mean asking whether she wants to make an appointment for a store visit or maybe even a consultation at her home or business. You want to walk away from the conversation with something that brings you closer to a sale. Oh, and whether the prospect accepts or refuses, remember to thank her for her time.

✔ **Monitor your company's live chat conversations:** If someone in your company other than you engages in business chats, review those conversations for purposes of quality control. This isn't spying. This is making sure that your business is properly and professionally represented. Happily, most chat software applications let you store and retrieve transcripts; some of them even send these transcripts to you automatically via e-mail.

Effectively Using Interactive Elements

One proven way to inspire action, improve customer conversion rates, and boost sales is by using *interactive goodies* (or bells and whistles). These can run the gamut from the purely functional to the fun and flashy, though the two most common are

✔ **Online coupons:** Coupons may seem like a throwback, but they still work very hard and very well. Apparently, the get-something-for-nothing-or-at-least-for-less impulse is coded into human DNA. This is excellent news for anyone who's selling anything.

✔ **Online video:** You can offer visitors an immersive multimedia experience that creates interest in and spurs involvement with your business. Plus, putting this kind of thing together can be fun.

Your first response to going the goodies route might be that they're bound to be too expensive or too complicated for a local business to use. Fear not: You'll find that these online technologies are well within the reach of even the most budget-conscious local business.

Online coupons

As more and more value-seeking Americans join the online community, the use of online coupons — like the one shown in Figure 5-5 — is rising exponentially. Coupon use helps incline people to try new products or services and most important, to cheerfully turn over their e-mail addresses and other contact information to the company offering the coupon.

In this brave new Internet world, businesses are also finding new and effective ways to put coupons to work. Often businesses send consumers a coupon by e-mail that they can then print out and take to a store. Coupons delivered in banner ads are another new wrinkle, and not unexpectedly, coupons are now showing up on mobile devices.

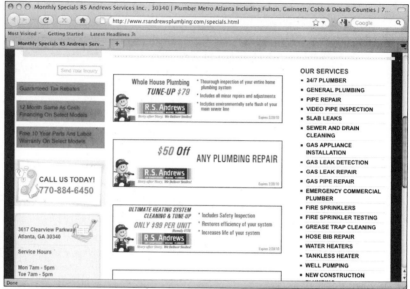

Figure 5-5:
Customers
like online
coupons like
these.

Ah, the power of coupons

Here are a few items you need to consider while you ponder the possible use of coupons for your local business:

✔ *Experian Simmons* (the *Bible* of the advertising industry) reports that 87 percent of all shoppers use coupons.

✔ According to The Nielsen Company, an independent marketing research firm, 95 percent of shoppers like coupons and 60 percent actively seek them out.

✔ Since 2005, online coupon usage has grown 39 percent, according to *Experian Simmons* Research and Coupons, Inc.

✔ The *Wall Street Journal* reports that coupon use rises sharply when the nation's economy declines.

Here are a couple more interesting little tidbits from *Experian Simmons*:

✔ Nearly 58 percent of online coupon users believe that the businesses offering coupons care about keeping them as customers.

✔ More than 70 percent of online coupon users say they'd be willing to provide their e-mail addresses and their first and last names to a business offering a coupon worth $2 or more.

✔ More than 70 percent of online coupon users say they're more likely to open an e-mail if a coupon is offered, and 64 percent are more likely to click a banner ad or search a listing if they know that the Web site is offering a coupon.

Businesses that use online coupons have a lot of good, practical reasons to do so. Here are six of them:

✔ **Online coupons can expand a business's marketing area.** This occurs because consumers will travel significant distances to redeem them (provided they see the coupons as valuable).

✔ **Coupons help entice new customers that have been shopping at competitors' sites.** Consumers will readily break with their routine shopping patterns to take advantage of a good coupon offer.

✔ **Coupons attract new residents of an area.** People who've just moved in are usually in high-consumption mode and are on the lookout for local product and service resources. Not only can coupons turn a newly arrived customer into a long-term one, but they can also help reactivate former customers if a business gives them a solid, value-rich reason to reconsider their earlier defection.

✔ **Coupons often have a ripple effect.** A customer who redeems a coupon for product or service A may consequently become sufficiently pleased with a local business to also buy products or services B and C — at full-profit margin — in the future.

✔ **Coupons build online traffic.** Consumers come to know that a business routinely offers coupons, so they keep returning to the business's Web site, and pretty obviously, the greater the traffic, the greater the potential for additional sales.

✔ **Online coupons are highly measurable.** You can relatively easily track the number of coupons that people have downloaded (and the number of those that have been used) and then judge the effectiveness of the offer. Coupon offers that haven't done as well as expected can then be refined to perform better next time.

Online video

Using online video to connect with and engage your customers is exactly the kind of thing — innovative, creative, and even a tad aggressive — that makes local businesses survive and thrive. Additionally, by posting your videos on sites like YouTube, you can get links to your site that can help search engine optimization (more on YouTube in Chapter 13 and SEO in Chapter 8). As an example of a Web site utilizing video, see Figure 5-6.

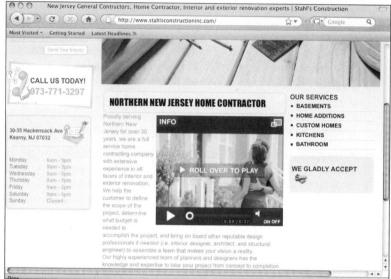

Figure 5-6:
A well-done online video can enhance a visitor's experience with your Web site.

Before you mentally tick off all the reasons why online video won't work for your business, take a close look at the reasons it will:

- ✔ **Video shows you're real:** We aren't talking Hollywood here. For local businesses, slick and polished production quality won't bring you customers because the secret in this case is to be real. A simple, down-to-earth production that lets customers really see you as the earnest company that you are is precisely what generates a personal connection between you and your customers.

  Different experts recommend different lengths for a short-form video, but don't let that confuse you. A good guideline is to aim between 30 seconds and 3 minutes long. Your video needs to be long enough to provide customers with specific information to act on, but not so long that you bore them. Just remember: You don't need to say everything in one little video.

- ✔ **Video doesn't cost much to make:** Local business owners can create effective videos and upload them to the Internet for just a few hundred dollars. Maybe you have a small handheld video camera that you use to capture the cute things your kids do. If not, you can usually rent (or borrow) one. That's virtually all you need.

Although you can easily point a video camera and hit the Record button, a lot more is involved in making an acceptable video. If you have any doubts about your ability as a filmmaker, you're better off having it done by someone with experience. Otherwise, you're likely to wind up with a piece that's pretty embarrassing.

Armed with your trusty video camera, here are five ways you can produce videos that are truly worth producing — and that can significantly move your sales needle:

- ✔ **Use product demonstrations:** Say your business sells lawn care products. Now, a lot of insecticides and weed-control stuff has to be used just right to do their job and produce a lush, beautiful lawn. The proper application of your products is a perfect subject for a video. (Better yet, you could make one application video for each of the kinds of lawn products you sell and then let visitors to your Web site view the video that demonstrates the specific product they're interested in.) In any case, providing this kind of show-and-tell instruction is likely to make a prospect much more likely to buy the product he needs from you. After all, you've already done him a service — and demonstrated that you really know your stuff.

- ✔ **Record your people:** A short video that introduces your staff and briefly profiles them can be an invaluable tool for establishing not just a comfortable familiarity with your employees, but trust in your company as well.

- ✔ **Spotlight your evangelists:** Are you lucky enough to have the kind of special customers who sing your praises to their friends and colleagues? Most businesses do. If so, plant them in front of your camera and ask them to talk. Obviously, you have to ask them very nicely to help you out, but if they're already big fans of your business, getting them to agree shouldn't be difficult. Even if they punctuate their onscreen comments with a lot of "ers" and "uhs," don't worry. Those can always be edited out later to make almost anyone sound brilliantly articulate.

- ✔ **Record special events you're involved in:** Does your business participate in fundraisers? Do you own a bookstore that puts on a Mystery Night every other Thursday? Do you sponsor a float in your town's annual Fourth of July parade? Great. Use video to share those events with your online visitors. As a bonus, your thoroughly winning personality also shines through — plus, you get brownie points for being a such a solid, reputable citizen.

- ✔ **Show prospects just what it is that you do:** Swimming pool owners will be very interested in seeing how your pool maintenance business accomplishes all the scheduled maintenance tasks that you perform. Dog owners will enjoy being walked step-by-step through the dog grooming techniques your pet store offers. And so on. You probably won't have to look far for inspiration either. Just take the most common questions you get from your customers and turn the answers into videos to put on your Web site. Here again, you establish your expertise and build trust. This can be a great way to differentiate yourself from your competitors.

Putting subjects like these into a Web-based video presentation isn't expensive, difficult, or particularly time-consuming. But it is a way to put the video medium to work for you, promoting your business, establishing customer relationship, and generating increased sales.

Of course, not everyone's a Fellini-in-waiting. Maybe you already wonder why the videos you shot on your last vacation came out too dark or too light, or the horizon was always crooked, or the sound was all muffled. And maybe that's making you think, "I'm really not up to this."

Pre-think and pre-plan

Shoestring budgets can produce impressive results, but only if you give the deal a little quality thinking before you take off the lens cap:

- **Try to see the finished video in your mind.** Are green trees in the background, an office setting, a blank wall, or a street in your town? Forage around in your head for what feels right, and odds are you'll know it when you hit on it.

- **Decide whether you'll hand-hold the camera.** A little (make that very little) movement in the camera's visual can be a nice effect. People who make documentaries do it all the time because it creates a certain genuineness and immediacy. If you think your video's going to suggest that you were shooting during an earthquake, use a tripod.

- **Make sure you know your camera and its settings.** Try it out at home. Record video of your family, your dog, a car going by, or the clouds in the sky. Figure out how to gauge the proper exposure (although most video cameras do this automatically). Listen to the sound quality you're getting. Is it too faint? Then move in. Is it muffled and hard to understand? Then, again, either move in or hook up a cheap microphone to that little input found on most video cameras and extend the cord so the mic is closer to the audio source.

- **Don't go nuts with zooming in and out, or panning side to side.** The object is to make a simple, credible presentation about your company and what it does, not to induce nausea.

- **Figure out ahead of time how you'll edit your footage.** Most home computers have at least a simple video-editing program built into them. A lot of inexpensive editing software is also available. *Remember:* As with all things highly technical, when in doubt, ask your kids how to do it.

Getting someone else to do it

Admittedly, everything so far about video may sound just a little too intimidating. Okay; no problem. You can usually find a local videographer or video company located in your zip code. (Hey, here's a wacky idea: You could search for one on the Internet!) On the other hand, even a good, experienced amateur is probably more than up to the job.

If you decide that only a professional will do, however, some great resources are out there. Companies like TurnHere, Jivox, and SpotMixer specialize in producing video for local and small businesses, and offer reliable turnkey solutions for video projects in a variety of formats and durations. They also tend to be modestly priced and excellent at giving you fast turnaround from planning, to shooting, to editing, to uploading onto the Web. Not incidentally, your video will end up looking and sounding really good.

Some quality providers include

- ✔ **TurnHere:** These folks can send one of their pros to your location to shoot custom videos. (www.turnhere.com)

- ✔ **ByteCaster.com:** They also shoot custom videos and are very reasonably priced (around $395 for a video that runs a minute or so in length). (www.bytecaster.com)

- ✔ **Jivox:** Jivox combines stock footage with your own still photographs to make interesting composite videos and offers some services to get your videos distributed as well. (www.jivox.com)

- ✔ **SpotMixer:** They offer the same kind of stock-and-stills video composites as Jivox. (www.spotmixer.com)

- ✔ **Adfare:** Adfare specializes in combining stock footage with your own video footage, which can work out very nicely. (www.adfare.com)

Hiring a pro won't cost you all that much money, especially considering they use their own equipment and editing facilities, so you're saved that expense. What's more, any decent video provider can upload the video onto your Web site.

And the best part of all? You come up with the idea, they sweat the details — and all's right with the world.

Capturing Customer Information

One of the things we keep hammering on is that in order to create customers, you first have to capture leads. Here are two basic ways to do that with your Web site:

- ✔ Use online forms (including, almost always, e-mail opt-in)
- ✔ Use virtual phone services

Online forms

Presenting Web site visitors with an online form to fill out is a proven and highly effective method of lead capture. The subject of the form can be anything from a simple Contact Us message to the acceptance of an offer (Sign Up and Get Your Dog's First Grooming — Free!), to a request for a price quote. The specifics of the offer almost don't matter, as long as it's appropriate to your business.

What does matter, though, is that you capture the information you need. One mistake that some local businesses make is to ask for too much information from visitors. Start asking for things like waist size and last vacation spot, and things can start getting a little creepy — and can promptly send prospects heading for the exit. On the other hand, you obviously need to gather enough information to make the prospect reachable later.

Generally speaking, the most common form fields that local businesses ask prospects to fill in are

- ✔ Name
- ✔ E-mail address (and opt-in check box)
- ✔ Phone number
- ✔ The best time to call

As we discuss in much greater detail in Chapter 10, include an opt-in device when you ask for an e-mail address. The way the law currently stands, you can e-mail someone one time whether he opted in or not. But after that one gimme, you can send e-mails only if you've already (and provably) obtained their permission. A lot of folks get tripped up on this, so it pays to be picky here.

Figure 5-7 shows a typical online form.

Figure 5-7: An online form is an excellent way to capture leads.

You can also ask prospects a few other questions to further enhance the quality of your leads or otherwise help you better gauge their level of interest. A caterer, for example, might ask, "How many people will be attending your event?" A guitar teacher could ask, "Which days or nights are you available for lessons?" A bath remodeler may want to know, "What budget range do you have in mind for the job?" And so on.

Thou shalt not ask too many questions, or thy prospects shall run away.

One other very important field you want to include, however, is a place for your prospects to leave their comments or questions (typically called — what else? — a Comments box). Many people will use it, and what they write can give you some very useful information as to who they are and what they're looking for. You can then address their needs and/or questions personally when you contact them — a great way to demonstrate that you are, indeed, paying attention to them as individuals.

Virtual phone services

Probably since its invention, the phone has been a primary tool for capturing leads with good reason. A conversation remains the best way to build rapport with customers. They not only get information, but they also get a sense of your winning personality and what you'd be like to work with. You get a sharper sense of what your customers are interested in and what their common questions and concerns are.

But a lot of smaller businesses just don't have enough staff available to take calls all day. For these companies, virtual phone services can be a tremendous help. No matter what the size of your business, they can turn your humble little telephone into a rip-snorting, data-gathering colossus.

A *virtual phone service* simply provides a remarkably easy and affordable way to accomplish phone-based online lead capture. (You don't even need to buy any additional hardware.) When you sign up for the service, you immediately get your own toll-free or local-area-code number; this becomes your front door. To really get the most out of such a service, you can sign up for multiple numbers, each of which can be used to track incoming calls from different parts of your Web site or keyed to different offers you've put there. This, in turn, helps you measure just how well your site is performing and to make improvements as needed.

Most virtual phone services offer other features as well. Probably the most popular of these are call logs that give you a complete record of who called, who they asked for, the number they used, the date and time the call was made, the call's duration and even, in some cases, what the result of the transaction was.

If someone called for a free quote but didn't leave a message, you have her number, and you can call her right back. You can listen to a recording of what was said on a given customer call (although the laws in your state may restrict this in some cases). You can have all calls coming from your Web site seamlessly routed to your cellphone, so you don't miss a single opportunity. In other words, no prospect is left to simply wander off.

A few of the more popular virtual phone service providers are

- **RingCentral:** www.ringcentral.com
- **my1voice:** www.my1voice.com
- **eVoice:** www.evoice.com
- **Virtual Phone Line:** www.virtualphoneline.com
- **Onebox:** www.onebox.com

Closing the Deal

After you've managed to generate qualified leads from the forms and phone numbers on your Web site, the natural question becomes how do you turn your potential customers into paying customers? In other words, how can you close the deal?

The simple answer: Be thoroughly professional, conscientious, efficient, knowledgeable, and polite in handling all the interactions that you have with any prospect. Fall down here, and all is lost (or at least that potential customer is). Whether it's in the promptness of the Thank You message you send when someone completes an online form or in how you answer an incoming call, realize that you are your business. You have to be at your best.

A few handy, time-tested rules for how best to handle the leads that come to you from your Web site follow:

- **Say thanks:** Use a confirmation page. This is the page your prospect sees within your Web site very soon after she's submitted one of the forms on your site. This confirms that you've received the form — and critically, it's where you do what Mom always insisted on: Say thank you. Perhaps you say, "Thank you for your interest," "Thanks for setting up an appointment," or "Thanks and expect a call back from us within 24 hours." Whatever. But manners are important, and no more so than right here, at the very beginning of the relationship you're trying to cultivate.

- **Use auto-responders:** An *auto-responder* is simply an e-mail that's sent automatically when a prospect fills out a form. What she gets back from you is an e-mail (in addition to a confirmation page that appears on your site). Your auto-response will generally say something like, "Thank you, we'll get back to you soon" just like a confirmation page, but an auto-responder is often used for other things, too, such as sending an Out of Office reply. Auto-response e-mails can also be generated to confirm the receipt of a comment or a question that was received on your Web site.

Confirmation pages and auto-responses are usually created from within your Web site design or as an option in your e-mail program. In either case, the content of your reply is almost always written beforehand, so you don't have to come up with something original each time you get a completed form or an e-mail. This prefabricated response just sits on your computer and shoots out when something comes in. In the case of a response to a completed form, however, you can create different responses to different types of input from the prospect. If, for example, he's selected the I Want to Make an Appointment check box, your message can be written to say, "I'll call you very soon to set up an appointment at your convenience." Or if he's asked a question on the form, you could have a response that says, "Thanks for your question. I'll be in touch shortly to answer it and any other questions you may have." The more personalized and individualized your response appears to be, the more likely you are to win over the prospect.

✓ **Answer your e-mail:** A growing stack of unanswered e-mails can bury you in more ways than one. How quickly you get back to a prospect goes a long way toward shaping her perception of your professionalism. So respond to form submissions and e-mail inquiries now. Delay and you give your prospects time to reconsider or worse, to go browsing through your competitors' sites while waiting to hear back from you. Also know that frequent Internet users have become trained to expect a response in less than 24 hours; they may tolerate one that comes up to 48 hours later, but after that, your name officially becomes mud, if it's remembered at all.

✓ **Answer the phone:** Here's a scary thought: An April 2006 survey by Fastcall411 of 5,000 local businesses showed that two-thirds of incoming calls went unanswered. A study by market research firm Synovate found that four out of five Americans regard immediate availability by phone as an important or the most important factor when selecting a local service provider. Put together those two factoids, and it quickly becomes clear that someone has to be available to answer your phone. Don't rely on voicemail to bail you out because statistics show that getting a voicemail makes potential customers far less likely to send their business to the offending company.

✓ **Reply to your voicemail:** The only time that using voicemail is less than a hanging offense is when it's used to field calls that come in after business hours. For that eventuality, keep your automatic greeting short so that callers don't get frustrated and hang up. And of course, when you get back to business each morning, check your voicemail messages and respond to them promptly.

Following these pieces of advice shouldn't be hard for any local business to do. None of them is really anything more than common sense. Taken together, they can definitely help drive your conversion rate ever upward.

Chapter 6

Analyzing Results for Long-Term Gains

*F*or generations, the people who ran advertising in conventional media (broadcast and print) knew that one ad generated business, and one didn't — but they didn't know why. Even today, the why of conventional advertising remains at least partially shrouded in mystery. (Spooky music goes here.)

But that is decidedly not the case with online advertising in general and Web sites in particular. That's because the tactics — and the content — of Web sites, and of the online advertising that drives traffic to them, can be changed so quickly, it's possible to figure out which elements trigger (or fail to trigger) a given response from consumers.

The primary tool that makes this incredibly useful new magic possible is *Web analytics,* which we discuss in this chapter.

Using Cutting-Edge Reporting Tools

Web analytics is the process of gathering and analyzing the behavior of visitors to a Web site. Like any kind of analysis worth its salt, the results of Web analytics are shown in the form of tables, charts, and graphs. An example of how results can be displayed is shown in Figure 6-1.

Figure 6-1:
An example
of how Web
analytics
data is
typically
presented.

Most importantly, using Web analytics enables a business, local or otherwise, to attract more Web site visitors, create new customers and retain existing ones, and increase the dollar volume that each customer spends.

It's the immediacy of the Internet itself that allows the feedback you get from your Web site traffic to be gathered and measured in a flash. Not surprisingly, the actual doing of this requires tracking. And tracking is what Web analytics is all about.

Although this chapter deals with Web analytics in significant detail, pay-per-click (PPC) analytics is a more complex subject than most other kinds. Metrics such as maximum cost-per-click, click-through rate, and a basketful of other considerations merit their own discussion, which is exactly what we give them in Chapter 7. You can read even more in *Web Analytics For Dummies* (Pedro Sostre and Jennifer LeClaire).

Web analytics in a nutshell

As a local business, you have goals for your Web site. You want visitors to request more information about your products or services, sign up for your e-mail newsletters, download a coupon you put on the site, or contact you by phone. In any and all of these cases, your overriding goal is to generate and capture leads — and to determine the efficiency and effectiveness of the investments that you made (and will make) in your site to get those leads.

Web analytics helps you accomplish all that by enabling you to

- ✔ **Measure and maximize your ROI.**

  - Identify which referral sources (search engines, banner ads, blog entries, and so on) generate the most new leads and the most new revenue.

  - Determine how (and how well) your online efforts are keeping up with your overall business goals.

  - Make sound and timely decisions as to which of those efforts are producing the results you want and which aren't, with an eye to retaining the former and jettisoning the latter in favor of something more productive.

- ✔ **Better target your advertising efforts.**

  - Define your visitor groups by the content they read, the actions they take, and even the referral sources they come from.

  - Show which of these visitor groups are most likely to be converted into customers or subscribers.

- ✔ **Optimize your conversion rates.**

  - Use click-path tracking to maximize the rate at which your Web site's visitors convert into customers or subscribers. (*Click-path* refers to the breadcrumb trail that visitors to your site leave behind them, in that it tells you where they started out, and the links they subsequently clicked to get them to where they ended up.)

  - Apply the results of your analyses to help you adjust the content of your site and the navigational paths that you built in.

That's a lot of stuff, eh? Make that a lot of good, useful, actionable stuff that can help you get your business exactly where you want it to go.

Right about now, you're probably thinking, "Yeah, but this whole analytics thing has got to cost a bundle." *Au contraire*. As competition in the Web analytics field has grown, costs have fallen. You can even find some very effective free options.

Then there's the learning curve. Web analytics has one. You need to figure out how to analyze the data that comes in if you're going to get the most out of it. The good news is that the curve isn't all that steep and that the rewards for climbing it are well worth the effort. (You do want to make more money in less time, don't you?)

And one more good, if sort of intangible, thing: It just feels really good to step out of the dark about what is and isn't working for you. It's empowering. (Oh, and did we mention the making more money part?)

Where the magic of metrics comes in

Here are all the things that Web analytics tools can help your measure — in other words, the metrics — and why you should care:

- ✔ **Visits:** The number of distinct user sessions that take place, which is fancy talk for how many times your Web site is visited. A lot of what you need to know flows from this number.

- ✔ **Unique visitors:** The number of user sessions that originate from different computers, from which you can pretty safely deduce the number of different people who are visiting your site. This isn't necessarily a true 1:1 ratio, however. Although people who visit your site more than once will usually do so from the same computer, the analytics tool can only identify computers' Internet protocol (IP) addresses, so it's like finding out which house on your block you're hearing noise from, but not knowing exactly how many people are inside it. Still, just knowing how many repeat visits you're getting from a single computer is useful information in itself because it indicates that folks are visiting your Web site multiple times, and that means you're doing something right.

- ✔ **Page view:** The total number of distinct Web pages downloaded — that is, the number of pages that are actually being seen by visitors on their computer screens.

- ✔ **Page views per visit:** The number of pages viewed divided by the total number of visits. This is important because the more pages seen, the longer a given user is on your site. If people leave after viewing only one or two pages, that's a pretty clear sign that your content is too little or too dull to hold their attention or to make them come back again — which tells you that your content's in need of a fix.

✔ **Time of day:** When you know what times people are visiting your site, you can make a highly educated guess as to whether they're doing so from home or from work. This information might be useful in knowing what kind of psychological state they're in when they visit: relaxed at home, or pressed for time at the office.

✔ **Day of week:** This is another piece of data that can give you insight into patterns of visitor behavior. For instance, it seems fairly common for people to visit Web sites on weekends, and then make a purchase on Mondays. And the advantage of knowing on what days and at what times you're getting the most visitors to your site is that you then have a clear indication of the best day or time to post a new offer or other promotion, or even just to freshen up your content.

✔ **Entry pages:** Generally speaking, your home page will be the most frequent entry point onto your site. The second most common are the landing pages that people arrive at by clicking on the URL where you put in an ad or that appears on some other site. Lesson here: Your home page and all your landing pages better be in great shape.

✔ **Referrers:** The Web sites or the other pages or sites that provided a link to your site.

✔ **Search engines:** Which search engines brought up a link to your site in the search results they generated. If you're paying an appreciable sum for PPC ads on a search engine that isn't producing much, stop doing that.

✔ **Search terms:** The words that a user entered into a search engine to find your site. Obviously, this is a critical thing to know for a few reasons:

- Search terms can help inform you as to the products and services that potential customers are most interested in, which is data you can leverage across other aspects of your marketing program.

- Search terms can help you discover where your local customers are coming from, in the sense that if someone searches for *salon in midtown manhattan,* there is a good chance that Midtown Manhattan is where that potential customer is located (or works or will be visiting).

- Popular search terms where people find you organically can help inform you what keywords you should be bidding on for your pay-per-click (PPC) campaign.

✔ **Conversion rate:** Typically expressed as a percentage of site visitors who actually took an action (such as completing an online form, sending an e-mail to you, signing up for your newsletter) versus the number of visitors who showed up and didn't do anything. Pay the closest possible attention your conversion rate. It's your bottom line talking.

Metrics tell you an astounding number of things. They focus you on what you're doing right and doing wrong, where you're wasting money, and where you've invested wisely, who your customers are (and aren't), and where your next and best opportunities lie.

Choosing a Web analytics provider

The first step in putting Web analytics to work involves choosing a software provider. The second step is to lift a few lines of code from that application and plug them into your Web site. Don't worry, most software providers make sure it's pretty easy to do.

A variety of Web analytic tools are available from a number of quality companies. And, as we mention earlier, several of these tools are free yet robust enough to serve any business well, be it local or large.

Table 6-1 gives several good, inexpensive options for Web analytic providers.

Table 6-1	Web Analytics Providers	
Name	*Web Site*	*Price*
Google Analytics	`www.google.com/analytics`	Free
Yahoo! Web Analytics	`www.web.analytics.yahoo.com`	Free
Woopra	`www.woopra.com`	Free and paid plans
CrazyEgg	`http://crazyegg.com`	Prices start at $9/month
Enquisite	`www.enquisite.com`	$49.95/month for the Pro package

The following list describes the Web analytics providers given in Table 6-1:

✔ **Google Analytics:** The free analytics tool that Google offers is simply today's best free analytic tool for any local business. It's very easy to set up and use. It offers basic analysis and reporting functions, which are capable of collecting standard metrics such as page views, unique visitors, time spent on the Web site, and the percentage of visitors who abandon your site rather than continue on to other pages. What's more — and terrific — is that Google Analytics (GA) runs on its own server, which is to say, it's hosted. That means you don't need to apply any in-house manpower to keep it up and running. All you do need to do is add some code to your Web pages, and Google walks you through that process step by step.

Because it's the leader of the pack, we view many of the subjects discussed in this chapter through a Google Analytics lens.

✔ **Yahoo! Web Analytics:** The Yahoo! folks are no slouches when it comes to the free analytic tools they offer. Like GA, Yahoo! Web Analytics can give you valuable insights in to the demographics and the interest level of your Web site visitors. It also gives you powerful and flexible *dashboards* (a jargon-y way of saying control panels), market segmentation tools, and campaign management features. And, like GA, it's very easy to implement.

✔ **Woopra:** Yes, it does kind of sound like a certain daytime talk show host, but actually, it's a great alternative to GA. Of course, it hasn't yet captured the sort of market share that GA enjoys, but that's because it's a relative newcomer to the field. Woopra is particularly useful for less-trafficked Web sites and blogs because in addition to offering all the standard metrics that GA does, it also has two really nifty features that can really only be applied to noncongested sites:

   • Real-time visitor analysis that tells you exactly which source a current visitor came from, the page of your site that he's now on, and the path through your site that he followed to get to that page.

   • Even more nifty is Woopra's built-in chat tool; this little gem lets you pop-up messages to a given site visitor while she's on the site, and start a real-time conversation. (Prompted chat is explained in Chapter 5.) Maybe you think this sounds a little creepy. These Woopra-ites would seem to be onto something here that could be huge.

✔ **CrazyEgg:** GA offers an overlay tool, and CrazyEgg offers a more advanced version of the same thing. An *overlay tool* gives you the ability to literally see where people are clicking on a Web page, and the results can be depicted on a *heat map* (a picture of a Web page with a transparent layer positioned over it). This layer registers clicks that occur on the various links, buttons, and other widgets on the page; the ones that get the most clicks appear in red (a hot spot), while those least clicked are shown in blue or have no color at all. This can tell you volumes about what's working on a page and what isn't. It can be so effective, it almost isn't fair. CrazyEgg offers a free version of this tool that gives a local business great insights into where visitors are going — and not going — on the Web site. There's also a fancier, paid version available.

✔ **Enquisite:** If you want much more detailed information about your regular search engine traffic and your PPC traffic, you really should take a look at Enquisite. It's an inexpensive tool for business owners who spend a lot of time and effort attracting Web site visitors from the search engine realm, and it allows you to do some great analysis that can help you improve the ROI of your online advertising.

Because many of the tools from these resources are free, there's no reason why you can't use more than one of them in combination. Let your specific needs be your guide in building your own personal Web analytics arsenal. What fun.

Understanding Key Metrics

As a local business owner who maintains a Web site, you need to keep your eye on only a few key metrics, but those few merit very close attention because they tell the tale on whether or not your online advertising program is doing its job.

Those key metrics (as expressed in nontechnical parlance) are

- ✔ Where are your site visitors coming from?
- ✔ What content are they consuming when they arrive at your site?
- ✔ Which offers are they most likely to take advantage of?
- ✔ What does it cost to get new customers?
- ✔ What is your lead-to-sales ratio?

Where are your customers coming from?

Knowing where your Web site traffic is coming from will help you refine your whole online advertising plan. For example, if it turns out that you're getting a lot of visitors from searches that people do on Google or Yahoo!, that tells you to further cement your relationship with those sites, and to try forging a relationship with similar sites (such as www.bing.com).

On the other hand, if you find that you're getting a lot of traffic from search engines based on particular search terms that don't reflect your business goals, you'll want to spend some time optimizing your site for other search terms. (If you own a dry cleaning service, for instance, you don't necessarily want to come popping up in search engine results when someone searches for *dirty sheets.*)

The metrics that are most relevant to sources are

- ✔ **Referring keyword data:** Checking your referring keyword data lets you infer the intent of your site visitors, understand how they typically search for the kind of products or services you offer, and determine whether you're getting the kind of traffic you think you should be.

This data isn't complicated. It simply tells you what keywords and phrases people have used in searching the Web, seeing your URL, and clicking it to arrive at your site. When you see how people are actually finding you, it becomes relatively easy to figure out which keywords and phrases generate the highest conversion rates for your business. Figure 6-2 shows a sample referring keyword report from Google Analytics.

Figure 6-2: A referring keyword report tells you which keywords and phrases bring visitors to your site.

Having this information is particularly important if you're spending a lot of effort and/or money on search engine optimization (SEO, which we talk extensively about in Chapter 8) because it makes no sense to use a lot of resources optimizing a Web site for keywords that fail to convert leads. For example, say you own a hair salon and you're optimizing your site on an ongoing basis for three sets of keywords — *haircuts, hair removal,* and *makeup.* All three of these drive a similar volume of traffic to your site. However, your Web analytics tells you that people who clicked after searching *haircuts* and *hair removal* are far more engaged with your site (they download coupons, sign up for you newsletter, and view a log of pages), but those who click *makeup* don't. As a logical business owner, what do you do? Simple. You stop focusing on *makeup* keyword from your PPC plan, saving time and potentially money overall or using your existing resources to optimize on new, more effective keywords.

✔ **Top referring sites:** As shown in Figure 6-3, here's the metric that tells you what other sites are sending traffic your way. Now look closely: Which of them are generating the most leads? Are you surprised at which sites are referring business to you? Do you have an existing relationship with each top referring site — and, if not, should you?

Knowing which sites are sending you traffic can really help you steer your online advertising dollars into the most productive channels. If a particular site sends you 50 unique visitors per day, and 25 percent of those convert (or take some positive action including filling out a form, signing up for a newsletter, or making an appointment), you're in great shape. And that should make you consider upping your spend on that site to increase your exposures, click-throughs, and conversions even further. On the other hand, if a site is sending you 100 unique visitors per month but none of them convert, what's the point? Better to shift dollars away from the dud site toward a bigger presence on a productive one.

Figure 6-3:
A top-referring site report makes clear which sites send you the most conversion-likely visitors.

What content are visitors consuming?

When you know where visitors to your site came from, the next logical questions are: What specific pages on your site are they visiting, and how well are your home and landing pages working? You know that you have lots of terrific stuff on your site, but are people going for that or for something else you never really expected would get much attention?

To keep your Web site running productively, you need to know what's working and what's not. To find out, take a close look at these metrics:

✔ **Site content popularity:** A lot of Web pros say that only about 20 percent of any given Web site's content gets consumed. Ah, but which 20 percent? Maybe people are heading straight for the page with your product's specifications. Or maybe they're making a beeline for your photo gallery. Or maybe it's your coupon offer that's generating the most readership. Who knows? Well, armed with your site content popularity data, you do. Then comes the next step. When you know where your site visitors go, make sure that you provide can't-miss links to those pages throughout the site, particularly on your home page. You might even want to feature a mention of that super-popular content in your advertising.

A report on site content–popularity will usually present the data in separate pieces, such as

- *Top content:* Shows you which of your Web pages are the most popular. You can then optimize those pages for even higher readership performance.

- *Content by title:* Gives you the most popular content views by page title, thus enabling you to spiff up the rest of the content on that high-traffic page.

- *Content drilldown:* Gives you a look at the content views by directory, which, in turn, lets you determine the most common patterns of user activity.

- *Top landing pages:* Shows which of your pages visitors land on the most. With this knowledge, you can optimize those pages. This data can also enhance your ability to figure out which of your online ads (or maybe your social network efforts) are delivering the best customers to your site.

- *Top exit pages:* Provides you with which of your pages is the most common place for visitors to exit your site. This metric can help you decide whether something in particular is wrong with that page and then fix it; it can also teach you more about visitors' general patterns of activity on the site.

- *Site overlay:* Shows you which areas of your site are most often clicked.

Every one of these metrics can help you optimize your site for more visits, longer visits, and more productive visits. And they're usually presented in a form that makes them easy to understand.

✔ **Bounce rate and time on site:** It's just a given that not all visitors to your site are going to like what they find there. Maybe they don't think it's relevant, maybe they find it confusing, or maybe they just don't go for the monkey motif. In any case, *bounce rate* is the percentage of entries on each page that resulted in an exit from the site, without the visitor's having clicked any deeper into the content.

Whatever the reason for a particular visitor's departure, knowing your bounce rate (or abandons) is very useful as a measure of how well a site page delivers its message. (See Figure 6-4.) Here are a couple of examples of how to put bounce rates to work:

- Say you offer dog walking services, and the majority of the visitors who come to your site using search terms like *dog walking* then exit your site as soon as they arrive at your dog walking landing page. There's something distressingly wrong with that page that needs to be fixed.

- It's possible that visitors have stayed around long enough to read your content, absorb it, and evaluate it; this is where the time on site metric comes in handy because it tells you how well your site engages visitors. If they're spending a long time on a page only to then fly the coop, odds are your content just isn't compelling enough and needs to be punched up.

Figure 6-4:
A typical presentation of visitor metrics from Google Analytics.

Which offers are visitors clicking with?

One of the best things about using Web analytics is that you track how well a particular offer or other incentive is doing in the real world. Is what you're offering leading to conversions? At what rate? Web analytics can give you the answers to those questions — and to the more important one: How can you do even better?

The time-honored, tried-and-true way to test the effectiveness of any given offer is to make it compete against another offer. The same thing goes for other kinds of inducements (such as free estimates) that can help you cross-sell and up-sell visitors to your site, or even softer incentives (such as comparison charts between your products and your competitors'). In a sense, these are all offers, and they can all be tested against other contenders.

It's natural enough to interpret this advice as "test offer A against offer B." Certainly, that keeps things manageable, but soon you'll want to test the winner of A versus B against offer C — and so on. If you can, you're better off simultaneously testing several alternatives because that will teach you more in less time. You might even find that although you definitely want to extend the most productive offer on your site, whatever came in second (or even third) might be worth including, too. Doing that couldn't hurt (provided the offers don't somehow cancel each other out), and it just might give your conversion rate a nice upward nudge.

Here are some of the kinds of offers that local businesses commonly use and that can easily be tested against one another:

- **Percent discount:** Straight percent-off or buy one month of dog walking, get one free offers nearly always drive lead capture; note, though, that they tend to have the most effect with customers who are in a "buy now" mode rather than with those who are just browsing.

- **Sales demo or appointment:** This can be a high-risk offer because it will chew up a chunk of your valuable time, but it can also work very well when your potential customer is already primed to buy.

- **Free estimate or consultation:** Like the demo/appointment approach, this one can use up some time. Similarly, though, it can be just what a prospect needs if he's teetering on the edge of making a purchase. This is particularly effective for products or services where a certain level of education is required on the part of potential clients or customers before they become clients or customers (such as legal services, medical procedures, and so on).

- **Sweepstakes:** This tactic can quickly build your volume of leads, but those leads might be of lesser quality than those you get some other way. One sure-fire way to make sweepstakes more effective is have them relate to your product or service (a spa can give away free facials, a bed and breakfast can give away a free getaway package). Sure, you're still giving away something for free, but you're also getting someone to try what you have to offer, and with luck, they'll become repeat (and paying) customers. A possible negative is that some states regulate sweepstakes pretty tightly, so make sure to stay in strict compliance with whatever laws apply.

✔ **How-to guides:** These can be a great way to educate consumers and give them a good feeling about your business. The guides don't have to be especially complicated; something as simple as "How to determine which perennial flower seeds you should plant when" can be more than sufficient.

Ideally, whatever offer(s) you're testing should also be included in the advertising that you're using to drive traffic to your Web site, and each offer should run for the same duration, just to keep things fair.

You might well be wondering how you can test multiple offers at the same time on the same Web site. The simplest way is to create different landing pages, each of which contains a different offer. You can split an e-mail communication, with half the recipients getting one offer, half getting the other, and the link on each version leading to its own corresponding landing page. You could also field more than one PPC ad, each touting a different offer, to drive traffic to the pertinent landing page. (You can read all about such techniques in *E-Mail Marketing For Dummies,* by John Arnold.)

It's terrific to have an offer start generating strong consumer interest in your business. Just keep in mind that interest by itself isn't really what you're after. Conversions are the goal. So, the metric that truly counts here is which offer produced the most positive, actionable responses from prospective customers at the most efficient cost. Sound familiar? Yep, it's our old friend, the conversion rate. Maybe one of your offers beat out all the others in its ability to induce your Web site visitors to fill out a form, call your business, or opt-in to your e-newsletter. Well, there's your winner.

Even your also-ran offers can teach you something, though. Look closely at them and the mechanics behind them. Were the offers too stingy? Were they so complicated that they couldn't be explained in simple terms? Did it take too much navigation to find them on your site? Was there something in the way the offers were expressed that wasn't compelling enough or that came off as too haughty — or conversely, too needy and desperate? You can fix any of those things. Then throw those new and improved versions back out there — and see how they fare this time around.

What does it cost to get new customers?

You want to bring in the most customers at the most efficient cost. The more formal way to say that is that you're looking for the lowest cost per acquisition. Your overall cost per acquisition (CPA) is what you get when you divide your total acquisition expenses by your total number of new customers. How simple is that?

How much is a customer worth?

We stress the importance of measuring your CPA whenever possible because it's one of the best metrics that you can use to determine whether the marketing you're doing is actually worth the time, effort, resources, and blood, sweat, and tears you're putting into it. The other side of that particular coin is determining just how much a new customer is actually worth to you.

Say you're a cosmetic surgeon who specializes in rhinoplasty, and the average nose job goes for $6,000. When you take out the direct costs associated with performing each nose job, you're left with $3,000 of gross profit. In business circles, this gross profit is often referred to as the *contribution*.

The whole deal looks like this:

Revenue ($6,000) − Direct costs ($3,000) = Contribution ($3,000)

Except that's not necessarily the whole deal. There might be other factors that you should think about when coming up with the true value of a client. Two of the most common of these factors are

✔ **Future sales:** Say that, on average, one out of two of your patients will come back for a facelift, and that the contribution for a facelift is $2,000. That means that the benefit to you of acquiring a new nose-job patient has a 50 percent chance of being significantly bigger than just the initial nose job itself. And, not surprisingly, there's a simple formula for that, too:

Contribution from a facelift ($2,000) × Probability of a facelift for nose job patient (50%) = Additional contribution from the nose job patient ($1,000)

✔ **Referrals from the client (patient):** Say that you're a really good cosmetic surgeon and that on average, one of every two of your prior nose-job patients refers another nose-job patient to you. That works out to be

50% of nose jobs done × Contribution from each referred nose job ($3,000) = $1,500 additional contribution from the original, referring nose-job patient

What you'd have is the contribution from the original direct sale ($3,000), plus the value of the future sale ($1,000), plus the value of the referred sale ($1,500), for a potential lifetime nose-job client value of $5,500, as opposed to the initially assumed $3,000. And because, seen as a whole, the contribution is higher, you can technically afford a higher CPA and still be profitable.

Well, the calculation is simple, and so is counting up your new customers. The more complicated element is figuring out just what your acquisition expenditures really are.

For example, if in one year, you spend $2,000 on a print ad in your local newspaper or on a Yellow Pages display ad and you acquire 20 new customers, that's a CPA of $100. If, on the other hand, you spend $2,000 on a PPC ad campaign for that same year and acquire 200 new customers, your CPA is $10. However, those might not be your only costs. How much did someone charge you to create your newspaper ad? How much did it cost you to maintain your Web site over that year? For that matter, what was the initial cost of having your Web site built, and how many years has the site been up? So what's the amortized yearly cost of your site's development?

The point is that some acquisition costs are easy to put your finger on, but others are less obvious. It takes some time (and probably some good documentation of what you paid to whom for what) to get all your costs totaled. The good news is that after you do that, the result of your customer-conversion-cost calculation will probably give you a crystal clear idea of where to keep spending your money as well as where to pull back or pull out.

Think very hard before you spend advertising dollars in a medium where results can't be reliably measured — say, like those ads that some businesses stick all over the town's lamp posts. Similarly, don't continue to advertise in a medium where use you can't justify in any measurable way.

What, then, is the goal here? Obviously, it's to generate the lowest CPA you possibly can. But there's another, long-term goal: to get that cost at least a little bit lower each and every year. Otherwise, you're not really making any progress. You should use this year's cost-analysis results to make next year's results even better. Tweak your Web site to make whatever's working work harder. Figure out whether there are other, better-chosen keywords you could be using in your PPC ads. Make your e-mails punchier. And keep doing it over and over.

Ultimately, you'll have an online advertising campaign that squeezes every nickel. You'll spend ad money with amazing effectiveness and efficiency. You will, in short, be bringing in each customer for a fraction of what you used to spend.

What is your lead-to-sales ratio?

An example will help demonstrate how to arrive at your lead-to-sales ratio, why it's important, and how some of the other metrics we've already discussed will come into play.

If you send an e-mail aimed at your target audience, you can determine exactly how many people saw it and then clicked through to your Web site. You can also figure out how many people actually became a lead via that e-mail and even see how many were then converted.

Say that your statistics for a given month are

- Cost of the monthly e-mail blast: $500
- Click-through number: 100
- Leads generated: 25
- Cost per lead: $20
- Lead conversion rate: 25%
- Sales generated: 5
- Lead-to-sales ratio: 20%

Now look inside these numbers:

- ✔ Of the 100 people who looked at your e-mail and then clicked through to your Web site, 25 filled out a form they found on your site or called you as a result of the e-mail.

- ✔ You calculate your cost per lead by dividing your total cost ($500) by the number of leads you got (25); in our example, that comes to $20 per lead. The lower this number, the better.

- ✔ The *lead conversion rate* is the result of dividing the number of folks who clicked through to your Web site from the e-mail into the number of leads that group generated; in this case, that's 25 ÷ 100, or 25%.

- ✔ Finally, if 5 of those 25 new conversions actually bought your product or service, your lead-to-sales ratio is 5 ÷ 25, or 20%.

Okay, 20% isn't bad — but it could always be better. The key is to increase your lead-to-sales ratio, which, technically speaking, you could do in either of two ways: Decrease your number of leads, but get more sales from that smaller group of people (not a good idea), or increase both your number of leads and the percentage of sales that you get from that larger number. In the latter case, you would have something that people with an MBA call a *growing business.*

The neat thing about breaking down the lead-to-sales calculations this way is that you can see each of the moving parts. You can monitor these numbers continuously and systematically, and steadily make smarter and smarter decisions as to where and how to spend your advertising dollars.

Optimizing for Improved Results

So here's kind of a scary-sounding word: optimization. All *optimization* really means is the process of making something better. And, using the metrics we discuss earlier in this chapter, you can make your Web site better in any number of ways, at virtually no cost.

You do this by continually testing the various elements that appear on your site to determine which could use some improvement. Then you make the improvements. Then you test the improvements. Not too complicated, really. What you're doing is optimizing your site to optimize your results.

Testing what, exactly? It's usually not a big thing. Maybe you move your contact information from the right side of the page to the left so that it's easier to find. Or put in a big red Download button to make it obvious what you want people to do. Or make your call to action (say, to complete a form) more visible or better phrased.

Whatever the specifics, Web site optimization involves trying and testing, and then drawing solid, evidence-backed conclusions. Every conclusion you act on improves the performance of your site.

The reasons you want to bother with testing is because it allows you to

- ✓ **Increase conversion rates and sales** by identifying the content and content combinations that best drive conversions and increase your ROI.

- ✓ **Improve landing page performance** by making it more interesting and compelling and thus reducing the number of people who exit the site at that critical point without going further.

- ✓ **Generate more leads** by streamlining your online lead-generation forms to make them easier to find, understand, and fill out.

- ✓ **Increase the time visitors spend on your site** by continually making it more informative, attractive, and engaging.

- ✓ **Eliminate guesswork from site alterations** by basing your changes on the real-world empirical data you get from actual visitors.

Split testing

We talk a good deal about testing the elements of your Web site to find out which are working and which aren't. But, how exactly you should *do* that deserves some explanation.

The typical method is *split testing* (or A/B testing). You probably remember high school science classes and the whole idea of comparing a control something-or-other against alternatives. Well, that's essentially what split testing is. Say you want to test the headline on one of your landing pages to see whether what you're using now is as effective as it might be. The one you already have in place is your control. Then you swap that out for a different headline on the same landing page, leaving every other element on the page as is. Then you do a *split run* — for instance, when one visitor clicks onto the landing page, he sees Headline A (the current one), and the next person who clicks on sees Headline B (the alternate). You let this split run go on for an appreciable amount of time, maybe two weeks or longer. Then you compare results: One headline will outperform the other in terms of increased response rate or of some other outcome you have as your goal. And that's your winner.

We simplify here in the sense that you'll probably want to split test Headlines A, B, C, and maybe even D at the same time, and there's no reason you can't. Doing so can save you a lot of time, and the general concept remains the same.

Testing page elements

When you think about it, you optimize other aspects of your business all the time. You paint your showroom a new bright color. You freshen a floor display. You improve your own computer system to give you more information, faster.

Optimizing your Web site represents exactly the same kind of beneficial tinkering except that it takes place in the online realm rather than the physical one.

The following steps outline the process you use to test Web pages:

1. Choose the pages you want to test.

   Your Web analytics point out areas of your site that are underperforming, so you then aim your efforts at these specific pages or elements.

2. Decide what elements to test.

   Look at an underperforming page. Why do you think it's falling short? You don't have solid data yet on specifics, so you need to hypothesize a little. Ask yourself these questions:

   - Considering your site's traffic sources, does it seem like the page matches up with the expectations that visitors would have? Does the page give them what you can surmise they're looking for? Did you make an offer in an ad that isn't clearly contained on the landing page?

   - Could you improve the continuity (or flow) from one page to another? Do all the pages look and feel like they're part of the same site? Would using the headline from your PPC ad as the landing page headline make for a smoother transition from ad to site?

   - What's missing from the page? Is there enough content there to pay off the visit? Or is there so much content that it's likely to be putting people off?

   - How well is the page organized? Is the information on the page organized in a way that can be easily followed and digested by a stranger?

   Several elements on any given page might call for testing, such as the headline, images, text, layout, and so on. Just make sure to test only one element at a time; otherwise, you'll never know for sure which change did the trick.

3. Test and measure performance.

   When your test is up and running, start monitoring the data you're getting from your site visitors. Are people spending more time on the revised Page X than they did on the old Page X? Are more people filling out the form on Page Y than they did before? Are you using a long enough time frame (a week, two weeks, a month) to make your determination? If the answer to questions like these are yes, you can consider your Web site now firmly improved.

4. Start the process over again.

   What's the next thing that could use some optimization?

For example, say you're a landscaper, and your Web analytics tells you that your Gardening Tips page is underperforming. It's the page that invites visitors to opt-in to receive tips from you via e-mail, but most people are abandoning your site at that page. You take a good hard look at the page and come up with a few possible reasons why it's not capturing users' interest. Maybe the headline "Gardening Advice" is too passive, and you realize that your call to action is pretty far down the page, too. You decide to test two new headlines: "Stop Killing Your Plants" and "How to Grow a Green Thumb." Bingo! The "Green Thumb" headline starts creating more opt-ins. Nice work. Now you try moving the call to action higher up on the page so people don't have to scroll down to find it. Double bingo! You're now getting opt-ins from nearly half the people who visit that page. Isn't optimization fun?

Google offers a fee tool — the Website Optimizer (`www.google.com/websiteoptimizer`) — that automates testing and makes it easy for you to fix troubled landing pages and put the new-and-improved ones up on your site. It's definitely worth taking a look at.

Optimization doesn't have to be complicated or difficult. It requires nothing more, really, than the application of good old common sense, and it's something that the world's biggest advertisers do every day because they've made a corporate commitment to leaving no stone unturned in their drive to create more and more business for themselves. It's the same kind of commitment you should make. It isn't hard, and it pays dividends, putting more of your business's future and fate firmly in your own hands — exactly where it belongs.

Part III
Doing the Advertising Part of Local Online Advertising

The 5th Wave   By Rich Tennant

© RICHTENNANT

"Make sure to pick keywords that people will associate with our brand."

"How about "sleazy," "tacky," "overpriced"..."

ONLINE ADV

In this part . . .

Advertising has always been an essential part of doing business. As a successful local business, you're almost certainly doing some kind of advertising — probably just not the online kind (yet). Online or offline, the basic principle remains the same: People have to know about you before they can bring their business to you.

This part covers a lot of ground, but that's only because it's all pivotal stuff that any serious online advertiser needs to take to heart and put to use. As you no doubt will.

Chapter 7 discusses — and Chapters 8 and 9 go further to explain — one of the cornerstones of advertising, search engine marketing. Chapter 10 gets into the important subject of using business e-mail. Chapter 11 explores the use of directories and lead aggregators. Chapter 12 talks about banner ads and online classified ads.

Then we step a bit outside the box, as Chapter 13 describes the marketing uses of social networks, such as Facebook and MySpace. Chapter 14 examines the ways in which online public relations efforts can come nicely into play. Chapter 15 closes out with a discussion of how you can augment your online advertising efforts by experience from your offline advertising channels and vice versa.

Chapter 7

Demystifying Search Engine Marketing

*H*ere's a secret: At its heart, local online advertising isn't all that complicated. In fact, mastering two key elements of the process is enough to get you up and running and pointed toward success. Those two elements are a good Web site and a solid handle on the use of search engines, because a Web site gives people a rewarding place to go, and search engines give them a way to get there.

In this chapter, we discuss searching organically and paid search engine marketing so that you clearly understand how they work and how well they can serve your business goals.

Understanding Organic and Paid Search

How do you look for information? You search the Internet, right? According to Marketing Sherpa, almost 134 million people in the U.S. regularly use search engines when looking for information online. That's the good news. Of those 134 million, 63 percent look only at the first page of search engine results. That's the bad news.

The objective for any ambitious marketer is to make sure your ad shows on that first page. And to do that, you need to put a number of search engine strategies to work for your business. Taken together, these strategies for paid search and organic search are *search marketing*.

Both organic and paid searches aim at getting highly qualified visitors to your Web site — and that means getting your site to rank near the top on search engine results pages when people type in the keywords you've chosen. Although either form of search, done correctly, can get you prime exposure on search engines, using both options may well be the most sensible and effective path for local businesses.

Organic search results

As we discuss in Chapter 2, *organic* (or natural) listings appear as a result of decisions that a search engine makes with its proprietary algorithms. The way to influence your placement or rank in an organic search is *search engine optimization* (SEO). (We deal with the actual nuts and bolts of SEO in Chapter 8, but what follows gives you a pretty good idea of how it works and what it can accomplish.)

SEO lets you actively direct the way your site is listed — and, consequently, the ranking it receives — by giving search engines exactly what they're looking for. They're looking for relevance to the user's search term so that they provide a useful consumer experience. The best way to understand SEO is to ask yourself, "How do I make it easy for Google to find my site when a consumer types in something relevant to my business?" Fine-tuning both the content and coding of your Web site will help. When the engines see your site as relevant, they place it among the top organic results when people search for the kind of products or services you offer.

Organic search is such a valuable advertising tactic; many search engine surveys and studies show that users are more likely to click organic search results than paid listings. Why?

- ✔ Organic listings are unbiased and not bought. As a result, users trust these results more than paid listings.

- ✔ People view organic search results as more permanent than paid ones. Paid listings remain in the results only when paid for, whereas organic listings remain ranked until the search engine changes its algorithm or ranking methodology.

That might make you think that SEO needs to be at the core of your overall online advertising plan. After all, the process is free (assuming you do it). And we just said that the organic results it produces are, in key respects, preferred by search engine users. So does that mean you can fold up the tent on this chapter and move on to something else? No. Because one of the major downsides of SEO for local businesses is that it isn't always a winnable proposition.

For instance, say you're a locksmith. If someone types **locksmiths** into Google, he'll find that the overwhelming majority of the organic search results on the first page don't show local businesses because *locksmiths* is just too broad a keyword; it produces a lot of category killers, such as directories, Internet Yellow Pages (IYP), and industry associations. These are sites that contain so much relevant keyword content that they tend to win out over any local competition for the same keywords. Figure 7-1 shows what a search results page like this looks like.

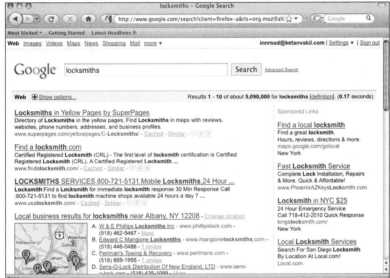

Figure 7-1: The top several results when searching for *locksmiths* are category killers.

You can try to localize your SEO efforts by attaching a geographic modifier to your keyword (such as *locksmiths.denver*), and Google would then dutifully produce just the organic results for Denver-based locksmiths. (See Figure 7-2.) Even then, any single Denver locksmith is likely to find it difficult to compete successfully with directories, IYP, and so on for a high-visibility ranking.

However, we do have one way you can relatively easily compete organically. The advent of local listings that come with those nifty little maps attached nearly always show up at the top portion of the organic results whenever someone searches with *local intent* (meaning she used a specific geographic modifier, such as a town, suburb, or zip code, along with her keyword or phrase). Additionally, some of the search engines have started serving local listing results using your computer's IP address. After all, if someone in Denver is locked out of his car, he'll want to find the locksmith located closest to the parking lot he's stuck in. And when a local mapped listing gives that to him, his search is over.

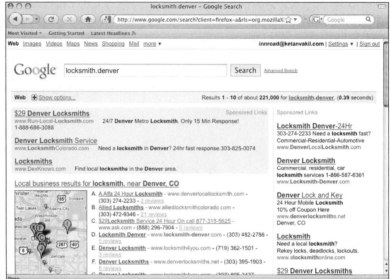

Figure 7-2:
Local business results gain more prominent placement with maps listings.

Paid search advertising

The vast majority of search engine users never venture further than the first page of their search results, and getting an organic, non-specifically localized listing to show up on the first page is a pitched battle that is often difficult for businesses to win. Put together those two factors, and it's pretty obvious that there has to be another way to ensure a high-visibility search engine presence. This is when paid searches enter the picture.

Do a Google or Yahoo! search and right off the bat, you notice a special type of listings situated around the organic results that appear on the page. These are paid listings (or sponsored or pay-per-click [PPC] listings), and they get their prominent position because someone paid to have them appear when someone types a specified keyword into a search engine. Also notice that these paid ads occupy space either at the top of the page or along the right side. Either location makes them almost impossible to miss — which is the whole idea.

To get accustomed to the idea of paying for search engine listings, you need to understand the tremendous advantages that paid search gives to local businesses:

✔ Paid search engine ads appear almost immediately, which means you can quickly start driving traffic to your site. You don't have to wait for your SEO efforts to get up to speed.

✔ With paid search advertising, you pay only for results. No matter how many times your ad is displayed, there's no cost to you until it's clicked.

✔ By tracking the results that your paid search advertising produces, you can easily figure out whether the business you're getting from your ad(s) justifies the expense.

✔ Paid search is a great testing tool. You can run several different paid ads simultaneously and then determine which offers and messages work best. You can also (and easily) test the effectiveness of your keywords, your product offerings, your ad headlines and sales copy, and even your price points.

Understanding How Consumers Rate Search Results

As you enter the wonderful world of search marketing, you need to understand how search users actually view a search engine results page. Generally speaking, well-ranked organic listings are more likely to be clicked by users than sponsored listings.

"Inside the Mind of the Searcher," a 2004 study by Enquiro, showed nearly 80 percent of the test subjects initially skipped over all sponsored listings and dove straight into the top organic results. Not only that, but in most cases, their eyes never went back to the sponsored listings. A 2009 study found much the same thing: Organic results still generate the majority of clicks. (Figure 7-3 shows a heat map that illustrates how people typically view a search engine results page.) Some industry gurus come at it a slightly different way, suggesting that 70–75 percent of actual clicks are organic listings and only 20–25 percent are sponsored ones.

Given the super-high, super-visible position that paid listings get, paid search may strike you as counter-intuitive. But arguably, searches all come down to trust. Many users know that the ads near the top and right are, well, ads whereas they seem to perceive highly ranked organic listings as having merited their position on the page. Merit apparently indicates trustworthiness to these users — and that's enough to get them confidently clicking away.

People who click organic results are more likely to be researching or browsing, whereas people who click paid listings tend to be ready to buy now. In fact, according to new research, 82 percent of the money spent as a result of search engine listings comes from paid listings.

Don't overestimate the importance of this distinction. Your best bet is to use both organic and paid search, to cover all your bases.

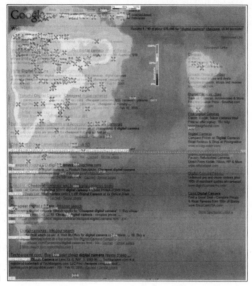

Figure 7-3:
You can tell
which list-
ings people
view the
most.

What is it about a particular result listing — whether organic or paid — that most often captures the click? In a word, *relevance.* Optimized Web site titles and descriptions are consistently identified as the top items that induce people to click one result over another. Of course, a listing generally has more pieces to it than just those, so here's how the overall hierarchy usually shakes out, in order of decreasing relevance to search engine users:

- ✔ **The wording of the title and description:** The same keywords people enter into their query show up here in boldface type (as shown in Figure 7-4).

- ✔ **Offers and product information:** Features, prices, special offers, product comparisons, reviews, and the like.

- ✔ **Consumer reviews:** Almost two-thirds (62 percent) of consumers read online merchant reviews and 82 percent say it impacts their purchase decisions.

- ✔ **Known and trusted business names and vendors:** Household names are the leaders of the pack.

- ✔ **Promises of added value:** Percentage discounts, free shipping, and so on.

- ✔ **The ability to book online:** Register for an appointment or sign up for a free consultation.

- ✔ **Trustworthy-sounding URLs:** Use a short URL with your name in it, such as www.davesautoservice.com instead of www.cheapcarrepairs.com.

When you're striving for success, you simply have no choice but to sharpen and fine-tune the way your business's search listings appear — at least if you expect to get stellar marketing results.

Figure 7-4:
People look
at a listing's
title and
descriptive
text.

303 **Locksmith** Services in **Denver** CO
303 **Locksmith** provide professional Emergency, Auto, Residential, Commercial, Rekey and
Lockout services in **Denver** - and other Colorado surrounding areas.
www.303**locksmith**.com/ - Cached - Similar - ⧉ ⊞ ⊠

Pairing Organic Search with Paid Search

Making organic search work well for your business, whether exclusively or
with paid ads, requires some serious competence in the SEO department. So
if your SEO skills aren't well-honed, relying on organic search will likely mean
settling, with the exception of those trusty local listings, for a weak search
engine presence.

Ultimately, the argument for using both search engine tools is just too strong
to ignore. Consider that leveraging organic results and paid search ads
together will bring you

- ✔ **More traffic:** Although searchers go straight to the organic results first
  80 percent of the time, 60 percent of searchers click paid ads at least
  sometimes, and 12 percent click them either always or most of the time.
  Leave paid search ads out of your online marketing plan, and you're sac-
  rificing a lot of traffic.

- ✔ **Better click-through rates:** Recent research shows that Web sites listed
  at the top of both the organic and paid search results commonly enjoy
  a click-through rate that's three times greater than Web sites appearing
  at or near the top of organic results alone. Experts attribute this to a
  second opinion effect: People who see a Web site appear in both paid and
  organic listings think that makes the site (and the business behind it)
  much more credible.

- ✔ **Greater penetration:** When you arrive at the right keywords and keyword combinations, you rank well in organic search results. PPC can
  spring into action almost instantaneously. And even though it comes
  with a price tag, PPC can be turned on and off as needed, depending on
  your budget and any special promotions you want to put a big effort
  behind.

- ✔ **More productive use of keywords:** Several tools are available (such
  as the Google Keyword Tool and Wordtracker) that let you do keyword research before you do any SEO or PPC work. As you make your
  keywords better and better, and thus improve your organic search
  rankings, you gain knowledge that can make your PPC response rates
  improve, too.

✔ **Increased visibility:** When your business's name appears in either PPC or high-ranking organic search results, people see you. Using both approaches means they see twice as much of you. Remember, just because people don't click your listings every time doesn't mean you're doing something wrong; at the very least, you have visibility for your company that you wouldn't have enjoyed otherwise. You never know when your name will spontaneously pop up in someone's mind at a later date thanks to the exposure you got in search engine results.

Among the ways you can use organic and paid search to create a unified and well-balanced strategy is to *refine your keywords*. We note earlier in this chapter that the primo keywords you arrive at through SEO can and should then be put into your PPC ads, but the reverse is true as well. You can run a short-term paid search campaign with the keywords you're considering using for your SEO and get a fast read as to which ones get the highest response rate. You can then use those keywords to optimize your Web site and consequently improve the results you get from organic search.

Another method is *frequency*. For success with paid and organic search, make sure that you sprinkle your best keywords liberally throughout your Web site. The more frequently (within reason) they appear, the better position you get through organic search. Search engines use frequency to determine what position you get among the other PPC listings that appear in your category.

Although the frequency with which keywords appear on your Web site has a big impact on the search engine ranking you get, don't go nuts. Slipping keywords into every other sentence makes it painful for readers to try to hack their way through your copy. (And they may well thank you for that by bailing out.) So, where your keywords fit naturally, great — by all means, put them in. But where they aren't a natural fit, do your readers a favor and leave them aside.

Chapter 8

Getting Web Traffic for Free: Practicing Search Engine Optimization

*U*sing search engines to attract visitors to your local business is a theme that runs throughout this book. There's a good reason for that: In all likelihood, more people will come to your Web site from a search engine than from any other source. Upwards of 80 percent of computer users visit search engines regularly, so indisputably, those engines represent the mother lode of potential customers for your local business.

Search engine optimization (SEO) is the practice that helps you take advantage of how search engines organize content in the organic results of the search engine results page (SERP). This organization happen automatically as an outcome of an algorithm (a program employed by the search engines), which means that you don't pay to get your Web site listed as you do when you run pay-per-click ads — see Chapter 9.

Essentially, search engines are trying to find the most relevant and most useful content for consumers who are searching. SEO done well, is the art of helping search engines be more effective and finding useful content. SEO done poorly attempts to trick the search engine into listing a Web site. In the long run, if a Web page does not provide value to the consumer, it will ultimately fail in its SEO efforts in that it clogs up the SERP with useless clutter — something search engine companies have thousands of engineers trying to figure out how to avoid. Create useful content and structure in a way that is search friendly, and you will achieve higher search engine rankings and SEO success. And that's what this chapter is all about.

Getting click-throughs from organic search results can enhance your ROI (return on investment) because there's no direct cost charged to your advertising budget. Plus, of the 80 percent of computer users who use search engines, 75–80 percent of those tend to click an organic listing first, rather than a paid one. (We discuss some of the reasons for this habit in Chapter 7.)

Boil down these ideas, and you get this simple two-part formula: Search engines are critically important for driving people to your site. And practicing SEO is one of the primary ways your site achieves the greatest visibility on those search engines' lists.

Leveraging Local Search Listings for Easy Visibility

Here comes a curve ball. The first subject we address in this SEO chapter is *local search,* a kind of search that doesn't rely on SEO in the strict sense. However, local search is still a form of optimization, and looking at this type of search now — before we get into the details of real SEO — makes sense.

With local searches, you get the kind of optimization that helps maximize your overall presence and visibility on the Web; with SEO, the goal is to get better and better rankings among the organic listings that appear in search engine results.

We know that the distinction between these optimization goals is subtle, which we hope to clarify for you in this section. First, know three key things about local search:

- ✔ It's (almost always) free.
- ✔ It takes relatively little effort on your part.
- ✔ For many searches it actually gives you a better position than all other regular organic listings that appear on the same results page.

That last point is where the optimization we're talking about comes into play.

Your (nearly) top-dog status

Figure 8-1 shows the Google search results page for a search with local intent (in this case, *roofer in denver*). The hierarchy — from top to bottom — on such a page is pay-per-click (PPC) ads, local listings, and then organic listings. But how, you ask, do you get yourself that nice, fat position with a local listing for your business? And why would search engines think it's a good idea to give local listings such special treatment (and for free, no less)?

The how part is easy. Search engines obtain local listings, not through crawling around Web sites looking for useful keywords, but through information that you submit directly to the engines. A key part of that information is your location, including city, state, and zip code. That's all the search engines really need in order to know that you belong in their local search results. Therefore, by submitting your location information, in effect, you are optimizing your exposure on the Web.

Because you furnish information directly to the search engines, you provide them with everything they need to give you a spot in their prominent local listings. Your business doesn't even need a Web site to get this preferential treatment. Yes, you read that right. The information you fill in on the search engine form is enough in itself to get you into the local search game.

Regarding why local search results are given such prominence, the answer is that, like most of us, search engines want to be loved. Each engine wants to be everyone's primary go-to resource because it can make more money that way. The major search engines realize that a huge and growing percentage of their users is looking primarily for local listings. Hence, they give those listings a super-visible spot.

So, yes, local search really is one of those rare situations where everybody wins.

Before you start jumping up and down and shouting "Eureka! I've found the holy grail of search engine strategies and don't need to know anything about SEO!" stop and consider that, first, you're scaring the cat and, second, you're leaving a whole lot of potential customers floating around beyond the reach of your online net. You should view local listings as additions to your SEO efforts if you really want to get the most out of organic search. In other words, local search should definitely be in the mix, but it can't be the mix.

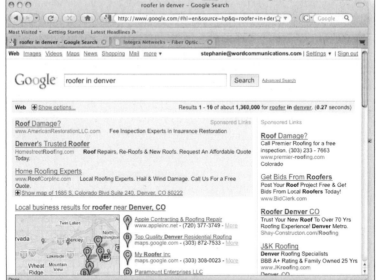

Figure 8-1:
Local search listings get the highest ranking among other organic search results.

Counting the reasons to hook up with local searches

Local listings get preferential placement; getting listed takes relatively little effort on your part; and the number of people who use the major search engines as their means of finding local businesses is steadily growing. Yep, local listings are very cool things. So cool, in fact, that you'd be woefully remiss not to put them to work for your business. Here are some more reasons why:

- ✔ **Invested time and effort is minimal:** Local listings increase your business's visibility and traffic, and they can do it with relatively little effort on your part. Just fill out the search engine form, and you're officially in the game. You don't have to do any Web site optimization (which, we admit, can chew up some of your valuable time).

- ✔ **Local listings find qualified customers:** Thanks to the nature of local listings and the information you provide when creating your listing, odds are excellent that you'll attract customers who live, work, or otherwise hang out in the geographic area you serve — which can be a big help in generating repeat business.

Anyone who's looking for a business like yours in your locality is also probably ready to contact you right now. If your listing doesn't show up on that person's local search, you're just kissing their business goodbye and driving them straight into the arms of a competitor.

✔ **You can reach mobile searchers:** Local listings display on cell phones and PDAs for the benefit of mobile consumers.

✔ **Tracking results is simple:** Even though local listings are less sophisticated than some other online advertising techniques, the major search engines can provide you with some robust reporting tools to help you track results. For example, you can tell how many customers are finding you through local search and what keywords they're using to find you.

✔ **You can supply more than your location:** In addition to posting your address and phone number in a local listing, you can include your hours of operation, photos and videos, and even online coupons. Some search engines charge a small fee for these fancier extras, but Google does not. An example of a Google form that lets you add extra elements is shown in Figure 8-2.

Figure 8-2:
A Google form helps you provide extra business information.

How to go local

Getting a local listing to show up prominently on a results page is very easy. You simply fill out a brief online form, and you're off to the races.

You get the form directly from the search engines you want your listing to appear on. (You can find a listing of search engine links in Chapter 2.) The simple stuff that you enter is your name, your company's name, and its address, phone number, and e-mail address.

Describe yourself in 25 words (or so)

Here's an example of how the description section of a local search listing form might function. Suppose that you sell and install car stereo systems, and you figure your primary service area is northwest Tulsa. On the description line of the form, you enter: *Brand-name car stereo electronics and speakers sold and installed at two locations in northwest Tulsa.* Your business might be found and listed if someone searches for

✔ *car stereo tulsa:* You have a good chance of popping up with this combination of terms unless Tulsa has an inordinately large number of car stereo businesses.

✔ *car speakers oklahoma* or *car stereo installation eastern OK:* With these combinations, your ranking won't be quite as high because a larger area (the state) is part of the search term.

The most important information that you enter is a description of your business; the words you use to describe what the business offers help trigger the appearance of your listing on a search engine results page. The words in your description combined with the address information you enter create the hooks that will snag a search engine's attention when a searcher enters some combination of those words and location as search terms.

Be careful with how your description presents your business. Keep your description brief, straightforward, and objective. Give the search engines the facts — just the facts. Search engines won't accept a description that sounds too much like an advertisement. The minute you start sliding in adjectives (such as *best, most experienced, lowest-priced,* and so on), you're probably just asking for trouble. If the search engines see advertising lingo, they smell spam, and they reject your listing.

When the type of business you're in has many competitors whose descriptions are similar, not all of the companies show up on any single search results page. Most search engines do a kind of random sampling of local listings to come up with the 5, 8, 10, or more selections that they list on any given page. Consequently, if the same user types exactly the same geographic modifier(s) again three seconds later, he'll probably get a different mix of local listings.

Can you give your company a leg up in the round-robin local search process in addition to simply claiming your listing? Some experts say that including reviews you receive from customers or clients will give you a certain degree of precedence, but that's not a hard and fast rule. Remember that your listing will appear on a regular basis. And it's not as if you're paying for the privilege, right?

Looking at local listing providers

Each of the major search engines has a somewhat different way of serving businesses that apply for inclusion in their local search results. The upcoming sections tell you how each of today's leading local search providers handles and presents the listings it posts.

Google Local Search

Not surprisingly, Google is considered by many to have the most powerful local search engine, in part because Google integrates a large and sophisticated map alongside the local search results. The map has overlaid balloon icons that show the exact locations of the local businesses listed. Click a balloon, and a larger balloon pops up showing that business' full address and phone number, plus links (when applicable) to the company's Web site, to customer reviews, and to driving directions.

If Google has already indexed your site automatically on the basis of your address and phone number, chances are you've already appeared in Google Local Search results (without those handy extra links). If that level of visibility is enough to satisfy you, you really don't have to do anything else. If you want to explicitly add your company to Google Local Search, you do that through the Google Local Business Center at `www.google.com/local/add`. You need to have a Google account to post your listing, but you can open one completely free of charge.

Yahoo! Local Search

Yahoo! Local Search also provides a map pinpointing the local businesses listed, but it's neither as large nor as sophisticated as the Google maps. Figure 8-3 shows a typical local results map on Yahoo!

Yahoo! and Google also have a different way of handling reviews. Google displays only pre-existing *reviews* that it gathers from other sites (for example, a site specializing in restaurant reviews), but Yahoo! lets anyone with a Yahoo! ID create a review directly on the local listing page where the business appears.

Yahoo! offers a basic, free service that provides you with a local listing. As long as you have (or get) a Yahoo! ID, you can add your local listing to their search engine, whether or not you currently have a Web site. If you don't have an ID, Yahoo! also offers a free, five-page Web site just for signing up, which you can do at `http://listings.local.yahoo.com/signup/create_1.php`.

Yahoo! also offers an enhanced local listing for $9.95 a month; fork over that fee and you can include more detailed information, links to your coupons, and so on. And the fee will, in most cases, guarantee preferential placement in the local results (provided, of course, that your listing is sufficiently relevant to the search terms a user enters). You can find more information about these enhanced listings at `http://listings.local.yahoo.com/#enhanced`.

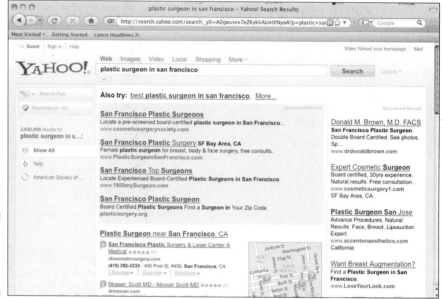

Figure 8-3:
A local
search on
Yahoo!

Bing Local Search

Formerly known as MSN.com, Bing is similar to Google in that your business already has an excellent chance of appearing in Bing Local Search results. But Bing goes about gathering companies' information in a slightly different way. The folks at Bing get most of their information about a particular business from local telephone records, so, if you have a valid business telephone listing in the *White Pages* or *Yellow Pages,* you'll show up on Bing Local Search. Of course, you can (and should) also explicitly add and categorize your company, and it costs you nothing to do it. You can learn more about Bing's Local Search program at the Bing Local Business Center, `http://ssl.bing.com/listings`.

Understanding How Search Engines Organize Content

We mention SEO in earlier chapters, but that just got your toes damp. Now we're talking up-to-your-eyeballs immersion — or at least waist-level wading — to get you on track to optimize your business's Web presence.

To get a handle on SEO, you need to understand exactly how search engines find and categorize the content that shows up in their non-local-search organic listings.

First, they crawl

Search engines rely on proprietary, automated software agents called *spiders, crawlers, robots,* and just plain *bots.* For simplicity's sake, we refer to all these agents collectively as robots. These robots are the seekers of content on the Internet, and the content they find on individual Web pages plays a key role in how search engines operate.

The robots may be smart little critters, but they're not human beings. They don't see pictures. They can't appreciate graphs. The only thing they can do is read what's on a Web page, and further, they can read and understand only the text that's laid out in a format that's already been tuned to their needs. The process of tuning all your Web site's pages to the needs of the various search engines is the core, the *sine qua non,* the beating heart of any success-ful SEO strategy.

Robots primarily look for links. After all, the whole idea behind the Internet is that related pages and sites should be linked together, and robots simply follow that paradigm. Robots will find the important content within your site if (and, generally speaking, *only* if) other credible, reputable Web sites link to it. This process is referred to as *building reciprocal links* with other topically similar sites, and it enables people to reach your site with a click. A majority of the SEO game involves linking up with reciprocal sites (a subject we deal with in greater detail in the later section "External linking strategies").

So, a robot is crawling around Site A where it finds a link to Site B. It follows that link and looks around Site B, absorbing the (properly formatted) text that Site B has to offer, including links to yet other sites. In the process, it reports to its search engine the URLs of the sites that it visits (and can under-stand). These URLs show up in that search engine's organic listings.

Then, they index

Search engines take all the goodies (URLs and key text) that the robots bring back and create an index or database. Each search engine has its own rules and algorithms that it uses to evaluate and score the information that its robots collect. After the search engine finds, evaluates, and deems your Web site worthy under its rules, it includes your Web site in the index. Therefore, your site is available to appear in the organic results when a searcher enters the relevant keywords in her query.

The search engine takes a searcher's query and, at the speed of a finger snap, goes through a series of steps to determine which sites are the most relevant to that particular search. Those sites appear in the search results, which, considering the roughly three bazillion Web sites on the Net, is a pretty nifty accomplishment.

Disappearing ink: A major search engine taboo

Did you ever play with disappearing ink when you were a kid? You'd write something in blue or black ink on a white piece of paper, and your writing was legible — but not for long. In 10 minutes or so, the ink had magically disappeared into the paper.

A Web page equivalent of that funky old novelty is *hidden text,* and the people who use it are almost invariably spammers. In fact, the practice of using hidden text is often called *search engine spam.* The text is hidden by making it the same color as the background; human readers can't see it, but search engine robots can. The robots simply register the fact that text is on the page and report the content back to the search engine whence they came.

What the spammer is trying to do is fool the search engine into thinking that a Web site has content that it really doesn't have. For example, a site that sells used farm equipment adds hidden text about new farm equipment even though the site contains nothing readable (by humans) about new merchandise. And (use your imagination) some spammers get a lot more dastardly than that.

The bottom line is that hidden text can make a search engine's results look un-useful and can ultimately degrade its overall performance and reputation. So the use of hidden text has — thankfully — been made illegal.

Good old disappearing ink, on the other hand, is probably still available out there. Somewhere.

Next, they rank

Even the highly relevant site listings that the search engine gleans from its index don't just appear willy-nilly on the search results page. They're ranked according to that search engine's own particular, private, top-secret criteria.

We can't know the top-secret criteria for sure, but Table 8-1 shows what we deduce as characteristics of ranking criteria from each of the three major search engines' observable behavior.

Table 8-1		Search Engine Ranking Behavior
Search Engine	*Rank*	*Observations*
Google	1st	Regarded by many to be the most accurate in terms of relevance; good at weeding out duplicate and irrelevant sites; favors *off-page SEO* (optimization based on links from well-established third-party sites) in determining rankings; good at filtering out sites built to artificially boost rankings (a form of spam)

Search Engine	Rank	Observations
Yahoo!	2nd	Criticized by some as less accurate than Google or as aggressive at filtering out potentially deceptive sites; favors *on-page SEO* (optimization based on a site's own page content, page titles, and so on) in determining rankings; uses paid-inclusion listings, which can create a bias for or against a given site
Bing (formerly MSN)	3rd	Newer to the game than Google and Yahoo!; favors *on-page SEO* (like Yahoo!); some experts claimed that MSN wasn't as good as Google or Yahoo! at avoiding spam sites or obviously artificial ones; however, all the changes to Bing with the new release make broad generalizations difficult at this point.

Making Your Site SEO Friendly

SEO helps search engines determine what your site and its pages are about, where they fit in the engine's index, and how prominent a ranking they deserve. The better and more polished your (or your consultant's) SEO skills, the greater the rewards. SEO can eventually get your business a place among the search engines' most liked and list-worthy sites.

SEO is — and has to be — an ongoing, all-touching kind of strategy. Very little of a Web site's content and structure can't be optimized. Then, after a time, you revisit and re-optimize. When done correctly, your SEO efforts focus on everything from your content and tags to your links and filenames to your site map and coding. You can consider all these elements of your Web site as oars rowing in the same direction. They all represent the same unique and important subject: your business.

SEO greases the wheels of commerce and makes the cash register ring. You simply, truly, seriously can't afford to ignore it. Similar to the considerations regarding your business Web site that we discuss at length in Chapter 4, the SEO process is something you (probably) shouldn't tackle on your lonesome. Unless you've built your own site and can bring some serious optimization chops to the table, you'll benefit immensely from the assistance of a professional SEO consultant. We think you'll understand why we make this recommendation as we present the major elements that come into play in any search engine optimization strategy.

Selecting keywords

Consider this message carved in stone: Keywords form the nucleus of any proper SEO effort, and carefully selecting the right keywords is absolutely critical to your success.

The process for selecting keywords has two parts:

- ✔ **Creating a list of possible keywords.** Review your site content to identify which keywords (word combinations and phrases) describe the main categories of your business. Write down every relevant keyword under each category you find. Expand the list by including all of your brand and product names, as well as plurals and synonyms for each word or phrase on your initial list. Also, remember to think like your customers: How might your customers ask for your product or service?

- ✔ **Narrowing the list to the best keywords.** Delete generic keywords on your list that could relate to a wide spectrum of products or services; and because one-word keywords are likely to be too generic, try using two- or three-word phrases. Also, delete keywords that aren't closely related to your primary landing page themes. (See Chapter 5 for more about landing pages.)

Maybe you think this selection process sounds easy, but it isn't. It's not exactly astrophysics either; we help you take the steps that turn plain old, average, everyday words into big, bright search engine signposts.

Creating a keyword list

Start by putting yourself in your customers' shoes. It's probably safe to assume that they see your business somewhat differently than you do. After all, you're on the inside; you know the jargon; you know what's really important and what isn't.

But your customers only know that they need the kind of product or service your business offers. Consequently, the words they pump into a search engine are probably simple, basic, down-to-earth, and, in the eyes of insiders (that's you), amateurish. Your customers choose different, non-jargony words because they're on the outside of your business. Time for you to think like an outsider, too.

Suppose that you're an optician. As someone familiar with an optician's business, you might search for *diopter, astigmatism,* or *flexible titanium alloy temples.* But your average customer is probably going to look for *glasses, eye tests,* or *contact lenses.*

Your prospective customers aren't professionals in your field. They go for the simple, direct, painfully obvious words to describe your products or services.

Fortunately, you don't have to fly blind to come up with a list of the keywords your customers might choose. Basic research can get you on your way to building a solid keyword list. You can

✔ Take advantage of excellent sites where you find free keyword tools, including

- *Wordtracker:* Helps you identify the keywords you need to rise above your competitors in the search engine rankings. (`www.wordtracker.com`)

- *Google Keyword Tool:* Offers you an easy way to generate a list of relevant keywords and phrases. (`https://adwords.google.com/select/KeywordToolExternal`)

✔ Find out what keyword tags your competitors are using; you'll find them through the source code link on their Web sites, as shown in Figure 8-4.

✔ If you already use keywords, check your site analytics to find out which words work best to drive traffic to your site.

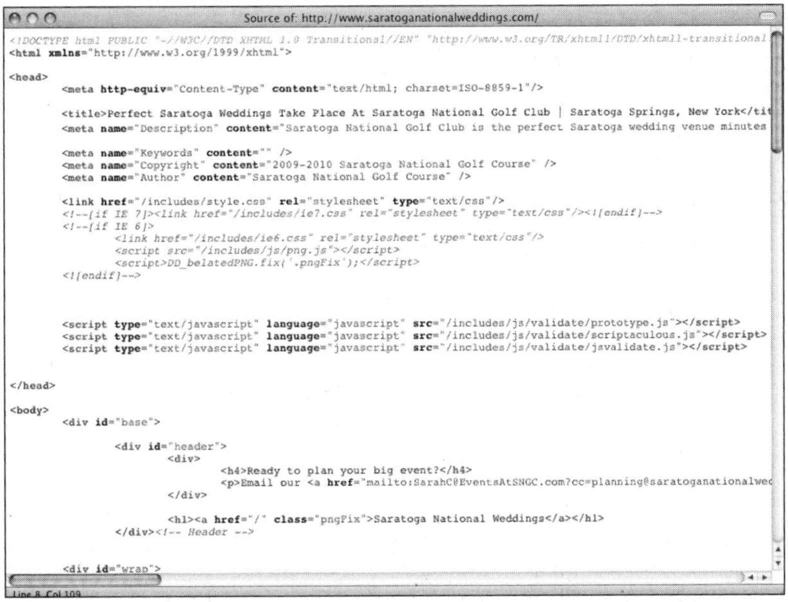

Figure 8-4:
A source code page, showing the keywords the site uses.

```
Source of: http://www.saratoganationalweddings.com/
<!DOCTYPE html PUBLIC "-//W3C//DTD XHTML 1.0 Transitional//EN" "http://www.w3.org/TR/xhtml1/DTD/xhtml1-transitional
<html xmlns="http://www.w3.org/1999/xhtml">

<head>

    <meta http-equiv="Content-Type" content="text/html; charset=ISO-8859-1"/>

    <title>Perfect Saratoga Weddings Take Place At Saratoga National Golf Club | Saratoga Springs, New York</tit
    <meta name="Description" content="Saratoga National Golf Club is the perfect Saratoga wedding venue minutes

    <meta name="Keywords" content="" />
    <meta name="Copyright" content="2009-2010 Saratoga National Golf Course" />
    <meta name="Author" content="Saratoga National Golf Course" />

    <link href="/includes/style.css" rel="stylesheet" type="text/css"/>
    <!--[if IE 7]><link href="/includes/ie7.css" rel="stylesheet" type="text/css"/><![endif]-->
    <!--[if IE 6]>
        <link href="/includes/ie6.css" rel="stylesheet" type="text/css"/>
        <script src="/includes/js/png.js"></script>
        <script>DD_belatedPNG.fix('.pngFix');</script>
    <![endif]-->


    <script type="text/javascript" language="javascript" src="/includes/js/validate/prototype.js"></script>
    <script type="text/javascript" language="javascript" src="/includes/js/validate/scriptaculous.js"></script>
    <script type="text/javascript" language="javascript" src="/includes/js/validate/jsvalidate.js"></script>

</head>

<body>

    <div id="base">

        <div id="header">
            <div>
                    <h4>Ready to plan your big event?</h4>
                    <p>Email our <a href="mailto:SarahC@EventsAtSNGC.com?cc=planning@saratoganationalwed
            </div>

            <h1><a href="/" class="pngFix">Saratoga National Weddings</a></h1>
        </div><!-- Header -->

    <div id="wrap">
```
Line 8, Col 109

Combine the words you find through your research into a large list of potential keywords for your site. The list no doubt contains many more keywords than you can actually use, but that's okay. Doing the research helps build a list of qualified words to choose from. The following list gives an example of the potential keywords for a plumber in Brooklyn, New York:

> 24 7 plumber greenpoint
> 24 7 plumbing service park slope
> 24 hour maintenance plumber brooklyn ny
> 24 hour plumber brooklyn
> 24 hour plumber Clinton hill
> 24 hr plumber brooklyn ny
> 24 hr plumbing brooklyn
> 24hr plumber greenpoint
> apartment plumber park slope
> find a plumbing company brooklyn
> general plumbing brooklyn
> kitchen remodeling plumber brooklyn ny
> licensed plumbers Williamsburg
> local plumbing business brooklyn
> maintenance plumber brooklyn
> plumber brooklyn
> plumber brooklyn ny
> plumber park slope
> plumber Williamsburg
> plumbers Bedford
> plumbers brooklyn
> plumbers brooklyn ny
> plumbers bushwick
> plumbers red hook
> plumbers ridgewood ny
> plumbing company brooklyn
> plumbing contractor brooklyn heights
> registered 24 hour plumber brooklyn
> top plumbers brooklyn
> top plumbing company Bedford

Narrowing your keyword list

When you're ready to take the plunge into selecting your own keywords from the vast pool of possibilities, consider these important strategies:

- ✔ **Avoid broad keywords:** The more general and generic a keyword, the harder it will be for that keyword to produce a respectable rank on a search results page. Using the keyword *veterinarian* is fine if you personally have 300 clinics scattered around the country. But if you have only one and it's located just outside Cleveland, you'll rank a lot higher by using *veterinarian shaker heights* or *veterinarian 44120* instead. If you offer a not-too-common service (such as boarding), you can include that specific in your keywords, too. The combination *veterinarian boarding 44120* should work nicely.

✔ **Avoid vague keywords:** Some keywords can have alternative meanings, so beware. A person searching for *pipe repair* might be looking for a plumber, someone to clean a pipe organ, or fix an antique briar smoking pipe. So if you run a plumbing business specializing in repair, try using *kitchen pipe repair* or *bathroom pipe repair* as a keyword combination to attract the right searchers.

✔ **Use keyword modifiers:** Use modifiers that allow your pages to be found under a variety of searches and give you a higher ranking. Table 8-2 shows various modifiers — some obvious and others not so — that you might consider using.

Table 8-2	Keyword Modifiers	
Most Searched	*Money Related*	*Geographically Specific*
Your company name	Your rates	Your city
Your services	Your product pricing	Your city's surrounding suburbs
Professional	*Deals*	Your state
Best	*Affordable*	Your county
Top	*Package(s)*	Your zip code
Leading	*Offer(s)*	
Solution	*Value*	
	Discount	

Adjusting site structure

Search engines use cues from you to determine how best to index your site for Web searchers. These cues usually include everything from what you name your Web pages to how they're linked together to how a searcher might be expected to navigate from one page to another. The net result is that how your Web site is structured affects its ability to attract the attention of search engines and influences how good a ranking it gets in the search results.

Pay attention to the names you give your site's pages. Don't give your pages generic, computer-geek names like *page1.html*. Instead, use filenames that include the keywords you're trying to rank with. So, if your page is about Chicago florists, name the page *chicago-florists.html*. Assigning meaningful page names is the sort of little tweak that can make a meaningful difference in your search engine rankings.

Filling up your footers

In the footer section of your Web site, including anchor text links to important pages on your site is a good idea. *Anchor text* is the visible, clickable text in a hyperlink. For example, rather than using *Click here,* which tells the search engines nothing, a plumber might use anchor text such as *Troubleshooting Common Household Plumbing Problems.* Such links help tell search engines what the linked to page are about. (Just be careful not to overdo it and look like you're trying to stuff keywords that have no real purpose into the footer.) The footer is also a great place to include your full contact information, including your phone number, and company information like privacy policies, terms of use, and so on. This kind of link helps search engines tie your Web site to a certain location and helps you rank better in localized searches.

A lot of things in life are annoying, but right up near the top of the list are Web sites that make finding the business contact information about as easy as finding cattle in Manhattan. If a customer needs help now, don't make them truck through a bunch of links or pages to find your phone number. By the time they do find it, chances are they won't be in a pleasant mood — and won't be much fun to talk to. Put your business contact information in the footer so it's available from any page.

Including site maps

A *site map* is a page within your Web site that clearly lays out the hierarchy of your site. Think of the site map as a sort of outline of your site's content. Having a clear site map readily available makes navigating your site easier for both visitors and search engine robots alike.

A good free tool that can create an effective site map for you is available at www.xml-sitemaps.com. After the tool completes the creation part, you simply upload the site map file to your Web site and put a link to it on each of your pages.

Making good use of tags

Web site tags fall into four basic categories, each of which has a potential to affect your site's SEO positively:

- ✔ **Meta tags:** Each page on your site should have unique meta tags that encapsulate — briefly and precisely — what the content of that page is about. You can use up to 10 keywords in a meta tag, but don't repeat the same word over and over or the whole meta tag gets watered down into uselessness, and search engines ignore them. A good meta tag example is shown in Figure 8-5.

✔ **Meta descriptions:** A meta description is a short summary of each page's content, and each page should have its own unique summary. (See Figure 8-5.) Meta tags contain the keywords that help your site get noticed, but perhaps more importantly meta descriptions contain the copy that will often show up verbatim on a search engine's results page (depending on the exact search). This copy can often have a huge impact on whether or not a searcher ultimately clicks on your listing in the organic results. You usually draw the meta description text from copy that already exists within your site; it can be up to a few sentences in length and will include your keywords within it.

✔ **Title tags:** Each page on your site should have its own unique title tag of 65 characters or less (no cheating), and the title should include two or three keywords that you want to be ranked by. Figure 8-6 shows a sample title tag.

✔ **Alt tags:** Search engines can't read images that you use on your site, but they can read the alt text that's associated with each image. This alt tag is simply a label that you hang on each of your site's images. It describes (with the inclusion of some keywords) what that image shows. Alt tags can help both organic search as well as when someone searches specifically for images (on Google for instance you can do this at `http://images.google.com`). Figure 8-7 is an example of a good alt tag.

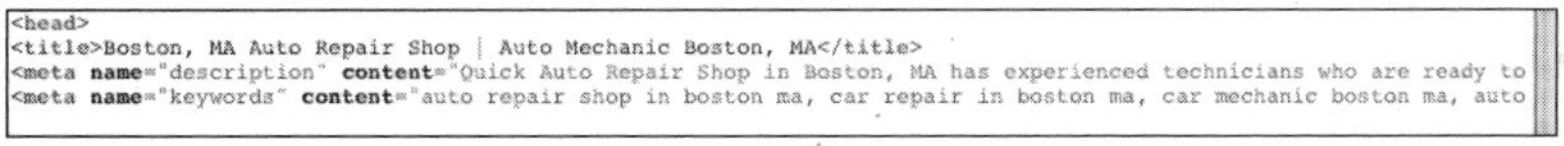

Figure 8-5:
Meta tags and descriptions describe contents.

```
<head>
<title>Boston, MA Auto Repair Shop | Auto Mechanic Boston, MA</title>
<meta name="description" content="Quick Auto Repair Shop in Boston, MA has experienced technicians who are ready to
<meta name="keywords" content="auto repair shop in boston ma, car repair in boston ma, car mechanic boston ma, auto
```

Figure 8-6:
How a title tag affects the heading.

About Quick Auto Repair Shop | Boston, MA Auto Muffler and Exhaust | 617-379-2623

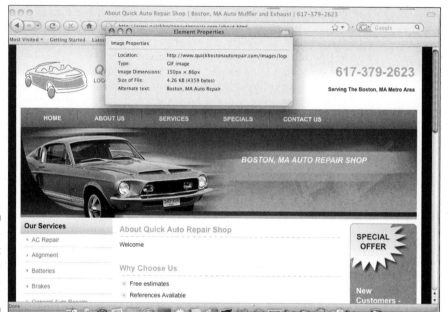

Figure 8-7:
A sample alt
tag, used to
describe an
image.

At the risk of sounding like we're pulling the old bait-and-switch routine on you, we need to tell you that as widely used as tags have been in the past, they're becoming less and less important to search engines *themselves*. At one time, search engines relied heavily on tags to order their search results. But they've become victims of too many unscrupulous people who use tags to try to game the search engine system. (Google, for one, is good and sick of this play, and many experts suggest that they are on the verge of implementing a little doohickey that will make most tags irrelevant to the ordering of their search results.) Nevertheless, tags are still *very* important to the businesses that appear in search results because tags are often, in essence, the copy that searchers see as part of each local listing. To boil it down: Tags today mean less to the search engines themselves but remain highly important to the searchers who use the engines and to the local businesses whose listings they find.

Page optimization

Like your site as a whole, each *page* of your site can and should be optimized because such optimization has a lot to do with how well you'll be ranked. Search engines just love fresh and unique content — so much so that their robots routinely cruise your site to see whether you've done something new. As always, the more relevant your content is to your keywords, the better.

When you set about optimizing each page, keep these things in mind:

✔ **Sprinkle — don't drench — your site with keywords.** Include your keywords throughout your site's content — but don't go crazy. Write naturally and don't try to stuff 10 pounds of whatever into a five-pound bag. Ditto on a per-page basis: Repeating your keywords over and over on a page is annoying to readers. Search engines are smart enough to realize what you're trying to do — and will penalize you in the rankings.

✔ **Favor specific phrases over single keywords.** Forget about trying to rank well for globally applicable, one-word keywords (such as *dentist*). Getting properly noticed by using single keywords runs the short gamut from incredibly difficult to completely impossible. Concentrate instead on two- or three-word phrases (such as *family dentist Philadelphia* or *dental veneers 19104*), and you'll get better rankings and better-qualified visitors.

✔ **Limit the number of keyword phrases used on any one page.** Be aware that search results are based on a number of factors, a primary one being the relevance of those results to the terms the searcher is using. If you're targeting 10, 20, or 30 search terms per page, your page loses focus and really winds up not being about anything. A better SEO practice is to concentrate on just one or two phrases per page. For this practice, less is invariably more.

✔ **Keep your content fresh.** Remember that the robots are out there, looking and feasting. Give them something new and tasty to feed on.

✔ **Mind the look and position of keywords.** Put your keywords in bold or italicized type, as search engines will give these more importance. (Again, don't go crazy with keyword repetition, or the page will look, well, awful.) Generally, the higher your keywords appear on the page, the better the score you'll get from a search engine.

✔ **Break down your content.** Use headlines, sub-headlines, and bullet points to present your page content. Don't think narrative stream, think chunks. Include your keywords in these elements, too, because that will only help your ranking.

✔ **Avoid borrowed content.** Search engines have a way of remembering everything — including content they've seen on another Web site. If that same content suddenly shows up, word for word, on yours, they won't turn you over to the authorities, but they may decide to dock your rankings big time.

Figure 8-8 illustrates how keywords can be used effectively — but judiciously — on a sample Web page.

Figure 8-8:
Use
keywords
sparingly
and in the
right places.

Internal linking strategies

Linking to the other pages within your Web site is a good way to help both visitors and robots find their way around. Such links are often found within *anchor text,* and are descriptive so that the links seem to occur naturally. The links themselves blend in with the message presented in the anchor text.

For example, having this anchor text (with link) on your Web site

> Check out our many <u>plumbing services</u> and let us know how we can help you.

is much better than having

> Click <u>here</u> to see our plumbing services.

Also, links that appear within a block of text tend to have higher search-ranking value than links that are isolated. Like keywords, the higher a link appears on the page, the more weight search engines give it.

External linking strategies

Search engine rankings are a lot like a popularity contest. If your site is linked to by several credible third-party sites, a search engine will think you never have trouble getting a prom date, and they'll give you a nice healthy spot in their rankings. To gain the right kind of popularity, these other sites must be credible. A credible third-party site is one that has an identifiable brand name (Wikipedia, *The New York Times*, and so on), strong organic rankings of its own, lots of traffic, and plenty of inbound links.

Getting linked to by spam sites, for example, can actually harm your site's reputation — and your rank. So, to protect your site's reputation and its search engine rankings, you'll want to have your Web site linked to from as many other quality (what we call *credible*) sites as possible.

How exactly do you pull off this linking magic? Here are a few ideas:

- ✔ **Have excellent content.** Build a Web site with content so interesting, unique, or indispensable that other sites will *want* to link to you. It really is a case of "if you build it, they will come." Remember that those other folks want to make their sites interesting, unique, or indispensable, too, and they'll be looking for links that make them look good. Some easily implementable ideas for content formats include videos, blogs, or a tip of the day. (See Chapter 5 for more on online video and Chapter 13 for a discussion on blogs.)

- ✔ **Ask.** (There's a wild and crazy idea.) Go to the owner of another, related site, and simply ask to add a link for your site on his or her site. The price for this link will likely be a reciprocal link on your site — but, hey, fair's fair.

- ✔ **Submit press releases to some of the many PR sites.** Just make sure that your release actually contains some news of real interest. (No one will care, for example, that your basset hound just had puppies.) But when you've recently become a dealership for some new product, done a service job of note, or won a commendation or award, submit that information. PR folks eat up that stuff.

- ✔ **Submit your Web site to the directories that list companies like yours.**

- ✔ **Participate in blogs, and link back to your site from your signature.** You'd be amazed how many clicks you can get from doing this — and the search engines will duly note your link, as well.

For super, double-good rankings, make sure to include your target keywords in the link that other people put on their site. Search engines will see it and give you points for your keywords, thus killing the proverbial two birds with one link.

Domain names and URLs

Search engines like domain names that include keywords within them. So, if you're trying to get rankings for the keyword phrase *Phoenix Electricians,* www.phoenixelectricians.com would be a better, stronger URL than www.wiredelectricians.com. Even if your primary URL won't comfortably accommodate a keyword or two, you can always register a secondary URL designed to house your targeted words nicely.

Looking at Rankings with the Proper Perspective

After your Web site is built, optimized, and online, your next step is to sit down. Breathe deeply. Put your feet up. And be patient.

Neither Rome nor Des Moines was built in a day, and so it is with getting search engines to list you. Back when search engines were new and only a few intrepid souls had figured out how to use them, a listing would appear in no time at all. Today, the wait for a decent listing position can be weeks, months, even (gasp) a year or more. Because search engines favor great content and inbound links so much and getting those things takes time, it's important to understand that SEO is, by definition, a gradual process.

You may also experience delayed gratification because of the pecking order. Your site may well show up within a few weeks but fall on page 73 of the listings where no one will ever find you. Slowly, you'll climb as other sites fall off. Maybe a little more optimization can help you leapfrog some sites between you and the top, but even that takes time.

Here are a few things you can do while you're waiting:

- **Search your own keywords on the various search engines.** See whether your local competitors have a decent position in the rankings. This exercise gives you a real-world understanding of exactly what you're up against (which may not be much of a comfort, but it's better than *not* knowing, right?)

- **Add new content to your site on an aggressive, ongoing basis.** Think about how you might incorporate tips, case studies, reviews, or other new elements that will spice up the information on your site and keep the robots interested. When these added features repeat your keywords, extra search engine brownie points will probably come your way.

✔ **Don't kid yourself.** If you were smart enough to figure out a foolproof way to rocket yourself up to the top of the listings, you'd be smart enough to pull off a massive Swiss bank heist and wouldn't need a Web site to begin with. No, Virginia, there are no shortcuts. The major search engines have already seen many scams and have cut the scammers off at the knees. (Anyone who tells you he can successfully cheat the system is pulling your leg.)

✔ **Don't take it personally.** How well your Web site ranks has little to do with how well you run your business and do your job. Ranking is a reflection of how good your *site* is on its own and in relation to your competition's sites. More accurately, ranking really reflects how good a bunch of search engine people you've never met (and never will) think your site is. In times of distress, repeat to yourself 20 times in rapid succession: "Pffft. What do they know?" When it comes down to your business and your industry, the answer is: A whole lot less than you do.

Getting Help Optimizing Your Web Site

Here's that pesky subject again: Should you or should you not get SEO help from a professional? This question is as relevant to SEO as it is to the initial building of your site. (See Chapter 5 for that lengthy discussion.)

In either case, put the question into context before you make a decision. The two most meaningful contextual issues are

✔ **Time:** How much do you have? Maybe you run a busy dental practice and, between seeing patients and doing paperwork, you barely have time for lunch much less for noodling with SEO. If so, get a pro.

On the other hand, maybe your business is small and seasonal. In that case, going the DIY route may make perfect sense.

✔ **Expertise:** Do you have it or not? If you have a lot of experience with computers and the Internet, you could be a great candidate for handling your own SEO. If you don't, you're probably not — so put a pro on the case.

Some DIY resources

Deciding to go with DIY SEO doesn't mean that you have to do it all alone. Here are some great resources to help you get started:

✔ **Google SEO Starter Guide:** Besides taking pride in having one of the galaxy's longer URLs, this is a 22-page guide from the mouth of Google that walks you through how to improve your sites' interaction with users and search engines (that is, move up the SERP). (`www.google.com/webmasters/docs/search-engine-optimization-starter-guide.pdf`)

✔ **Search Engine Watch:** According to their meta description (remember those?): "Search Engine Watch is the authoritative guide to search engine marketing (SEM) and search engine optimization (SEO), offering the latest news about search engines." (http://searchenginewatch.com)

✔ **SEOmoz:** A hub containing education, tools, and resources for SEO. (www.seomoz.org)

✔ **Local SEO Guide:** Local SEO expert Andrew Shotland's informative blog. (www.localseoguide.com)

✔ **SEO Book:** Offers training programs on a variety of SEO topics. (www.seobook.com)

Using an SEO professional: Some tips

If you decide to go with an outside SEO consultant, proceed with caution. You'll find a lot of consultants and companies offering SEO services so do your research — your due diligence — before you sign up with any SEO professional. You should

✔ **Ask for references and examples of work they've done for other businesses.** And when you get references, call them.

✔ **Ask how much experience they have working with businesses in your industry.** After all, you want to pay them to make (and keep) your Web site optimized, not to start learning about your business, industry, and customers from the ground up.

✔ **Ask them how long they've been in the SEO business.** And confirm the answer you get. (**Hint:** If the answer is "Since 1947," move on.)

✔ **Ask what type of service and periodic reporting to expect.** Also, find out whom you can speak to if you have questions or problems.

✔ **Ask how they gauge success.** Do they measure success by good rankings? Number of clicks? Conversion rates? It matters because you don't want to work with someone whose definition of success is markedly different from your own.

✔ **Ask them if they require that you sign a contract and find out what the terms of that contract are.** How long is the contract term? What's their cancellation policy? Are there any money-back guarantees? If the answers make you queasy, step out for some air. And keep going.

 Don't let the number and tone of the questions you need answered strike you with fear and loathing regarding the use of SEO professionals. We believe that some very good consultants and companies can take a great weight off your shoulders while earnestly and efficiently fostering your success. Here are some great resources for finding the kind of SEO consultant or company you're really looking for:

- ✔ **SEO Consultants Directory:** A directory of SEO consultants from around the world. (www.seoconsultants.com)

- ✔ **oDesk:** A great place to source top-flight talent for projects averaging $5,000. (www.oDesk.co)

- ✔ **ExactFactor:** An automated SEO service starting as low as $29 per month. (www.exactfactor.com)

- ✔ **WebsiteBreaktrhough:** A great resource for SEO services, training, and education. (www.websitebreakthrough.com)

- ✔ **Local Splash:** An SEO provider focused on small, local businesses. (www.localsplash.com)

Happy hunting.

Chapter 9

The Nuts and Bolts of Search Engine Advertising

*T*hink of search engine marketing as a friendly two-headed creature. One head is *organic listings* (see Chapter 8), which are the non-paid, just-sort-of-happen-when-you-set-up-your-site-right listings that make up the vast majority of search engine results. The more effectively you optimize and refine your Web site, the higher the rank that search engines will give your listing on their search engine results pages (SERPs). The other head is *paid search advertising* (or pay-per-click [PPC] ads or sponsored listings), which is what this chapter is all about.

Paid search advertising is the crown jewel of search — and rightly so — because it's one of the fastest and most effective ways to bring customers who are ready to buy straight to your Web site. Paid search is fast because, after you set a ceiling on the amount you'll spend per click and per day, if that ceiling is high enough to make you competitive with others bidding on the same keywords, your ad will appear immediately among the most prominent listings on a SERP. (Organic listings, on the other hand, will often rise in the rankings much more slowly as your optimization efforts take hold.) As for effectiveness, paid search allows you to specifically target people searching for the exact products and services you offer in the exact location you offer them. Additionally, paid search allows you to specifically tailor your message depending on the exact keyword the consumer searched for. How's that for effective?

Sponsored listings have a couple other things going for them, too. They're extremely easy to measure, so you can keep track, on a nearly real-time basis, of how well your investment performs. You can also tweak your listings for better and better performance as often as you like.

Using a Proven Strategy for Small Business

Organic listings are great, but you face long odds of getting ranked among your top competitors on a SERP unless your optimization efforts have been sharpened to a fine edge. That's why you should seriously — and we mean *seriously* — consider coupling your organic listings with a paid search campaign.

Paid search has the following benefits:

- **Low initial risk:** If you have reservations about paying for a search engine listing, you can dip your toe in the water by allocating a modest initial investment to see what happens. If your Web site starts buzzing and your phone starts ringing, great. Invest more in paid search advertising. On the other hand, if the results are pretty anemic, you can either work on improving your listing to make it more compelling or go back to relying on organic listings alone.

- **Control:** With paid search, you can control exactly which search queries (or keywords) you want the appearance of your ad(s) to be triggered by, and depending on your budget, you can also control how high up on the SERP your ad appears. In any case, you completely decide the maximum amount you're willing to pay for each click and the total amount you're willing to spend each day. Paid search also lets you control exactly what your ad says.

- **Speed:** Search engines post your paid listing about as quickly as it took to type this sentence, and you can remove your ad just as quickly. Speed is a major distinguishing factor between paid and organic search. In the latter case, even the best search engine optimization (SEO — see Chapter 8 for more information) efforts can take weeks, even months, to pay off.

- **Measurability:** The major search engines' (Google, Yahoo!, and Bing) paid search platforms produce a ton of data on everything from how many impressions and clicks you're receiving on a specific keyword, to how much each keyword costs, to the average position your ad gets on the page for each keyword that searchers use. You can also track how many people (again, on a keyword basis) fill out forms, claim coupons, or contact you by phone or e-mail, turning themselves into leads. That gives you a way to figure out your cost-per-lead (CPL), which in turn helps you figure out your return on investment (ROI). (For more on how to calculate CPL, ROI, and other handy metrics, see Chapter 6.)

✔ **Highly qualified traffic:** Studies routinely show that although the lion's share of clicks go to organic listings, all clicks aren't created equal. People who click sponsored listings are far more primed to buy. With paid listings, you sell to folks who have their hands on their wallets. (The fact that this may make it a little difficult for them to type shouldn't concern you.)

Following a Step-by-Step Guide to Paid Search

Done on a basic level, running a paid search campaign is surprisingly easy. Doing it on the most advanced level, however, pretty much takes either a degree in differential calculus or a highly excellent and comprehensive resource like *Google AdWords For Dummies,* 2nd Edition, by Howie Jacobson.

In this chapter, we give you a solid understanding of the all-important basics: how paid search advertising works and the simple tools you need to get started. Like most things having to do with search engines, the first and foremost provider of paid search listings is Google. When you understand the mechanics of Google AdWords, you'll know just about all you really need to know about basic paid search. So we spend a lot of time looking through the Google AdWords lens; from there, you get a good sense of how other major search engines like Yahoo! and Bing do it, too.

When it comes to paid search, the single most important factor is *relevance,* meaning that each of your paid listings must relate tightly to your keywords, your ad copy, and your landing page. Done right, the flow from one to the next will be seamless. The simple truth is that relevance is about good old-fashioned marketing.

For example, if someone searches for *teeth whitening* and you serve him up ad copy that talks about *teeth pulling,* he's probably not going to click your ad. That can't be blamed on Google or a search engine algorithm; it's just that potential customers are, by nature, looking for ad copy that is both relevant to their search and that makes it easy for them to recognize that relevance. Give them those two things, and they'll be disposed to buy. Don't do it, and they'll be disposed to flee.

Setting up an account

Getting an account set up with one of the major search engines is easy. Go to the main site and navigate to the ad department, where you'll find the instructions you need to get up and running with a paid search account.

Of course, the major search engines are in constant competition for your advertising dollar and will try to entice you into their own corral with slightly different features and tools. Here's a look at some of the things they offer:

✔ **Google AdWords:** There's no way around the fact that Google is the king of PPC. Not only does Google provide sponsored listings on its search pages, but the Google Search Network also supplies paid search ads to second-tier search engines, such as Ask.com and AOL, and its Content Network does the same for subject-specific sites such as WebMD and HGTV.com. Google AdWords offers the Keyword Tool, which lets subscribers see exactly how often Web users search for a particular word or phrase, and then provides an estimate of the cost-per-click (CPC) for that word or phrase. AdWords give you other tools, too. Content Match, for example, allows subscribers to broaden their marketing reach within Gmail and other sites that have signed on with Google to share PPC advertising space, whereas Geo-Targeting lets you specifically target those customers who are looking for local services. (`www.google.com/adwords`)

✔ **Yahoo! Search Marketing (YSM):** This may stand in the shadow of the Google colossus, but YSM is still an important player in the search engine field and shouldn't be ignored. Yahoo! offers its set of tools to help you manage your paid listings, including one that forecasts the number of clicks you'll receive based on your maximum CPC. (`http://advertising.yahoo.com/smallbusiness/ysm`)

✔ **Microsoft adCenter:** The father of Bing, MSN takes a somewhat different approach than the other two and lets its users select the target-audience demographics (such as location, household income, age, educational level, and so on) that they especially want to cater to. (Demographic targeting has been the foundation of the conventional advertising industry since, oh, forever.) (`http://advertising.microsoft.com/search-content-advertising`)

After you sign up with one or more of these search engines, you take the following steps before launching your account. We address these steps throughout this chapter, but for now, here's a very general overview (see Figure 9-1 for a visual representation of these steps as seen from the viewpoints of businesses, consumers, and the metrics you use to measure it all):

1. **Select your keywords and match type.**

   See the sidebar, "The match game," for more about match types.

2. **Organize the keywords into campaigns and ad groups.**

3. **Write your ad copy.**

4. **Create a relevant landing page for each ad.**

5. **Most important, attend to your new customers.**

The following sections describe these steps in greater detail.

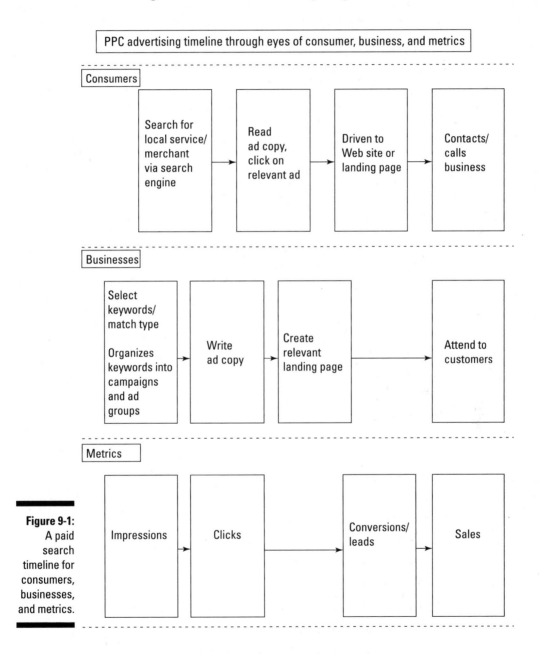

Figure 9-1:
A paid
search
timeline for
consumers,
businesses,
and metrics.

Google's Quality Score

When figuring out just how relevant a certain paid listing is to a given search query — and therefore, how prominent a position that listing will get — Google factors in a *Quality Score.* Admittedly, the Quality Score is sort of an intangible factor, but it's very important nonetheless.

Other major search engines have their own versions of the Quality Score, which kind of serves as an equalizer to the auction-based ad placements so that the results that appear toward the top are relevant, even though they're paid for. If that wasn't the case, the highest bidder would always get the best position, and you'd see some icky sites at the top of a given SERP. Eventually, users would revolt and use another search engine, and the offending engine would lose money.

So Google (and the others) also gives ads a kind of bonus for their degree of relevance. The idea is that a high Quality Score entitles a listing to a higher ranking on a Google SERP than a given bid amount (with a lower Quality Score) would warrant. Some of the factors that go into the awarding of a specific Quality Score are

- ✔ **Your click-through rate (CTR),** meaning what percentage of people who see your ad are actually clicking it.

- ✔ **The structure of your ad groups, or how your keywords are organized.** (We dive deeper into the subject of ad groups later in this chapter.)

- ✔ **The relevance of your ad copy to the keyword searched.** This is a judgment call on Google's part, and although it knows what its reasons are for making a specific determination, those reasons are deliberately kept undisclosed so advertisers can't easily game the system.

- ✔ **The relevance of your landing page to the keyword searched** (another factor whose calculation method Google keeps pretty close to its vest). But worth mentioning is that Google will stop running your ads if it determines that your landing page's relevance falls short.

To demonstrate how a Quality Score works, take the teeth whitening example from earlier in this chapter. Obviously a query for *teeth whitening* is dead-on in relevance. But what about *teeth cleaning, elective dentistry,* or *brighter smile?* They're all relevant, kind of. But surely they aren't all equally relevant. And that's what the Quality Score sorts. Google uses all the factors described in the preceding list and arrives at an order of relevance.

Developing a keyword portfolio

Keywords are what searchers type into a search engine to find you. When selecting keywords you want to be found with its critically important that you think like a consumer, not like a business owner.

Your customers are people, and a lot of folks aren't so good at typing, spelling, grammar, punctuation, and so on. To be on the safe side and get as many ad-clickers as you can, consider bidding on keyword aberrations that take these innocent mistakes into account.

Choosing the keywords you're willing to pay for in a sponsored listing
really no different than choosing them for your unpaid, organic listing.
both cases, you need to

- ✔ **Identify your target audience:** Who are you trying to reach? Which of these people are the most likely to buy soon? Where do they perform searches — at home, at work, or both? As the owner of an ongoing local business, you can probably intuit a lot of this. But, particularly where you're looking to expand the breadth of your customer base, let your imagination do some of the work. Imagine who your new target is. Is she well-educated, part of mid-to-senior-level management, into sports, into cooking, into bird-watching? Or is she probably none (or only a few) of those things? In any case, try to create a three-dimensional persona for her in your head — then, with your innate smarts, take an educated guess as to what search terms someone like that would be likely to use. (Truth be told, it's not just important that you do this, it's also kind of fun.)

- ✔ **Brainstorm:** What are all the formal/informal/colloquial/technical ways to describe your service or product? How do customers phrase what they're looking for when they call your business on the phone or email you? Brainstorm and write down as many keywords as you can possibly think of that your target audience might use to get to you. Don't edit that list — at least not yet. Come back to it later and see whether the keywords you already have inspire you to come up with still more. Then, don't edit those either. You probably won't bid on them all, but doing this kind of mental core dump will shortly prove to be an important step.

- ✔ **Review your log files:** The Web server that hosts your site keeps log files of each and every visitor who comes to your Web site, and these files can be invaluable. Analyze this data using a log file analyzer or basic Web analytics (some places you can do this include `www.weblogexpert.com`, `www.sawmill.net`, or `www.splunk.com`) to find out which search engine(s) your visitors came from, what keywords they used, what time of day and which day they visited, what browser they used, and so on. These are all highly good and illuminating things to know.

- ✔ **Research and analyze the top-ranked sites in your category:** Put each of your keyword candidates (see the earlier Brainstorm bullet) into a major search engine. What appears? Anything useful? Eventually, a word here and a word there will generate results that include highly ranked sites. Now, go to those sites and look at their *meta tags* (which we discuss in Chapter 8; these are usually the title, description, and keyword tags) by following these steps:

    1. *With the site you wish to view loaded in your browser, choose View⇨ Source (Internet Explorer) or View⇨Page Source (Mozilla Firefox).*

    2. *In the code that appears, find* `<meta name = "description">` *or* `<meta name = "keywords">` *and look at the keywords and phrases located within the quotation marks.*

If these top-ranked sites have good keywords that apply to your business as well, add those keywords to your list. If they're already on your list, circle or highlight them. These are definite keepers.

✔ **Research and analyze your direct competition:** A lot of the top-ranked sites aren't going to affect your own business all that much. Either they serve a different locality or their goods and services are at a different price point or quality level than yours. What you really want to know is what keywords your direct competition is using. Back to the meta tags you go. What are the title, description, and keywords you find there? And what's in there that you, too, can use?

Metadata is, in effect, in the public domain because its purpose is to inform search engines' robots as to the subject matter of the site. So, unless a keyword is an individual's name or a trademarked word or phrase, feel free to use it.

Testing your keywords

Use one of the commercially available keyword tools both to identify additional promising keywords and to get rid of some of your turkeys. Two of the most popular keyword research tools are

✔ **Google AdWords Keyword Tool:** Type one of your keyword candidates into the text box and then out comes the number of searches for that word that Google has counted to date. This tool also takes an educated stab at providing you with other associated keywords, including combinations and permutations of them. (`http://adwords.google.com/select/KeywordToolExternal`)

✔ **Wordtracker:** This tool offers a large number of keyword phrases that are related to the keywords you enter into the text box. Wordtracker also comes in two versions: free (`http://freekeywords.wordtracker.com`) and paid (`http://wordtracker.com`). The free one gives you up to 100 related search phrases, which helps you determine the most popular keyword phrases currently being used to find products and services like yours in search engine queries. If you're going to be administering a significant PPC campaign, use the paid version, which you can do on a monthly or annual subscription basis. Because the PPC universe is constantly shifting, today's best keywords won't necessarily be tomorrow's, and you want to be able to use a good keyword tool again and again.

The last step in building a keyword list (for either organic search engine optimization or a PPC program) is to sort and filter your list. This means subjecting each of your prospective keywords to at least two different filters:

✔ **Relevance:** If a keyword is too broad or ambiguous, traffic will be unpredictable and will most likely surface higher in the buying funnel. (That's fancy talk for the tire-kicking stage.) If the keyword is specific enough, though, the people who enter it are probably more likely to buy.

  • For instance, *surgeon* is too broad, whereas *rhinoplasty surgeon* is nice and specific (assuming you do nose jobs).

  • If you're selling tankless water heaters, just using *water heaters* is likely to be too broad, so *tankless water heaters* is definitely the way to go.

✔ **Popularity:** This can be looked at as search volume combined with popularity amongst advertisers. Some keywords may have such a high frequency of being used in searches and are so valuable to advertisers (hence, high CPC bids), it'd take an enormous budget to get and maintain a highly ranked position among the other PPC ads that those words bring up on the page. But how can you know just how popular a given keyword is? Google to the rescue. Its Keyword Tool can give you an estimate of both the average CPC that that keyword will require for your listing to show up on the first page of a SERP as well as the number of clicks you can expect, which is another way of indicating its value to advertisers and search volume, respectively. Then, armed with that information, you can decide whether to play. For the details, go to `http://adwords.google.com/select/KeywordToolExternal`.

For example, if you're bidding on *NYC dentist,* good luck. Your competition is going to be stiff and (probably) awash with loose cash. On the other hand, *upper west side family dentist* is almost certain to be less popular (because it's far more specific) — and thus, less costly to compete for. Additionally, due to the specificity of the keyword, those less expensive clicks are much more likely to actually turn into new patients. Double good!

Organizing your keywords

After you determine what keywords you want to bid on, decide how you want the search engines to match them to the user queries that come in. To do that, you have to get your keywords organized. (We go more deeply into this later in this chapter, but the subject deserves some attention here as well.)

To organize your keywords, you need some (figurative) baskets. Take your master keyword list and start breaking down the keywords into individual baskets, or what Google calls *ad groups.* After you load these baskets, write highly targeted ad copy that incorporates each basketful of keywords. And the better job you do of this, the higher your CTR, Quality Score, and conversion rate — and the lower your cost-per-conversion — and new customer.

Here's how to sort your keywords:

1. **Separate your keywords into groups based on product or service.**

2. **Break out these groups further on the basis of similarities in language/wording.** Remember to keep then as targeted as possible.

3. **Create a group of *negative keywords*.**

   These are words that although closely associated with those on your final keeper list are also associated with the kind of queries you don't want.

   You don't want these keywords because they're highly unlikely to bring you any conversions, and you'll just end up paying for pointless clicks. For a plumber, these might include *supplies, training, class, classes, certification,* or (the ever popular) *water*.

Preempt the possibility of coming up in the results for these undesirable words by registering them into the search engine's do not use list. On Google, for example, you can add negative keywords within your ad groups by clicking on the keywords tab and scrolling down to the Negative Keywords field. (We cover ad groups in the "Organizing your account" section, later in this chapter.)

The match game

No matter how thoroughly you've thought through your keyword choices, searchers throw words into a query that don't quite match your keywords. Search engines have seen this happen a couple billion times, so most paid search platforms include match types that allow you to choose how the engines should handle your ad in the event that one of these near-miss queries comes in. Generally, these match-types options are

- ✔ **Broad:** Your ad is shown for search queries that Google (for instance) deems to be semantically related to your keywords. This is the default option. For example, if your keyword phrase is *bankruptcy lawyer*, Google would still bring up your ad in response to queries for *bankruptcy, lawyer,* *lawyer for bankruptcy, filing for bankruptcy,* and *going bankrupt*.

- ✔ **Phrase:** This filter requires that the search query contain the entire keyword phrase in order. For the *bankruptcy lawyer* example, the ad in question would show up for say, *bankruptcy lawyer in Phoenix* or *best bankruptcy lawyer,* but not for *lawyer for bankruptcy* or *Cleveland lawyer for going bankrupt*.

- ✔ **Exact:** Ads are shown only for queries that match keywords exactly. So if your keyword phrase is *bankruptcy lawyer,* only a query for *bankruptcy lawyer* will do. Even a variation as slight as *bankruptcy lawyer in Portland* won't cut it.

Organizing your account

Three levels of organization are required for your paid search account on Google — the account, campaigns, and ad groups — and each level gives you different ways to control your advertising. The account is where you have control over user-defined administrative items like login, billing information, and global spending limits.

The campaign

The *campaign* is the largest organizational unit in your Google AdWords account. At the campaign level, you set your daily budget, your geographic and language targeting, and your Google network distribution preferences (we talk more about these in the "Network distribution" sidebar). If you want to keep all these settings the same across all your paid advertising, you need only one campaign. This is another way of saying that each unique combination of settings requires an additional campaign.

Setting a daily budget

When you set your daily budget in the campaign section, Google does its best — which is generally very good — to see that your ads display when and where they'll be most effective without exceeding that budget. Two things are important to know here:

- A given day's budget isn't a hard cap. Some days you'll exceed it by a little, and some days you'll fall a little short.

- In any given billing period, Google doesn't charge you more than the number of days times your daily budget.

Targeting locations

What locations should you target? As a general rule, target at least the entire area that your business serves. If you plan to start expanding your business's reach, you can add on more (usually contiguous) areas. In any case, Google lets you select your targets on a country, state, metro area, city, or even zip code basis, so your aim can get pretty precise.

You may wonder how search engines determine which users are where? Simple. The Internet service providers (ISPs) maintain Internet Protocol (IP) addresses showing the approximate physical location of every computer that logs on to the Internet. (We know that may sound a little creepy, but this is really no more sinister than the government knowing your mailing address, and no one seems to have a problem with that.)

Anyway, this data is just that precise. So if you target, say, a small city or group of cities that extends just a few miles from a central, specified point, your ad will nevertheless be seen by users whose actual physical locations are a bit outside that range. Many Web advertisers actually set up their targeting in the opposite way: They'll specify an area that's larger than their actual target market to ensure that they have all their targets covered — and any extra, non-targeted users they happen to pick up in the process are just considered gravy.

Another way to target your audience geographically is to include geographic modifiers in your keywords. So a local dentist who runs the keyword phrase *dentist in Montpelier* may well have his ad run nationally on Google, though it will appear only when someone types that exact keyword phrase from wherever she happens to be at the time. A simpler way to express this, perhaps, is to say that the tactic allows users who are themselves located nationwide to see listings that are essentially local. (A local limo service, for example, might well be eager to reach people who will be flying into the local market and will need transportation from the airport when they arrive. In other words, they're not here yet, but soon will be.)

The ad group

An *ad group* is a list of keywords associated with certain ad variations. In general, create a group of any keywords that logically share the same ad. Each ad group is then assigned to a campaign.

For example, say that Saratoga National Golf Club (in Saratoga Springs, NY) uses PPC ads to attract wedding business to its location. Two of its ad groups are Saratoga Weddings and Golf-Themed Weddings. Some of the keywords in the first ad group might include *saratoga springs weddings, wedding receptions saratoga, wedding venues saratoga,* and *wedding locations saratoga springs NY.* The second ad group might include *golf weddings saratoga, saratoga golf course weddings,* and *golf course wedding sites saratoga springs.* The two ad groups are similar enough to rationally belong to the same owner, yet different enough to attract business in two distinct ways.

Which keywords should share an ad? Well, an ad group needs to contain keywords that are very closely related in meaning and that can be assumed to answer queries that have similar intent, as shown in the following ad examples. What's more, whenever searchers use one of your keywords and phrases in their query, that word or phrase appears automatically in your ad in **bold.** This makes it easier for users to scan for those ads that best represent what they're after — and research shows, significantly increases the odds that a given ad will get clicked.

Poorly organized ad group

Ad group: Services

Keywords: *haircuts, color, blow-drying, pintura, pedicure, manicure, massages, hair removal, massage, facials, waxing, tanning, DevaCare shampoo, conditioner, styling gels, lipstick, cosmetics, nail polish, blow-dryers, diffusers,* and *curling irons*

Ad: Salon Services Galore
Great prices on everything from
haircuts to massages and lots more!
www.EdenSalon.com

Well-organized ad groups

Ad group 1: Hair services

Keywords: *haircuts, color, blow-drying, pintura, conditioning treatment, extensions, permanents,* and *thermal straightening*

Ad: Save Big On Your Hair!
Haircuts, color, permanents, blow-
drying, and more, all at 20–40% off.
www.EdenSalon.com

Ad group 2: Salon services

Keywords: *manicure, pedicure, massage, facials, waxing, tanning,* and *botox*

Ad: Experience Eden For Less
Save 20–40% on facials, massage,
waxing, tanning, and more.
www.EdenSalon.com

Ad group 3: Products

Keywords: *DevaCare shampoo, DevaCare conditioners, DevaCare cleanser, DevaCare styling gels,* and *DevaCare firm-hold conditioning gel*

Ad: Salon Products For Less
Save 20–40% on DevaCare shampoo,
conditioners, styling gels, and more!
www.EdenSalon.com

Landing pages

Because we discuss landing pages in detail in Chapter 5, in this chapter, we only make a couple points regarding the relationship of these pages to paid search. Ideally, each separate piece of ad copy you use needs to send searchers to a different landing page, and this is especially advisable if each version of your ad copy is different enough in subject matter to demand its own more-thorough explanation. (If on the other hand, all the versions of your copy address the same subject but are worded differently, routing a visitor who clicks any of the ad versions to the same landing page is sufficient.)

Most important, however, is that any landing page — and the ad copy that leads to it — needs to contain as many of your keywords as you can include. This accomplishes two things:

- ✔ Increases your Quality Score and therefore helps lower your CPC.
- ✔ Improves your conversion rate.

Optimizing your Quality Score

We mention earlier in this chapter that the biggest factors that influence an ad's Quality Score are CTRs, ad copy, and landing-page relevance. Optimizing these elements is important. Here a few guidelines as to how you can accomplish that:

✔ **Optimize ad group structure:** Use small, tightly focused ad groups with just a few keywords in each.

✔ **Optimize copy:** Create compelling ad copy that contains keyword phrases and that is likely to be clicked.

✔ **Optimize landing pages:** Your landing pages need to repeat text from your ad copy (especially the keywords in that copy). Also, do everything you can to ensure that each landing page loads quickly, and that it has enough text content to give a visitor a solid understanding of the subject being addressed.

Why? Because the more consistent and seamless the transition from a keyword query, to your ad copy, to the corresponding landing page, the easier it is to establish relevance throughout the whole chain of communication, and the more effective it will be in convincing a prospect to become a customer.

Writing effective ad copy

Effective ad copy doesn't just drive up your CTR (and consequently, your Quality Score), it also helps separate the qualified leads you want from the unqualified ones you don't. (*Qualified* meaning leads with the right geographic location, set of needs, financial ability to buy from you, and so on.)

Here's the rub: The character limits placed on ad copy are tight. Google, for instance, allows you just 25 characters for a headline and 70 characters for the copy itself, with the latter prohibited from running longer than two lines. So guess what? You have to work hard to say the most you can in the most efficient way you can. This is likely to require some work; as you scribble copy, edit it to its essence, see if it still makes sense — then crumple it up and start over. (You'll get better and better at it as you go.) If you really want to make the most of your paid search advertising, each of your ads needs to present a unique value proposition regarding your product or service, and do so in a unique way. Just settling for some bland, generic-sounding copy is going to bring subpar results.

Your ad headlines are the most important elements to get right. Research based on heat maps shows that searchers' eyes spend more time on headlines than on any other part of the ad. Headlines have to grab attention and contain information that helps to pre-qualify your prospects.

Also critical is your call to action. What exactly do you want the readers of your ad to do? Buy? Call? Drive to your place of business? Whatever your call to action is, you have to ask searchers to do it — and give them some kind of incentive to follow through. This is usually a coupon or a promotional offer (such as Call Now and Save 10% or Buy One, Get One Free), but other unique selling propositions, such as The Area's Only Authorized Dealer of Smedley Lawn Tractors, may also work well.

Keep all your ad copy as keyword-rich as possible, and concentrate on the tightly focused language groups (your *baskets*) that you came up with beforehand.

You can also determine what display URL to use in your ad. Folks often forget that they can add, after the slash in their URLs, keywords that link to a specific landing page(s). Because a URL is shown in bold type in an ad, so will the words you add to it. For instance, rather than just using a display URL of `www.deaverdental.com`, try `www.deaverdental.com/teethwhitening`. As the saying goes, every little bit helps.

Network distribution

We note earlier in this chapter that one of the settings you can choose at the campaign level is whether you want your paid ads to be distributed to the Google Search Network and Content Network. By using the Search Network, your ad will appear in response to appropriate queries made on AOL, EarthLink, CompuServe, Shopping.com, ATT.net, and Ask.com, among other places. The Content Network by contrast places your ads on relevant non-search sites like About.com, *The New York Times,* and HowStuffWorks.

Going onto the networks does involve some incremental cost, but only in the sense that you're paying for clicks, and the networks will — or at least *should* — generate more clicks. (The good news here is that network bids are set at the ad group level.) And because, extensive as it is, the traffic quality generated by the networks (particularly the Content Network) usually isn't as high as that of the traffic that comes directly from plain, old Google, the cost included is nominal. That's why a lot of small businesses balance the extra cost against the wider exposure and figure, reasonably enough, "Okay, sure, why not?" And if your budget allows, you probably should, too.

You also have a safety net because when you're on the networks, you can always test to find out how much additional traffic they actually bring you. If the amount and quality of that traffic doesn't seem to be worth the incremental cost to you, you can always bail out.

Check out your competitors' ads for ideas. Look at their ads and see how you can differentiate from them. You may find that some of the language they use is indispensable — for instance, *lawn tractors* — but some is language you can use that they don't or can't, such as *exclusive Smedley dealer*.

Another tip is to write in *camel case* — capitalizing the first letter of every word you use. This makes your copy stand out more and commands more attention.

Naturally enough, each search ad provider has its editorial guidelines that you're required to follow, or risk having your ad rejected. Check each provider's Web site for their ad guidelines. A few of the most common guidelines are

✔ Only one exclamation point is allowed in ad copy and none in the headline.

✔ You can't include Click Here.

✔ You can't use superlatives (best, most, highest, and so on) unless that claim is supported by a third-party reference on the landing page.

✔ You can't use any foul or offensive language, or any drug-related content.

✔ You can't use excessive capitalization, but camel case is both permitted and common.

✔ Only certain information can be included in the ad (for example, Google allows ad copy to include a phone number, whereas Bing does not).

Write a variety of ads per ad group. The search engines give you the option to have them automatically favor (in terms of number of appearances) the ads that generate higher CTRs. The following examples show a poorly written ad and a well-written one.

Poorly written ad

Save $30!!!
SAVE BIG on lawn care services.
Your lawn will thank you.
`www.greenthumblandscaping.com`

Why that ad fails:

✔ Too many exclamation points, and in the wrong place (the headline)

✔ Too many capital letters

✔ Very generic in content

Well-written ad

Save On Lawn Care Service
Go Green with Our 25 Years' Experience.
Save $30 On Your First Appointment!
`www.greenthumblandscaping.com/lawncare`

Why that ad succeeds:

- ✔ Strong call to action

- ✔ Use of keywords in headline

- ✔ Promotion is showcased in headline

- ✔ *25 Years' Experience* is a competitive differentiator

Make sure that the URL you include in your ad leads to a landing page that has a direct logical connection to at least the first two-thirds of your ad copy. Also, although a good idea is to use different variables in your copy and then test to see which versions are earning you the most clicks, give each variation a statistically significant length of time to run before you make a judgments as to its effectiveness. (For most businesses, for example, a 48-hour run isn't long enough.)

Managing your bids

When time start bidding on a given keyword, concentrate on two things:

- ✔ Setting your initial bid
- ✔ Optimizing your bids

Setting your initial bid

Although you may ultimately use testing, measuring, and various optimizing techniques to determine your initial bids for a keyword, we assume here that this is your very first venture into keyword bidding, and so we concentrate on the universal basics.

A few different philosophies float around in the Web as to how you should set your initial bid. Three of the most prominent are

- ✔ **Just do what Google tells you to do:** Google can estimate what your bid would have to be to earn first page placement. That criterion makes sense because most search users never make it past the first page of search results. On the one hand, this is a reasonably sound basis from which to get a good ballpark figure for your initial bid. On yet another hand, going this route, in effect, puts the auctioneer (Google) in the position of offering bidding advice — and this auctioneer makes more money from higher bids. So is this approach helpful? Yes. Impartial? Uh, not so much.

✔ **Be very conservative:** This approach can be summed up as bid low and see what happens. If, as a result of this method, your ad gets poor position and hardly ever gets clicked, you can start raising your bids until you hit that magic point where you're happy both with the number of clicks you're getting and with the amount of money those clicks are costing you. Here are two possible downsides:

- • This approach is hard to budget because it may or may not actually cost you more than you planned on.

- • If you get a crummy position and a paltry number of clicks, you've wasted money.

✔ **Be aggressive:** Some paid search experts insist that bidding high very early in the process has a substantial benefit. Their thinking runs like this: A high bid brings a high position, a high position leads to a good CTR, a good CTR earns a higher Quality Score, and a good Quality Score lets you lower your subsequent bids and still get excellent placement. To which we say, maybe, maybe not. Google, for one, throws cold water on this idea, claiming that when it assigns a Quality Score, it normalizes for position. Yet many people nevertheless swear by this approach. Our best advice is that if you adopt this strategy, establish and closely monitor your daily spending caps; otherwise, you can burn through a lot of money in no time at all.

Optimizing your bids

Like optimizing your Web site and your paid and unpaid search engine listings, optimizing your bid strategy is largely a matter of trial and error. You test approach A against approach B, and then test the winner against approach C. A couple of general truths to keep in mind when you consider changing your bids are

✔ Increasing your bid on a keyword will usually also increase your CPL.

✔ Conversely, lowering your bid will generally lower your CPL, but it will also (probably) lower your SERP position, hence your visibility, hence the number of clicks you get and leads you gather.

Bid optimization on a keyword basis is nearly always a tradeoff between traffic volume on the one hand and profitability on the other. To optimize then is to find the balance between the two that best suits you and your business.

Before you can effectively optimize your bid strategy, understand clearly and fully the various steps that make up a paid search campaign. These are core principles:

1. Consumers search for products or services in your category and are presented with your ad (each of these ad presentations is an *impression*).

2. When a consumer sees your ad, she decides whether to click it.

The more people who click, the higher your CTR.

3. Clicking brings the consumer to your landing page, where she decides whether she wants to take any further action.

   Examples of this action could be filling out an online form or contacting your business by phone or e-mail. Consumers who take such an action become *leads,* and the percentage of your total visitors who become leads is your *conversion rate.*

4. You and/or your employees turn as many of these leads as possible into actual paying customers.

   The success level you have in doing this is your *sales rate* or *close rate.*

After you have a grasp of these steps, it becomes much easier to figure out what the root causes of a specific performance problem are. For instance:

✔ **Problem:** Not enough impressions

- *Root causes:* Not enough search volume in the area you're targeting, keyword portfolio isn't broad enough, or bids are too low, resulting in poor position on SERP

✔ **Problem:** Impressions are sufficient, but not enough clicks

- *Root cause:* Ineffective ad copy

✔ **Problem:** Impressions and click rates are good, but not enough leads

- *Root cause:* Landing page conversion is weak

✔ **Problem:** Leads are sufficient, but not enough sales

- *Root causes:* The leads are weak or just not sufficiently interested in your products, services, or offers; or poor lead handling

✔ **Problem:** Volume of leads is good, but they are too expensive to generate

- *Root causes:* Bids are too high, CPC is too high, or Quality Score is too low; or landing page conversion is inefficient

Tracking and refining results

The simple — and perhaps, obvious — fact is that you can't test what you don't track. Fortunately, you can track just about everything. The challenge is to identify the things you want to track when you're running a paid search campaign. This tells you which elements of your campaign are working well and which aren't. That, in turn, tells you which approaches are worth your investment and which are simply a waste of money.

The elements of a paid search campaign you're most likely to need to track are

✔ **Conversions:** This is the single most important metric because it's the last step before an actual sale. Conversions can be tracked in several ways, including:

  • *Actions taken:* When a user takes a desirable action on your Web site (for instance, downloading a newsletter or submitting a contact form), you can generally track that event back to the specific keyword and ad text that brought that user to your site. Keeping records of these two source elements over time tells you which ads and keywords do you the most good and therefore deserve more of your resources in the bidding stage.

  • *Conversion values:* If you have multiple conversion pages and/or use multiple conversion events (usually offers of some sort) on your Web site, you can track each page's or event's performance versus its cost to you.

✔ **Web site behavior:** These metrics tell you about the behavior of your site's visitors after they get there, such as

  • *Pages per visit*

  • *Bounce rate;* this is people who leave the site after viewing only one page

  • *Time spent on the site*

If you can't directly tie behavior on your site to actual conversions because those conversions tend to happen off-site, you can still use the traffic metrics listed previously to get a good idea of which keywords are generating the best behavior happening on your site. As always, keep the productive keywords and lose (or alter) the unproductive ones.

✔ **Queries:** The keywords people use to arrive at your paid ad and then, hopefully, to come to your Web site. Among the important query metrics are

  • *Session logging:* Web analytics can tell you which keywords were queried and then induced people who used those words to visit your site. Knowing this helps you refine your keywords as well drop those that result in unproductive queries. (For example: You run a catering business, and one of your keywords is *catering jobs.* The metrics subsequently tell you that many of the queries using *catering jobs* fall off your site quickly, and you deduce that those folks are looking for employment, not catering services, and drop that keyword.)

  • *Google's Search Query Performance report:* If you're using AdWords, this report shows you (among other metrics) every query that generated a click. Here again, you can use this information to weed out unproductive, though clicked, keywords to improve your CTRs.

When you use tracking to test one paid ad against another, don't mix apples and oranges — you aren't going to learn much unless the competing ads are similar enough that you can determine the exact factors that create good or poor results. For example, you might want to test a percentage savings offer against an actual dollar-amount savings offer to see which one results in more clicks. On the other hand, testing great prices versus prompt service tells you pretty much nothing. (However, if you're testing keyword against keyword, testing prices against service might make sense.)

One of the biggest challenges for local businesses that want to use online tracking is that many people looking for local businesses aren't going to fill out an online form. Instead, they're going to travel to the company's place of business or call them on the phone. So the problem becomes how to tie an offline action to an online behavior. The situation gets even stickier with paid search in which you really want to trace conversions back to the actual keyword that was searched and that then brought each lead to your door. Sadly, no easy way exists to do this, but the situation isn't entirely hopeless. Some local online advertising companies (such as www.yodle.com) use advanced algorithms that essentially timestamp clicks and phone calls, giving local business owners a way to identify a presumptive correlation between ad clicks and offline response. Small businesses can adopt a somewhat more cumbersome version of this technique on their own if they use a virtual phone service (as we discuss in Chapter 5). Metrics tell these businesses when individual clicks occurred, whereas the phone service tells them when calls were made. This approach is far from perfect, but it's better than nothing.

Finding and Using Resources for DIY and Outsourcing

As with Web site creation (see Chapter 4), a small business owner who wants to get into PPC campaign management has a fundamental choice: To do it yourself or to hire outside help. And as with site-building, the decision regarding PPC campaign management largely comes down to how much time and expertise the business owner has.

Getting a paid search campaign up and running the right way can require a significant chunk of your time. Although much of this effort generally comes at the front-end of the process, keeping track of your bids and your metrics on a frequent and regular basis can chew up valuable hours as well. (*Google AdWords For Dummies,* 2nd Edition, by Howie Jacobson can be a valuable resource for determining just how much time and effort a well-run campaign is likely to require.)

Tempted as you might be to set up your campaign and then leave it on auto-pilot, you really can't afford to. Unless you keep a daily (or even several times a day) eye on your bids, your PPC budget can quickly spin out of control.

Meanwhile, the expertise question is pretty much self-explanatory. Either you have significant experience in online marketing or you don't. Resources like the aforementioned book (not to mention this one!) can help you acquire a lot of the necessary knowledge, but reading about doing something and actually doing it are often quite different things.

So the DIY versus getting outside help question remains. To help you decide, the following sections describe the kinds of professional service providers you need to check out before arriving at your final answer.

Don't feel even the slightest embarrassment about getting outside help with your paid search engine advertising. Just consider how long this chapter is and keep in mind that it's only an overview of the subject. The details of paid search could fill several books.

Chapter 20 of this book lists several questions you need to ask a potential vendor before hiring him.

A number of great service providers are out there who can take a lot of the paid search burden off your shoulders. Because a thorough examination of each of their individual rosters of services would likely make you nod off, we simply categorize the different types of help you can get:

- ✔ Independent consultants (including small agencies)
- ✔ Internet Yellow Pages (IYP) companies
- ✔ Full-service local online advertising companies
- ✔ Technology platforms

The following sections take a brief look at each.

Independent consultants or agencies

To get a feel for just how many consultants and small agencies offer search engine marketing (SEM) services, just Google (or Yahoo or Bing) *SEM agency for small businesses* or *SEM consultant.* Don't be surprised to find a veritable sea of them. (If nothing else, the sheer volume of vendors at loose in the world gives you a good idea of just how important a tool SEM is in today's grand scheme of things.)

Although many — even most — of these agencies and consultants are highly reputable, we're sure a few less-than-straight-up players appear, too. Always ask for references and then follow up on them.

The upside of retaining one of these companies to help with SEM is that they'll help you with SEM. One of the possible pitfalls, however, is that having someone else run your SEM program is just about as labor-intensive as it would be for you to do so. That means that many vendors aren't convinced easily to work for anyone without a hefty budget. Don't lose heart: There may well be some kind of arrangement possible that won't break your personal bank.

Yellow Pages companies

A few years ago, many *Yellow Pages* companies simply offered SEM services as a kind of secondary revenue source to supplement their primary, paper-based *Yellow Pages* business. Back then, their paid search offerings usually consisted of so-called *click bundles* in which they'd charge a preset price for a preset number of clicks. While some of these were a great value, the potential problems arose in that some clicks are much better than others for a local business — and at times, (so the critics said) some of the *Yellow Pages* packages might supply the volume of clicks promised without too much regard to the quality of those clicks.

Over time, reality struck. More and more people started using search engines to find goods and services. As a steadily increasing number of local businesses started clamoring for quality SEM solutions to get themselves in front of the growing legion of online searchers, many *Yellow Pages* companies altered their approach.

The result is that several *Yellow Pages* companies have either developed their own robust and sophisticated SEM operations or formed alliances with local online advertising firms that can provide their *Yellow Pages* client base with extensive search marketing services.

That leaves you with this bottom line: If your local business is still committed to advertising in the print *Yellow Pages* because it's still a good source of quality leads for you, it can make good financial and hassle-avoiding sense to buy all your advertising services and placements from one company. That way you can just carry on with your paper *Yellow Pages'* campaign and supplement it with the *Yellow Pages'* SEM solution. Doing so makes for a certain efficiency, and that may well translate into overall savings.

However, be careful with this approach. Because although a *Yellow Pages* company may put a fancier, tech-sounding name on what they offer, that doesn't necessarily mean they're offering a great package. So you have to sniff around. Ask questions. You may find a great deal, or you may find not much in the way of real help. Before you do any of that though, check out all the options that are available in your area.

Full-service local online advertising companies

Full-service companies specialize in helping local businesses get found online. In many cases, they offer relatively sophisticated solutions that involve at least some level of automation to optimize their efforts (and serve their accounts) efficiently. One of the primary benefits of working with these companies is that they often have their own built-in distribution networks that extend a local business's reach and exposure well beyond that of the three major search engines (Google, Yahoo!, and Bing).

Most local online advertising firms give local businesses the ability to track their local search performance (that is, the number of clicks and calls they get, as well as the dollars spent), and many also provide a virtual phone service that permits call recording and tracking. The tracking feature is particularly nice in that it lets you know not only how many calls are coming in, but also what the quality of those calls is (meaning, are these calls turning into actual business?). Many local online advertising companies also offer ample SEO services.

Because the local online advertising company field is a relatively young industry, the competitive landscape changes constantly. Nonetheless, as this book is written, the major players in the arena include (in alphabetical order)

- **Local Marketers:** www.localmarketers.com
- **OrangeSoda:** www.orangesoda.com
- **ReachLocal:** www.reachlocal.com
- **WebVisible:** www.webvisible.com
- **Yodle:** www.yodle.com

    Disclosure time: One of this book's authors is a Yodle guy, but Yodle is a biggie in the field, so fair's fair, right?

Using a local online advertising company can be an excellent decision for a local business owner who simply doesn't have the time (or can't afford to put in the time) necessary to run a paid search campaign properly. As a bonus, the fact that most online advertising companies use automation to assist in the setup and optimization of online campaigns means they can often have you up and running in a as little as a few days. As to cost, because these companies have very efficient operations and are designed specifically to help local businesses, they're eminently aware that modest budgets don't have to be an obstacle to the success of paid local search campaigns.

Technology platforms

A few, recently emerged companies offer *technology platforms* (essentially software that integrates with your paid search accounts) to help local business owners more easily run, measure, and optimize their campaigns. The biggest benefit that comes from using one of these platforms is that you save the cost of having someone else manage your paid search campaign for you while still getting help in the form of automated advice and bid management as well as powerful tracking and reporting capabilities. The obvious flipside is that you still run your own campaign.

If you have a burning desire to run your own campaign, check out a few of these platform companies. Some of them offer free trials, so you can decide whether you like the platform before you start paying for it.

Clickable (`www.clickable.com`) is probably the best-known technology platform company. To find other platforms, just let Google be your guide.

Chapter 10

Saying It with E-Mail

*Y*ou will — or you have already — put a considerable effort into building your company's Web site. And, via modern wonders, such as search engines, people will manage to find you.

But not *all* the people you want to reach will come to your site from a search engine, which is where e-mail comes in — big time.

You may, in fact, find that your site gets more *conversions* (which occur when your visitor takes concrete action, such as scheduling an appointment online or calling a number listed on your Web page) from the links in your e-mail messages than through search engines. After all, e-mail is more personal than search ads, while offering more onscreen "real estate" to sell your company's goods and services. We also discuss how you can use *metrics* — which is a dressy way of saying *measurements* — to find out which source your Web site visits come from.

In any case, your e-mails can create significant Web site traffic — if they're planned and executed well. And we show you just how to do those things *very* well in this chapter.

Building the All-Important Address List

Obviously, you can't send e-mails until you have a list of addresses to send them to. (And we can almost hear you say, "Well, duh.")

The first step in your e-mail marketing program is to build a permission-based e-mail address list of your prospects and customers. *Permission-based* means that your addressees have given you explicit permission to e-mail them; they can do this by physically filling out a card or form at your place of business, or by entering their e-mail addresses on your Web site. Either way, you have a record of them giving you permission to send messages.

After you build a list that's big enough to justify sending e-mail *blasts* (or *mass mailings*), you can expect that list to grow by an additional 5–10 percent each year as new customers find you via word of mouth, search engines, or even the phone book.

Now, 5–10 percent a year may not sound all that impressive, but when you consider that it reflects relationships you actually established, it's invaluable. The people on your e-mail list are highly qualified potential buyers and consequently, are more likely to respond to the messages you send.

In this chapter, we often discuss the importance of getting permission from your e-mail addressees before you send them anything. We can't stress this point enough because failure to get the required permission can actually result in all sorts of unpleasant, government-imposed penalties and punishments. You can find much more on this subject in the section, "CAN-SPAM Compliance and the Opt-In," but we advise you to keep it in mind while you read this chapter and create your address list.

Finding the value of your e-mail list

Many small businesses find that their permission-based e-mail address database generates cost-savings and increases their return on investment (ROI) that far exceeds their initial expectations. Why? These businesses use their e-mail list to

- ✔ Open an additional and reliable channel for reaching their customers
- ✔ Increase their sales with little effort and at minimal cost
- ✔ Significantly reduce their customer *acquisition costs* (the cost of creating a customer who actually buys from your business)
- ✔ Allow them to easily measure the impact of their marketing campaigns and, incidentally, to sniff out — and capitalize on — trends and preferences among their customers more quickly than ever before
- ✔ Boost their customer participation and *retention rates* (the rates at which customers return to do more business with you)
- ✔ Attract and retain customers at far lesser cost-per-person than they could by using direct mail (plus, no paper cuts)

Why bother with an e-mail campaign?

If some skeptic asks you why you're involved in "this whole e-mail thing," you might find these facts to be a very eloquent answer:

✔ The number of e-mail users is projected to rise to 1.6 billion by 2011. (The *Radicati Group*, October 2007)

✔ As a direct result of receiving e-mail, 67 percent of respondents researched a specific offer. (*Epsilon*, 2009)

✔ Sixty-three percent of those respondents clicked a link in the e-mail to learn more. (*Epsilon*, October 2008)

✔ Forty-four percent of e-mail users said e-mail inspired at least one online purchase; and 41 percent said it prompted at least one offline purchase. (*JupiterResearch*, "The Social and Portable Inbox," 2008)

✔ Sixty-six percent of those surveyed had made a purchase because of a marketing message received via e-mail. (*ExactTarget*, "2008 Channel Preference Survey," 2008)

✔ E-mail's ROI in 2008 was $43.52 for every $1 spent on it. (*DMA*, 2008)

Creating the address list

You have three options (well, two-and-a-half) when it comes to compiling your database of e-mail addresses: create your own list, buy a list, or both.

Creating a do-it-yourself list

As a small business, it may actually be easier (and far cheaper) for you to obtain your customers' e-mail addresses than it is for a Fortune 500 company. The people you do business with probably comprise a manageably sized universe — that is, dozens or hundreds, not millions.

These people are also doing business with you because they *want* to. In other words, they've shown that they trust you, which makes it likely that they'll give you their e-mail information. But you have to do one critical thing first: Ask.

You can give those folks an incentive to say yes in several ways. If you're starting a list from scratch, tell your customers that you're introducing a new, exclusive e-mail program that will periodically provide them with one or more of the following:

✔ **Special limited-time discounts available only to them.**

✔ **Useful information:** For example, if you own a doggie spa, you could offer the convenience of regular doggie care reminders, such as letting them know when Tinkerbell needs her teeth cleaned.

✔ **A new product or service.**

- ✔ **The opening of a new location, or the expansion of your current business.**
- ✔ **Customer testimonials.**
- ✔ **An invitation to take part in a survey.**

The important thing to keep in mind is that you know your customers. And that means you probably also know precisely what sort of inducement they'll be most interested in — and that's the one you need to offer.

In any case, if you've properly read your customers' needs and wants and offered something they're really interested in as a reward for signing up for your list, hand them a simple sign-up card (like the one shown in Figure 10-1) to fill in with their e-mail addresses if they're physically present at your location or give them a way to subscribe on your Web site.

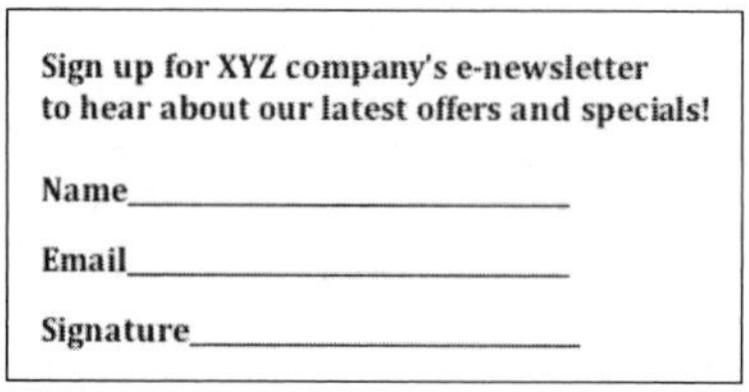

Figure 10-1:
A typical
sign-up card
for custom-
ers who visit
your place
of business.

> Sign up for XYZ company's e-newsletter
> to hear about our latest offers and specials!
>
> Name_____
>
> Email_____
>
> Signature_____

You can also get a lot of names and addresses from your Web site. Just include a check box on your site for a visitor to give you the necessary permission to contact him and then give him a space to enter his e-mail address if he wants to receive future valuable and informative mailings. You can also ask for his name to personalize the e-mails that will follow.

But how do you drive potential customers to the sign-up page on your site? You really have only two options:

- ✔ **You can put the sign-up section right on the home page.** A *home page,* as shown in Figure 10-2, is the page visitors first come to when they type your Web address.
- ✔ **You can put something on the home page that acts as an inducement to go to a separate sign-up page.** This can be modest offer for, say, a coupon or for more information on a subject that you mention on the home page.

Including a place on your Web site for people to fill in their e-mail addresses —
and thus knowingly give you permission to send them messages — is a pretty
simple step. Just include whatever sort of offer you want to, uh, offer, either
by putting it into a different typeface or in a special box, with a clickable
Subscribe link below it that takes customers to a sign-up page. Some people
insist on putting this right on the home page, but that runs the considerable
risk of looking a little too aggressive (or greedy, pushy, and desperate). If you
use a professional Web designer, just tell her that you want your site to contain an address-gathering page and let the designer take it from there.

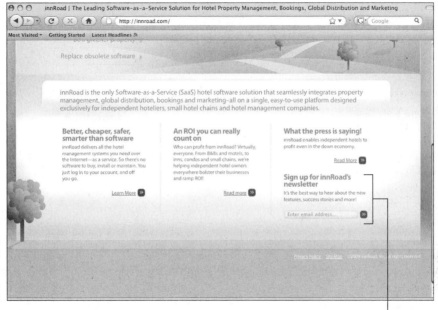

Figure 10-2:
A typical
e-mail opt-in
section.

An e-mail opt-in

So, because you can give customers a sign-up card in person or let them subscribe via your Web site, it's really pretty easy to generate your own quality
list of e-mail addresses. And, with any luck at all, it's a list that will just keep
getting longer.

After you compile your list, protect it. Do not sell or distribute the names for
others to use (or, just as likely, misuse) unless you've already given your customers fair notice on your Web site or on some other sign-up document that
you intend to pass their information along. Selling e-mail addresses without
permission isn't just tacky, it's illegal.

Going with the pros

You can rent e-mail lists from companies, and those lists can be honed to target the customers of specific business types, to reflect a particular demographic profile (such as age or gender), or even to reach a specific zip code.

Many of these companies can also handle the mailing details — for a fee, of course. Two such list-rental companies are CityTwist (`http://citytwist.com`) and infoUSA (`http://infousa.com`), though you can find many others.

This option can be a very good way to go, or it can turn into a screeching nightmare. A reputable list-renter is extremely careful to ensure that every person whose address it provides has given his permission to receive e-mails. This keeps you on the right side of the law and can save you an enormous amount of time. On the other hand, using a slapped-together list, where few, if any, of the addressees have given permission for e-mails is just asking for a threatening letter from the Feds. And you can't duck it by blaming the list-renter because the offending e-mails go out with your name on them.

The best ways to make sure your experience with a list-renter is a good, clean, and legal one are to

- ✔ **Insist on getting a guarantee** *in writing* **from the list company that all the names they provide have agreed to receive mailings from third parties, such as you.**

- ✔ **Ask the offering company how and where it acquired the names and addresses you want to rent.** If its answer sounds fishy, it's best to walk away.

- ✔ **Never use bulk lists (often offered on CD-ROM).** These typically contain names of people who haven't agreed to receive unsolicited e-mails, who have long since changed their e-mail addresses, or who are, alas, dead; in the case of people who haven't consented to unsolicited mailings, they can complain to your Internet service provider (ISP), who can then promptly shut down your account (ouch!).

- ✔ **Manage your expectations.** Based on the personal experience of many list-renters, your response rate from a third-party list is likely to be pretty low (2 percent or less on average). Considering the relatively non-targeted nature of such lists, that should come as no great surprise.

Don't let the pitfalls we note here deter you, however, from the idea of renting an e-mail list. Like any business, this one has its share of bad apples — but also big bushels full of good ones. And those can save you a lot of time in getting together an address list.

The expense? Figure the cost of renting a list ranges from $50–$150 for every thousand names you get.

Combining the two

You could use a reputable list-rental company t
gradually phase out that relationship as your (
longer.

First and foremost, determine whether your
fied customers to your business and whethe.
a strong return on your investment (ROI). If so, why ʌ
attrition occurs with any list, so continually replenishing it ʌ.
just makes good business sense.

On the other hand, if the opt-in device on your Web site does a great job of
growing a qualified list and driving a strong ROI, you may decide it's simply
no longer worth it to pay for a rented list.

Ultimately, using metrics to figure out what's working — and what isn't —
is the easiest way to decide where and how to invest your money wisely.

Creating an Effective E-Mail Blast

After you compile (or rent) a good-sized collection of *permitted addresses*
(sorry to keep harping, but it really *is* that important), what's the next step?
Easy: You have to actually send them e-mail.

For a small business, the window for sending your first mailing is no more
than six months. After that, your list of addresses can turn pretty stale. People
change e-mail addresses, forget who you are, or forget they ever consented to
getting e-mails from you in the first place — none of which is good.

In reality, you're best off sending your first e-mail message as soon as possible, thereby striking while the proverbial iron is plenty hot. Even after about
three months that iron definitely has cooled.

We get pretty specific about content in some of the sections that follow, but a
few quick and tidy guidelines for composing your e-mail blast message are

- Make it fresh.
- Make it brief.
- Make it interesting.
- Make it actionable.

In other words, give your e-mail recipients a powerful reason to open your
e-mail — and then give them something interesting to do after it's opened —
rather than to automatically hit the dreaded Delete button.

A lot of things can work. For instance, offering tips can be a very effective door (and e-mail) opener. If you're say, a landscaper, you could send an e-mail that presents Five Easy Ways to a Healthier Lawn, or maybe Three Kinds of Weeds That Will Happily Eat Your House, or some other piece of advice that your average e-mail recipient would be nuts not to open, read, and heed.

And although giving your mailings something that compels prospects to open them is important, it's even more critical now, with so much junk mail and spam clogging so many inboxes.

We break down the structure of an e-mail into two pieces: what your recipients see when your message shows up in their e-mail inboxes and what they find when they actually open the message.

Considering what customers see in their inboxes

The parts of an e-mail that a recipient sees in her inbox are collectively known as the *header,* as shown in Figure 10-3. These parts include the From and Subject lines as well as the date the e-mail is received. The date hardly requires any explanation, but the other parts definitely do.

Creating an effective "from" line

Your first hurdle comes right off the bat: Identifying yourself in a way that swiftly moves your recipients from seeing your message to actually opening it.

Obviously, you want the From line to clearly identify you and/or your company as the e-mail sender. You don't have a whole lot of ways to jazz up, say, Ferguson Kitchens or Muffins by Meghan, so don't waste your time trying.

Because you have a local business that's accustomed to dealing with people on a by-name basis, a really nice, personal touch is to add your name to your company's; for example, `Eddie@PremierCleaners.com`. See? Already you're on your way to starting a conversation rather than just giving a blunt company ID.

Unless you've rented a list of e-mail addresses from a third party, you're not coming into folks' inboxes as a total stranger. They know who you are. They willingly signed up to be on your list and they're expecting to hear from you. So just make sure they know that it *is* you when you come calling.

Never try to hide your real company name behind some seemed-really-clever-at-the-time pseudonym. So if you're Carlton Mufflers, for instance, don't make your e-mail appear to come from Mr. BoomVroom (unless you're also prepared to be thought of as Mr. HalfWit). It's just embarrassing . . . and it'll make your recipients think you're untrustworthy.

Figure 10-3:
What the
customer
sees in her
inbox.

Writing great subject lines

Here the plot really starts to thicken. What can you say to make your recipient say, "Ooh, I've just gotta see what this is about" — and click to open your e-mail?

Here again, don't get cagey or cute. You literally have just one second to set the hook, so if you're offering a special sale or discount, just say it. For example, This Week: 2 Shirts for the Price of 1 is miles better than Have I Got a Deal For You!

Whatever you say, make it about *him,* your prospect or customer, not you. People, whether they admit it, want to know what's in it for them. And when you consider how much spam and other junk getting delivered to people every single day, it's obvious that you have to say something that communicates, "Hey, this one really is worth opening."

What makes one subject line work well whereas another one is completely ignored? Here are some pointers that many successful e-mail marketers treat as musts:

- ✔ Keep Subject lines short and simple. Fewer than ten words is good, and fewer than five is better still.

- ✔ Focus on the benefits that are important to your reader rather than on the features that are important to you.

- ✔ Avoid using *you* in the Subject line, even though it is about the recipient. *You* is used to death by spammers. Better to use the "imperative case," as in "Get A Free Donut Now" or "Win This Big Fluffy Thing." (One slightly odd note: Although using "you" is generally avoided by the pros, *"your"* shows up fairly often in their work. What a difference a letter makes, huh? Go figure.)

- ✔ Avoid using two other spam flags: Exclamation points and words ALL IN CAPS.

A few more pieces of advice that many e-mail pros swear by are

- ✔ Don't use blank subject lines or *Re:*.

- ✔ Capitalize the first letter of each word, even prepositions (such as all, for, through), conjunctions (but, or, and), and articles (a, an, the). For example: "Take A Flight To And From The South Of France."

Table 10-1 lists some hypothetical Subject lines that will and won't work to get people to read the message.

Table 10-1	Examples of Subject Lines
Subject Lines That Won't Work	*Subject Lines That Will Work*
FREE CAR WASH OFFER!!!	Complimentary Care Wash From Andy's Auto
Save 15%!	15% Discount On Swedish Massage Ends Saturday
Monthly Newsletter	Cancer Care For Your Dogs And Cats
Save on everything in store!	Surprise Dad! Father's Day Is This Sunday
Big Bango Bucks Special Deal!!!	Our 24-Hour Sale Starts 9 A.M. Today

Composing your message

After you persuade your reader to open your e-mail with descriptive From and Subject lines, you need to write the content of the message. The following sections break down the parts of the *content* section (that is, the message in the body of the e-mail) and provide tips for writing effective marketing messages.

Writing the key elements in the content section

The content of a marketing message can be broken down into the following key elements (see Figure 10-4):

- ✔ **The masthead:** This is the information that appears at the very top of your e-mail so that your customer sees it first. The general rule of thumb for mastheads is that your logo goes in the upper-left corner, and your phone number and Web address go in the upper right.

- ✔ **The body:** This is the element that follows the masthead and contains the *substantive* part of your message. The body requires a balance between the amount of text you use and the number and size of any images you include; as for the text (or copy) itself, be aware that most e-mail readers simply scan your message rather than read every word, so make your copy easy to process by using short sentences and devices, such as headlines, sub-headlines, bullet points, and, by all means, a background color light enough to make dark copy read easily.

- ✔ **The footer:** This is the space at the bottom of the e-mail page where you should display your phone number, your physical mailing address, and your Web address even if you've already included them in the masthead of your e-mail's masthead; the repetition never hurts and often helps boost your response rate. Figure 10-4 shows several common elements of a proper footer.

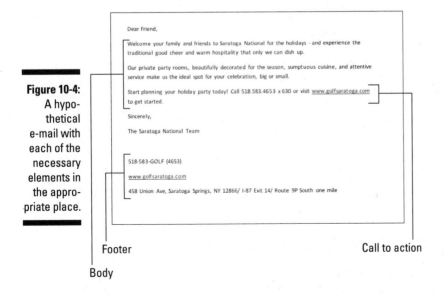

Figure 10-4: A hypothetical e-mail with each of the necessary elements in the appropriate place.

Dear Friend,

Welcome your family and friends to Saratoga National for the holidays - and experience the traditional good cheer and warm hospitality that only we can dish up.

Our private party rooms, beautifully decorated for the season, sumptuous cuisine, and attentive service make us the ideal spot for your celebration, big or small.

Start planning your holiday party today! Call 518.583.4653 x 630 or visit www.golfsaratoga.com to get started.

Sincerely,

The Saratoga National Team

518-583-GOLF (4653)

www.golfsaratoga.com

458 Union Ave, Saratoga Springs, NY 12866/ I-87 Exit 14/ Route 9P South one mile

Footer   Call to action

Body

✔ **The call to action:** Even though this element shows up last on our list, it's actually number one in importance because this is where you tell your readers exactly what you want them to do. Sign up for a catalog? Buy something? Take advantage of a special deal? Whatever it is and whether it shows up at the top (which is preferable), in the middle, or at the bottom of your e-mail, it *has* to be there — made visually impossible to miss or to be misunderstood.

In most cases, an effective e-mail presents the call to action and then directs readers to a Web site link that takes them directly to a landing page you've created. (A *landing page* is where people arrive when they click an online ad or search listing. The landing page is designed to be highly relevant to the e-mail, ad, or search listing that prompted the reader to visit your site.) Importantly, responding to your call to action brings these visitors straight to the specific information about your offer without making them through menus and links on your home page.

To learn more about creating highly effective landing pages, please see *Landing Page Optimization For Dummies* by Mike and Martin Harwood.

The landing page could let customers print an e-coupon or head to your online merchandise shop, or it could provide them with a form to give you their postal mailing addresses so you can send them your quarterly catalog. In any case, you'll likely actually close the sale on the landing page.

"Okay, fine," you say, "But I really don't want to spend time creating a separate page just for people to land on. They can get to the info well enough through my home page." Sure. But they can also get impatient, confused, and frustrated — and then just give up and go somewhere else (like your competitor's Web site). Why take that chance?

Writing effective marketing e-mail messages

Think of the following three rules as carved in granite or some other Igneous rock for writing effective marketing messages:

✔ **Make the content valuable to the reader:** If you accomplish nothing else in your e-mail, make crystal clear what's in it for them.

✔ **Be direct:** No need to beat around the bush; just say, "Here's a bush."

✔ **Be concise:** Write plainly and keep your messages to the point. Try not to say "utilize conversational devices in a communicative way" when you can just say "talk."

Your recipient has precious little time (a few minutes at most) to spend on your message. Say it simply, say it informatively, and then stop writing.

And, as with your Subject line, don't go over the top. S~~ ~~
Our Biggest Sale Ever) and exclamation points don't s~~ ~~
just scream. Avoid them and settle for being your nice, cal~~ ~~
credible self.

A lot of e-mail experts all seem to agree on some critical basics for the
content section:

- ✔ **Use strong, direct action and value words:** For example, Save, Get,
  Learn, Buy, or Call.

- ✔ **Don't use multiple punctuation marks or symbols:** For example, ***,
  \$\$\$, ###, and especially not !!!.

- ✔ **Don't use LOTS OF CAPITAL LETTERS:** It comes across at best, as
  shouting; at worst, as desperation.

- ✔ **Use short, punchy sentences, and bulleted lists (like this one) to make
  for easy reading.**

- ✔ **Create a sense of urgency:** For example, For a Very Limited Time, 3 Days
  Only, Available Only until Midnight, June 12th.

- ✔ **Use powerful, colorful, and descriptive adjectives:** For example, *amazing* instead of *special, huge* instead of *big, wonderful* instead of *nice,
  unmatched* instead of *low, immediately* instead of *fast.*

- ✔ **Proofread your copy for misspellings, grammar, punctuation, and
  other miskates.**

Keep in mind that your e-mails reach people who already know at least a little
about who you are and what you do (otherwise, they wouldn't have signed up
to hear from you). So don't use this valuable opportunity to bore them with
how many centuries you've been in business or that your Great Uncle Donald
(rest his soul) founded the shop and passed it on to your father Louis, who
passed it on to you and your brothers Hewey and Dewey. Because, know what?
Your readers won't stick around long enough to be bored. They'll be gone.

When people encounter your e-mail messages, it should feel a lot like it does
when they encounter you personally. If you're the homespun type, make your
e-mails homespun. If you come off as an always-on-the-cutting-edge kind of
person, your e-mails need to reflect that.

Choosing between plain text and HTML

The previous two sections describe the elements of an e-mail message and
provide tips for writing effective marketing messages. This section discusses
how the message *looks* — that is, whether you should use plain text or go the
bells-and-whistles HTML route. Here, briefly, is the difference:

✔ **Plain-text messages** are ordinary, unformatted e-mail messages that are readable as textual material without much processing. Most of the day-to-day, conversational e-mails you send from your home computer are plain-text messages.

✔ **HTML (HyperText Markup Language) messages** use the same language as Web pages to allow the display of rich media content in the e-mail message. This means you can write messages that contain all kinds of razzly-dazzly stuff like links, images, film clips, and interactive forms.

Some e-mailers like to use plain-text messages (refer to Figure 10-4) and maintain no significant difference in readership rates occurs between plain-text e-mails and those done in HTML. These folks, however, are a minority. Most e-mail pros rely on research showing that HTML readership is *overwhelmingly* greater than that generated by plain-text formats. So you have two schools of thought in the plain text versus HTML debate, but the HTML school has about 50 times more students.

That lopsided preference, however, doesn't change the fact that using HTML has several downsides:

✔ It's typically more expensive to produce.

✔ It requires more *bandwidth* (the amount of data a given computer can successfully download all at once).

✔ It often carries viruses.

✔ It may not always reproduce properly on the screen of every e-mail recipient because some e-mail programs simply don't show graphics unless the sender's address is already on the recipient's approved sender list.

The plain-text crowd also argues that e-mail is about content, not design, and that given the possibility of technical problems we describe in the preceding list, not everyone can or even wants to receive HTML e-mail.

To satisfy both sides, most e-mail service providers (ESPs) send multi-part format e-mails that let the recipient choose either plain-text or HTML versions. (The subject of ESPs is discussed in the "Getting Professional Help with Your E-Mail Campaign" section, found later in this chapter.)

The ability to make two versions available is made possible through the use of *MIME (Multipurpose Internet Mail Extensions),* an Internet standard for formatting e-mails. With MIME, e-mails are sent in both plain-text and HTML formats, and the recipient's own, pre-specified e-mail client preferences dictate which version automatically shows up on his screen.

Finding the right tone and look

Personality in print, whether in an e-mail or in some other form, is a function not just of what you say, but *how you say it* and *what it looks like.*

For example, starting a message with Hello (not that you really should) is completely different than starting with Dear, Sir (which you definitely shouldn't). The first says "I have something to share with you;" the other just says, "I want something from you." Which one do you suppose is going to get a more welcome reception from your reader? The challenge here is to find that fertile middle ground between being overly familiar and overly formal. Let your usual (charming) personality be your guide.

The look of your message is also important. If you make your message look as "stiff" as a business letter or report, you may as well not send it at all. On the other hand, gluing together a whole bunch of different, boxy chunks, each in a different color and with a different typeface, looks like a ransom note. In the former case, you appear too boring to bother with; in the later, you come off as too silly to take seriously.

Want to know what your e-mails should look like? Well, we suggest you start with the kind of e-mails that appeal to *you* when you open them. Try figuring out *why* they have that appeal. Then go from there.

If you're not working with an ESP though, you're probably best off sending plain-text e-mails at least initially to make sure *everyone* gets the message. You can always branch out into HTML later as you become more familiar with your recipients' tastes and technological capabilities, and as your own computer skills expand.

Getting Professional Help with Your E-Mail Campaign

Creating your own e-mail mailing list — and having total ownership and control over it — may sound appealing. But it can become extremely cumbersome and time-consuming (not to mention, frustrating) to manage.

Unless you have an automated system in-house linked to both your Web site and your databases, you'll have to make all necessary changes manually (such as removing Mrs. Brown's address at her request). And when we discuss *metrics* (measurements of effectiveness) in the following section, you see that that beast alone can be a killer for a non-specialist to handle. Which leaves you with your best option: *Don't* do it yourself. Use an ESP instead.

ESPs are companies whose whole reason for being is to make effective e-mail campaigns possible for the average local (and even larger than local) business owner. And the service options they can offer are so various and cost-effective that it just doesn't make financial sense *not* to use one. After all, you specialize in what you do, not in e-mail technology. So let them specialize in their field — which starts with saving you a whole hopper-full of headaches.

Just about any reputable ESP can do the following:

- Provide templates, either for free or at low cost that you can customize with your own logo, photographs, and colors.
- Handle the actual mass-sending of e-mails.
- Help you get the *white listing* seal of approval. (ESPs can't work for black-listed clients.)
- Ensure high delivery rates.
- Help you with multi-part formatting of your e-mails.
- Personalize the content.
- Host your chosen images.
- Handle unsubscribes.
- Generate custom reports, including the metrics you want.
- Help ensure that your e-mail campaigns are compliant with CAN-SPAM. (For more information, see the section, "CAN-SPAM Compliance and the Opt-In," later in this chapter.)

Highly useful though they are, selecting an ESP can be tricky. A search online quickly demonstrates that ESPs vary in their sophistication, from the simplistic to the complex.

Your best bet is to demo a few vendors to see what works for you and what doesn't. Any competent and reputable ESP has some sort of test-flight program you can take advantage of, and if one doesn't offer that, look elsewhere.

Don't be afraid of what you don't know. No one expects you to be an e-mail expert (otherwise, why would you need them?). So ask questions and see how much guidance and expertise the ESP is willing and able to share. More is better — and will make you that much more comfortable with your ultimate partner choice.

In any case, shop around to make sure you're getting the features you need at a price that makes sense for your business. Table 10-2 shows some of today's most popular ESPs, along with a few helpful details about each one. And, of course, many more companies can be found — where else? — on the Internet.

Table 10-2   Popular ESPs

ESP Name	URL	Primary Services	Demo Available	Estimated Cost
Constant Contact	www.constantcontact.com	Campaign creation, customizable templates, auto-responder, list management, delivery, tracking and reporting, campaign archive, coaching, and support.	Free 60-day trial for lists below 100 subscribers.	Plans as low as $15/month for up to 500 subscribers.
Campaign Monitor	www.campaignmonitor.com	Customize or build a template, manage e-mail lists, access reports, and create charts and private labels.	Unlimited free trial for lists below 5 subscribers.	Flat fee of $5 per campaign, and $.01 per recipient.
MailChimp	www.mailchimp.com	Everything from e-mail templates, list management and delivery, to reporting and optimization tools.	Unlimited free trial for lists below 100 subscribers.	Starts from $10/month for up to 500 subscribers.
iContact	www.icontact.com	Free templates, list management and delivery, integrated surveying, reporting, and auto-responders.	Free 15-day trial for lists below 250 subscribers.	$9.95 monthly minimum, including unlimited e-mail lists.
Emma	www.myemma.com	Templates, list management and delivery, proofing links, surveys and forms, triggers and follow-ups, and reporting.	Free test account.	$99 setup fee (includes customized template), plus $30/month for up to 1,000 subscribers.

Using Metrics to Gauge Your Success

As with any medium, you can never know how well e-mail works for you if you don't track it. This doesn't mean that you have to tie every e-mail you send to the specific dollar amount it costs you to drive a customer through the door (unless that's what you want to know). But identifying what your e-mail program's objectives are and then measuring against them to determine your actual success are keys to using the program to your maximum benefit.

Your goals in using metrics can be as simple or as complex as you want — anything from achieving a 50-percent *open rate* (which we discuss in the following list) for a particular offer to tracking every conversion to the penny with the objective of reaching an ROI of say, 5:1.

The basic e-mail marketing metrics are as follows:

- **Deliverability:** The number of e-mails actually delivered (not including those that were bounced or otherwise filtered).

- **Open rate:** The number of e-mails actually opened (which is significant in that it both validates the e-mail addresses used and indicates at least some level of interest on your recipient's part).

- **Click-through rate (CTR):** Tells you not only how many people have opened your e-mail, but how many have then gone on to click one of the links you provided (say, to your landing page).

- **Conversion rate:** The number of unique e-mails that resulted in a *conversion* (after clicking a provided link, the recipient took some further action). This is similar to the CTR, but because it involves even more action on the recipient's part, it's considered an even more significant measure of a customer's interest in buying.

- **Unsubscribe rate:** Tells you how many of your subscribers have opted out (jumped ship) and asked to be taken off your e-mail list. At best, this is due to a lack of interest; at worst, you did something that didn't sit well with them.

- **Return on marketing investment (ROMI):** The revenue actually generated by your e-mail campaign. This is usually calculated by dividing the incremental revenue attributable to your e-mail effort by the total cost of producing that effort.

Using metrics obviously can tell you a lot about what you're accomplishing with your e-mail efforts. But, as they like to say on TV, "Don't try this at home." Doing the necessary diagnostics to deliver quality metrics — not to mention coming up with the mega-geek-class algorithms that make the whole process possible — is something best left to a professional e-mail company.

When in doubt, test it!

One of the best things about the e-mail medium is that it allows you to do a lot of testing — with minimal effort — to find out what works and what just flat out doesn't. Here, too, your ESP can prove very helpful.

For example, say you're going to send 100 e-mails promoting the same deal or offering the same information. You can send 50 with one subject line and 50 with another subject line. Unless the two lines are really, really similar, you get a very quick read on which one works better because it gets the greater response.

Or you can try two (or more) different layouts, color schemes, or typefaces. Or try personalizing one group and not personalizing the other. As long as you only use two variables in a single test, you'll probably be surprised what a difference the little things can make.

Do enough of these tests — and take the results to heart, even if they don't quite line up with your initial expectations — and you can quickly become a very effective e-mail marketer.

CAN-SPAM Compliance and the Opt-In

There is one primary source of potential trouble for anyone who markets their business via e-mail, and there are two things about it that demand your close attention: It's *federal* law, and it's a doozy.

The federal CAN-SPAM Act (your own joke goes here) of 2003 essentially rewrote the rules of e-mail marketing to inhibit *spamming* — that lovely practice of indiscriminately sending unsolicited e-mail messages. (Recent Congressional amendments have, however, somewhat loosened the opt-in requirements; for an explanation of that wrinkle, a good source is www. marketingsherpa.com/sample.cfm?contentID=2555). In any case, CAN-SPAM compliance is a tricky beast. Here are a few of the mandates that apply most directly to the small business owner:

- ✔ **Misrepresentation:** Don't try and lure your e-mail recipient into opening your e-mail with false information in the Subject line or misrepresent who's sending the e-mail.

- ✔ **Company address:** Your e-mail must include your company's physical address; P.O. boxes are not acceptable.

- ✔ **Disclosure:** If you're sending a commercial e-mail to people who haven't asked to receive it, you must state that the e-mail is an advertisement, using precisely that word. Of course, if your recipients have already opted in, you're exempt from this rule, no matter how advertising-like your message may be.

- ✔ **Unsubscribe:** Recipients must be able to unsubscribe easily from your e-mail; you must then remove them from your mailing list within ten days of their request.

- ✔ **E-mail sharing:** You can't share the e-mail address of a person who has unsubscribed from your list.

- ✔ **E-mail harvesting:** You can't collect non-permitted e-mail addresses from other sources or randomly generate e-mail addresses.

Fun, huh? But it *does* address (no pun intended) a serious problem — spamming — that's been giving the whole e-mail marketing world a black eye for several years now. So it's not like Congress is saying "Eat your peas" just for the heck of it. And who knows? It might actually do the trick.

The bottom line is that compliance with CAN-SPAM is simple: Just do what it says. Include a valid unsubscribe method that requires only one click to activate, promptly unsubscribe people when they ask you to, present your physical mailing address in your messages, don't steal e-mail addresses, and don't be misleading. After all, when you think about it, it's really just common sense. But whether you like the rules or not, they apply to *every* business, large or small, that sends e-mail. Period.

Getting permission is still the safest way

All the information in the section, "CAN-SPAM Compliance and the Opt-In," earlier in this chapter, notwithstanding, the regulations currently being issued under CAN-SPAM are beginning to trend more toward opt out than opt in as the preferred e-mail model. But don't get too excited because you ignore the original act at your peril.

By not working with permission, you risk alienating the audience that you're trying so hard to reach. You're invading their privacy. You're choking their inboxes. You're just basically coming across as a pest. So, even if you think you've found some wiggle room in the law, don't wiggle. Stay within the bounds of the act as written, and nobody gets hurt.

And remember: No matter what the law says, in today's world of e-mail marketing, opt in and permission still starkly separates the legitimate marketer (like you) from the dratted spammer. So be smart, be compliant, and prosper.

Chapter 11

Linking Up with Directories and Lead Aggregators

In This Chapter

▶ Discovering the strengths of directories and lead aggregators

▶ Recognizing how directories differ from search engines

▶ Understanding how directories and lead aggregators work

▶ Identifying the best directories and creating an effective profile

▶ Using local listings, including community sites, to build your business

▶ Going with a lead aggregator, or not

Do you need to search for restaurants in a particular neighborhood, look up a phone number for a local repair service, or are you planning a weekend getaway and want to compare hotel rates? These activities probably motivate you to use a search engine (along with 90 percent of Web users), or to rely on a directory (such as Internet Yellow Pages or Yelp) or a lead aggregator (such as ServiceMagic.com).

Directories present Web users with listings of participating local businesses, often organized by business type. They're popular because they represent one-stop shopping for people who want to do business with a company located in their area. Related to (but not quite the same as) directories are *lead aggregators*. They do pretty much exactly what their name suggests: They bundle customer leads that they acquire on the Web and then market them to local businesses for follow up.

In this chapter, we dig into what makes directories and lead aggregators tick — and why they motivate so many Web users to click.

What's So Great about Directories and Lead Aggregators?

What can directories and lead aggregators do for your business? Potentially, a lot because they can bring you new customers in two ways:

✔ **By capturing search traffic:** Listing sites are the category killers we talk about in Chapter 7. These sites contain so much relevant content — and consequently attract so many clicks — that they tend to rank high in *organic search results* (see Chapters 7 and 8 for information about organic results) and push local business Web sites down the page. For businesses that rely solely on organic listings, this isn't great news. But for a local business that's included in these extremely potent sites, it can be wonderful news.

✔ **By delivering direct traffic:** Web users are becoming increasingly aware that local listing sites exist and go to them directly to find local products and services. Not only does this convenience save them the intermediate step of using a search engine, but it also often gives them value-added content, such as customer reviews and ratings.

Seeing that Directories Aren't Search Engines

Directories and lead aggregators can be lumped together into a set of Web tools known as *listing sites.* People often confuse listing sites with search engines, which is only natural because these Web tools work in similar ways and often work together. Understanding exactly how they differ is the key to using each properly.

Search engines are often the entry points to listing sites, and you can think of listing sites as the fulfillment engines that pay off a search. Figure 11-1 illustrates the relationships among three online resources: a search engine, a directory, and a local business Web site.

The general differences between search engines and listing sites include

✔ **Sourcing:** Search engines use software to crawl sites to find appropriate content (see Chapters 7 and 8 for more about crawling), but businesses submit their sites to one or more listing sites, where their business site is typically reviewed by in-the-flesh human editors. Unless something's really bizarre about your Web site, you aren't likely to have any trouble getting listed.

How Consumers Find Local Businesses through Search Engines

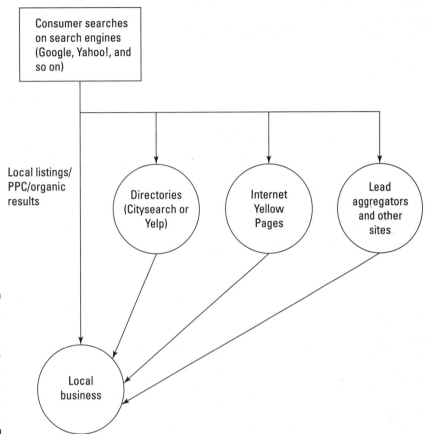

Figure 11-1:
Local busi-
nesses can
appear
in search
engine
results and
listing sites.

✔ **Organization:** Listing sites and search engines also organize their databases differently. Search engines score the sites they find on the basis
of relevance, but listing sites generally use a *hierarchical tree structure*
that zooms in from the general to the specific. For example, a listing
site might have a topical organization for listing electricians that looks
like this:

```
For the Home>Home Improvement>Electricians
```

When you submit your business for consideration by listing sites, identifying the right category is important; otherwise, you won't be found. The
categories are provided by each listing site and can differ slightly from
site to site. However, they're all based on simple common sense, so you
aren't likely to get trapped in some organizational corner where only
customers with bloodhounds can find you.

✔ **Landing:** This is a major distinction between search engines and listing sites. Listing sites usually list other Web *sites,* whereas search engines generally list Web *pages.* As a result, a listing site doesn't drive visitors to land on a specific page you've created; they simply arrive at your home page.

Exposing the How and What of Directories

Directories run on listings that local businesses submit directly to them, whereupon those lovable human editors step in to inspect the business sites and decide whether they're worthy of being listed. Happily, the worthiness bar isn't set all that high, but it serves to weed out the occasional wacko and other completely-in-the-wrong-category submissions.

The listings that survive this screening — which are the vast majority of them — are compiled into categories and listed alphabetically, starting with (what else?) A.

How directories get customer traffic

Directories use several techniques to attract visitors:

✔ **Organic:** Search engines sort through directories and index them to match various search queries. For example, if you type **plumber Memphis** into Google, a broad-based directory (such as Citysearch or Superpages.com) is nearly certain to produce several listings that match those search terms. Because directories with content that's rich in keywords — and therefore, eminently findable by search engines — are usually listed high in the organic search results, people tend to click them first and foremost.

✔ **Paid:** Some directories use pay-per-click (PPC) ads to buy their way into a prime search results position to take advantage of the chance that consumers will find at least one business in the directory to suit their needs.

✔ **Direct:** Many directories use traditional media, such as TV and radio, to drive consumers to their Web sites. A prime example of this strategy is illustrated by many of the Internet Yellow Pages companies. We take a look at such companies in the section, "Identifying the Best Directories," later in this chapter.

How directories get listings

The business sites submitted to directories aren't the directories' only source of content. Directories also often buy listings from data compilation companies, such as Localeze or infoUSA, because they want to provide searchers with a more comprehensive set of businesses and a better user experience. Additionally, having a more comprehensive set of business listings has the potential to increase that directory's overall presence in the organic results of the search engines.

That said, don't be concerned with a directory's content strategy. Focus on figuring out what directories have a strong online presence for your specific geography and industry.

The sort of information directories usually publish

In their listings, local directories typically include each business's name (obviously), physical address, phone number, and hours of operation. Some directories also let businesses include ratings they've received from customers. Businesses can often (for a price) mention their current promotions, upload coupons, and provide access to videos. The upshot of such extras is that businesses listed in the directory give their would-be customers a handy summary of the basic information they need to know.

Some directories organize and present their business listings using criteria other than alphabetical order. The most common of these other criteria is the strength of each business's customer ratings. If your business has good customer ratings, flaunt them (tastefully, of course) in your listing.

Inside the directories: What are your options?

You can take advantage of directories in a number of ways, and most cost you little or nothing. The options that directories usually give you include

- ✔ **Free listings:** What can we say? They're free. Upload your information to the directory, and they list you. However, you may start out (or heaven forbid, *stay*) at or near the bottom of the listings for a number of reasons. For example, you're the newest addition, your business's name starts with Z, or you don't (yet) get high user ratings. Practically speaking, this bad placement problem is a stumbling block only for local businesses whose geographic market area is huge and jam-packed with competitors.

✔ **Display:** Some directories sell banner advertising to their listers. The banner ad for your business shows on the directory's site and is usually priced on a *cost-per-thousand-views* (CPM) basis. The CPM generally ranges from $2–$20. (If that cost sounds a little steep to you, remember that you're paying for a *thousand* views per fee — which is a lot of exposure.)

✔ **Listing fee:** This option involves paying a monthly listing fee that can range anywhere from a few dollars a month to several hundred dollars a month. This fee ensures that you get a nice, fat, visible spot in the directory's listings (not unlike PPC ads on a search engine results page). Recognize that your chosen directory may not offer the listing fee option, and many businesses don't use it even when it's available.

If the listing fee cost is only a few dollars a month, it may simply be a no brainer. However, the only circumstance that justifies paying a fee of several hundred dollars per month is when you're fighting to get noticed among scores of other competitive businesses. Unless your geographic market is a huge city, this isn't likely to be the case. But, hey, it's your business, your money, and your call.

Identifying the Best Directories

Simply put, finding the best directories for your business usually comes down to how you want to be found. This list clarifies the various directory options you have available:

✔ **Internet Yellow Pages (IYP):** These online versions of the good ol' print mainstays you grew up with have inherent brand recognition among consumers, which can translate into significant customer traffic. People think of IYP as easy places to look up stuff, like with the paper versions. IYP often provide city guides and are starting to offer extras like user-generated content, including reviews and ratings. The most prominent IYPs are

   • *Superpages.com:* www.superpages.com

   • *Yellowpages.com:* www.yellowpages.com

   • *Yellowbook:* www.yellowbook.com

   • *DexKnows:* www.dexknows.com

✔ **Local directories:** Provide deep local content across a broad array of local business categories — as opposed to listing just restaurants or just building contractors. They often use reviews and ratings to help consumers wade through the listings they publish. Local directories are very similar to IYP, but without the familiar phone book heritage. Still, local directories are plenty successful, and they include the following sites:

- *Yelp:* Relies heavily on extensive ratings and reviews to help people find great local businesses. (www.yelp.com)

- *Citysearch:* Similar to Yelp with extensive reviews on local businesses. Owned by IAC, who also runs a number of other online properties such as the search engine Ask.com and lead aggregator ServiceMagic.com. (http://citysearch.com)

- *Local.com:* An easy way to find local businesses via features like top searches, local favorites, and local coupons. (www.local.com)

- *BrightPages:* Lets searchers find their favorite business listings, and organize, share, and store them, too. (www.brightpages.com)

- *Kudzu:* Designed to help searchers save time by featuring buying advice, buyer's guides deals, discounts, and more. (www.kudzu.com)

✔ **Vertical directories:** Present site listings for specific business categories, which are often referred to in the ad biz as *vertical markets.* Users who like vertical directories already have their desired category in mind, and their search is largely a matter of geography. They ask, "Which well-ranked businesses (in terms of ratings, if the directory includes them) are the most conveniently located?" Examples of vertical directories are

- *1800Dentist:* Enables searchers to find a nearby dentist by entering a zip code. (www.1800dentist.com)

- *Urbanspoon:* A popular local restaurant site. (www.urbanspoon.com)

- *newyorkdoctors.com:* Helps searchers find the local doctors their friends and neighbors recommend. (www.newyorkdoctors.com)

The not-really-all-that-difficult process of picking the right directory to list with

Start your search for the best directory (or directories) for your business to list with by searching for the keywords you think your potential customers would use to find you online and seeing what appears in the organic search results. Then dive into some of the sites you see with these questions in mind:

✔ **Does a directory rank in the top five of the search results?** If so, click through to the directory itself and have a look around. Does the directory look like a comfy fit for your business? If so, that one deserves big points – and serious consideration.

✔ **Does the directory contain authoritative content?** A directory's no place for vagueness or pussyfooting. Do these folks seem like they know what they're talking about? Do they give visitors solid information or just fluff? Obviously, you should prefer the former.

✔ **Does the directory have credibility?** The credibility factor results from evaluating a hodgepodge of characteristics. For example, does the directory appear to serve visitors efficiently and well, giving them useful information without making them jump through hoops to find it? Do you imagine that its service effectively instills confidence in users? Would you feel comfortable relying on this directory to accurately represent your business? All these factors are important to online searchers and need to be important to you.

Above all, use your own good judgment to evaluate directories. Remember that you're trying to assess the value of a directory based on how valuable you think its visitors find it. Do they see the directory as well-presented or clunky to navigate? Do visitors get a really good, thorough array of listings or do the offerings seem kind of lame? And so on. If you think the directory seems to be someplace visitors would and should like to visit, that counts for a lot.

So . . . are directories a good way to go?

As a general rule, listing your business Web site with directories is a solid advertising tactic. Their basic listings often gives you a free (or nearly free) way to drive traffic to your Web site. Also, if you have your business Web site placed on a number of directories, the search engines are likely to find your site and give it an individual organic listing on their results pages — which, of course, is also free and can drive even more traffic your way. Directories are also an excellent way to get the kind of external linking we discuss in Chapter 8, and that can help you merit an improved ranking for your site in search engine results.

The only downside to using directories is that directories individually often aren't guaranteed sources of a lot of traffic and seldom are sufficient to be your only source of traffic. Moreover, placing listings or buying space on a bunch of directories, unless you have the help of a local online advertising company, can in aggregate, eat up a lot of your time. Our recommendation is to focus on those directories you determine are most likely to have a real impact on your business instead of worrying about showing up on all of them.

Sharing Information with Your Chosen Directories

When you submit your site to a directory for listing, you're often asked to provide a company profile. Make sure this profile is a manageable-to-the-reader encapsulation of exactly what your business does, plus any (brief) selling kind thing you want to add. For example, state that you're the top in your market area or the longest-established business. You have to be fairly concise because directories don't give you all that much room to state your case. Then again, you have as much room as your competitors, so the playing field's pretty even.

How's your profile?

In preparing your profile, provide as much detailed information as you can within the limits imposed by the directory. Remember that you aren't writing your memoirs, just providing useful and compelling information.

Directory profiles, like the one shown in Figure 11-2, usually let you include a mix of content elements, such as

- **Basic business information:** This includes the name, address, phone number, business hours, and so on.

- **A succinct description of the products/services you offer:** Also include any industry affiliations or other relevant info, such as the number of years in business, that you think are worth mentioning.

- **Awards, reviews, and ratings you've received:** These can be from business organizations, local publications, or even from real customers. The reviews you publish shouldn't (and due to space limitations, usually can't) go on and on. Pick out the really good parts of the most flattering reviews.

- **Special promotions, coupons, discounts:** Mention any other offers you have going.

- **A reasonably sized photo gallery:** In some cases, also include access to video material.

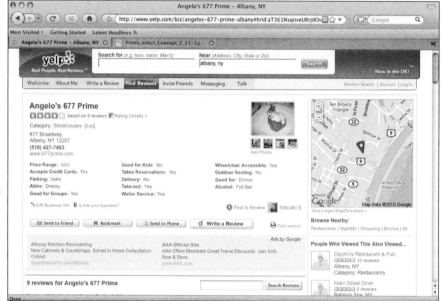

Your profile is a constant work in progress

Just like with your Web site, you must keep your profile current. For example, if your profile spotlights Louie as your most experienced and knowledgeable salesperson, Louie better still be on your staff when a visitor comes knocking. Otherwise, you risk looking like details aren't all that important — or worse. Ditto for the product lines you handle and the services you offer: They have to be kept up to date.

Keep refreshing your promotions and your customer testimonials, too. Make sure that any links to your site that you've given the directory still work. Sure, you may have a stellar profile on the directory, but if people click your link and nothing happens . . . well, that's the end of that.

Do some testing to help evaluate the effectiveness of your directory profile. If you already use metrics to track your Web site's performance, you can tell where your site traffic comes from, including how much comes through a directory. Tweak a few things in your profile to see whether that helps (or hurts) the amount of directory traffic you get.

Tapping into Community Sites: Craigslist and Then Some

Whether you just launched your Web site or have been at it for years, establishing a customer base within your local community is the whole point of your efforts. That makes local sites an invaluable way to drum up new business in your market.

Community sites are among the most popular of these local venues. They are a form of a directory that, as the name implies, give visitors a feel for what's happening in their community — a snapshot of who's doing what, selling what, and even in some cases, thinking what. Using community sites is a great way to get wide marketing coverage at little or no cost.

Many consumers prefer to do business with a local company, one with whom they can establish a personal relationship. This is especially true for consumers who don't have much of a comfort level dealing with businesses solely on an online basis. These potential customers want a local phone number they can call or a local address they can visit to get to know you and your company.

As for finding the *right* local portal(s), that's easy. Head to Google and type the name of your town or city. And presto! — there they are. By doing so, you're mimicking the behavior of your own local customers and prospects, and what better "teachers" could you ask for?

A grapevine for the 21st Century

Consumers love — don't just like, but *love* — using local Web resources. Nielsen NetRatings' statistics from 2001 show that community sites (and local search engines) are among the most often-visited kinds of sites for American Internet users. And the ever-growing use of portals like these is pretty easy to understand. People look for news and information that's relevant to them, and what's going on — and what's available — in their community could hardly be more relevant.

In short, local portals are gateways for the community's members. Because these sites provide a central point for them to find good local information, as well as locally based Web sites, they flock to them. This is good news for your business.

Some people know from experience which portals to use. Others get to these sites via a search engine (and search engines host plenty of local content, as we explain in Chapter 1).

We don't want to over-promise on the business impact from local portals. Although they're wildly popular among consumers, local portals don't drive unimaginable hordes of leads to local businesses. A lot of portal users just go there to see what's happening in their area and then move on to other things. Still, these sites can drive some additional, profitable leads to your door at little or no cost.

The local portals we're talking about include

- **Community sites:** These sites put all sorts of local information — from the recent birth of the Henderson twins to the local police blotter — under one roof. Many also offer services like e-mail and discussion forums where people in the city or town can communicate with each other about, well . . . stuff.

  Some examples are

  - www.alloveralbany.com
  - www.hellomemphis.com
  - www.americantowns.com/mn/minneapolis

- **Craigslist:** Unless you've been orbiting the earth for the last decade or so, you've at least *heard* of Craigslist. It is the Mother of All Local Portals, which may at first strike you as a little odd because it's a nationally run site. The Craigslist folks break down the listings they get into very specific geographical areas. These listings are really just online classified ads for practically anything: jobs, housing, personals, community events, local goods and services, resumes, discussion forums — and a few dozen other things.

  Most important from your standpoint is that the postings on Craigslist are gloriously free. If you haven't yet frequented the wonderful world of Craigslist, do — because if nothing else, it's something else. (Figure 11-3 shows Craigslist's somewhat charmingly chaotic home page, and Figure 11-4 shows a typical business listing.)

- **Angie's List**: Another major player in the community listings universe, Angie's List is one of many companies that aggregate consumer reviews of local businesses. Angie's List is unique among those other portals because it *charges* consumers to see the reviews. Huh? Why? Because the people at Angie's List believe that charging consumers adds *credibility* to the information they find there. (The fact that Angie's List is as successful as it is would seem to indicate they're actually onto something here.)

  Angie's List grades companies with an A–F report card based on consumer reviews and accepts advertising only from companies that score a B or better. Although consumers pay a membership fee, posting is free to advertisers, but only after an Angie's List member submits a report about her experience with the would-be advertiser's company. And nope, no cheating allowed: You can't pay your way onto Angie's List, although if you're already there and have a good rating, some advertising options for extra visibility are available.

✔ **Oodle:** An up-and-comer, Oodle is a directory of classified advertisings, including local business advertising. Oodle doesn't have a long track record, but postings are free and the portal has a decent reputation — so what do you have to lose?

Figure 11-3:
The home page of Craigslist.

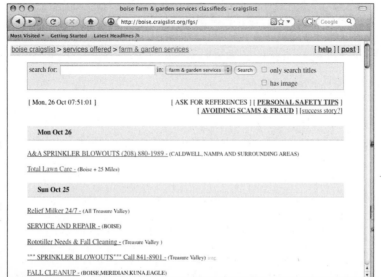

Figure 11-4:
An example of a Craigslist listings page and an actual business listing.

Some other local portals

If your business is located within a 30-mile radius of a major city, contact the premier newspaper that serves it and ask to have your site linked to the paper's portal. You can do the same with the newspapers located in smaller cities and towns, though these portals are likely to be a good deal less sophisticated than those offered by the big papers. And if you haven't done so already, become a member of your local Chamber of Commerce or Visitors Bureau so you can take advantage of these organizations' Web presence.

The upside of local portals is that there really isn't any downside. Such local portals can help as follows:

- **Newspaper Web sites:** These bring reputable, high-quality content and a loyal readership to the party, both of which can be beneficial to a business that wants to run a listing. To stay competitive with the kinds of portals listed earlier, the newspaper sites are also expanding into features like videos, blogs, and other user-generated content such as reviews and ratings. Most major-paper sites include a shopping guide, an event guide, and/or a directory, and inclusion in them is usually free. Depending on your location, you can use

  - *The Washington Post:* www.washingtonpost.com

  - *The New York Times:* www.nytimes.com

  - *The Seattle Times:* www.seattletimes.com

  - *The Boston Globe:* www.boston.com/bostonglobe

  - Or whatever big-shot paper serves your city.

- **Chambers of Commerce and Visitors Bureaus:** Because so many people go online for information these days, the Chambers and Bureaus now offer a number of reasonably priced services designed to promote their members' businesses and drive traffic to their Web sites. (Plus, with most Chambers of Commerce, you also get invited to a spiffy monthly luncheon where you can network your brains off and also, you know, eat.)

Considering Lead Aggregators

Lead aggregators are companies that generate *qualified leads* — meaning phone calls or Web inquiries — for local businesses. Although not technically directories, aggregators are another way in which local businesses can gather customers via centralized, business-related Web sites. A few examples include ServiceMagic.com (see Figure 11-5) or BidClerk.com for home improvement businesses, or 1800Dentist.com for — you guessed it — dentists.

Lead aggregators generate leads primarily using two of the proven traffic builders we discuss elsewhere in the book (organic search listings in Chapter 8 and PPC ads in Chapter 9), and they're a particularly useful tool for business owners who are just getting started in online marketing.

Generally speaking, lead aggregators use one (or both) of two models:

- **Direct aggregation:** Involves using either PPC ads or some kind of traditional media to drive consumers to navigate the lead aggregator directly. When someone clicks an aggregator's PPC ad or goes to its site, he sees its client's listings in all their glory. The business is then charged only when a consumer contacts them directly from those listings.

- **Indirect aggregation:** This model is kind of backwards. In indirect aggregation, the lead aggregator buys or otherwise, generates leads in a particular market category and then sells those leads to multiple local businesses within that category.

Figure 11-5: Service-Magic.com aggregates leads to then sell to contractors.

In both cases, the aggregator assumes all the risk for buying the leads. The business owner usually pays on a cost-per-lead or cost-per-referral basis, which puts the local business on the hook only for actual leads delivered — and that's a pretty good deal.

Looking at the pros and cons

As with just about everything else you can do in life, using lead aggregators has its plusses, its minuses, and its really bad minus-minuses:

✔ **The plusses:**

- You can buy leads that have a strongly predictable cost.

- You save labor, time, and money.

- You can buy what you need at the time you need it. Your own timeline is the determining factor in whether and when you use an aggregator.

✔ **The minuses:**

- Leads from an aggregator can cost more than DIY-created leads, though whether this is true usually depends on how adept a given business is at doing its online marketing.

- Especially with indirect aggregation, a lead is often passed to multiple businesses at the same time, which results in a race to reach the consumer. Some businesses see this as a challenge; others see it as a pain.

- With a bunch of businesses beating down their doors (or more accurately, ringing their phones off the hook), consumers can feel overwhelmed and get testy about the whole thing.

✔ **The really bad minus-minuses:**

- Businesses don't wind up with their very own name getting visibility because aggregators run generic category ads; for example, Funeral Homes in Warwick RI.

- Aggregators tend to go after the easy pickings rather than take the time to understand your business and thereby help you pursue more elusive, bigger-ticket customers. If nothing else, you don't want to rely solely on a lead aggregator to generate business because it's unlikely to feed you enough new customers to satisfy your goals.

- You know that race to reach the customers we mention earlier? Well, guess what else happens when *that* happens: price wars. If your margins aren't all that big to begin with, you probably don't want to get involved in any crazed race to financial ruin.

Deciding who needs to use an aggregator

As a general rule, lead aggregators tend to work best for *commodity-based businesses.* Companies whose services are widely available in the market — and whose customers can change suppliers seamlessly — may well find that having someone else generate good, numerous leads is a big help to their business. This may include businesses like snow removal services, lawn mowing companies, movers, storage operators, and so on.

If your business fits that particular mold, great: A lead aggregator could prove to be a real asset. But this path isn't completely strewn with roses because lead aggregation requires a few things from you that may or may not present a problem for you and your business, namely

- ✔ **Response speed:** Some competitors have trained and equipped themselves to respond to an incoming lead within one minute by phone or e-mail. (Wow.) Unless you have the resources to do the same (at least do so more often than not), your competitor has a serious advantage in getting the business.

- ✔ **Price sensitivity:** When more than one business responds to a lead, the customer holds a strong hand; he can play the companies off one another to get the lowest price and can get so into the game that he ends up putting price before quality in making his decision. The net result for you is that you can ultimately lose leads you've paid for to competitors who can better afford to cut prices.

- ✔ **Phone sales skills:** You'll be dealing with an incoming lead who is also talking to your competitors. Do you, or does someone on your staff, have the phone skills and savvy necessary to shuffle the prospect into your arms and close the sale? It's important that you do or that you learn these skills in a hurry.

- ✔ **Chasing (too) expensive leads:** In the crush of competition, you can easily lose sight of what your actual lead acquisition costs are relative to your actual sales conversion rate. This isn't helped by the fact that lead aggregators are in the habit of adding new lead sources to their own roster on a regular basis, and some less-than-stellar leads can result. You may have a hard time sorting the good leads from the hopeless ones, but you have to apply some cost-benefit (and time-benefit) analysis to your efforts to make sure you aren't *losing* money pursuing dead ends.

You might conclude from this discussion that using a lead aggregator is a bigger headache than it's worth, but why not find out? Contact and retain one for what you plan to be a limited time. If the leads the aggregator produces are profitable, great. If not, also great because now at least you know that this isn't the way to go about generating leads for your business. And that lesson won't have cost you much.

Chapter 12

Targeting Customers with Banner Ads, E-Newsletter Ads, and More

Search engine marketing — whether pay-per-click (PPC), search engine optimization, local search opportunities, or a combination — proves its effectiveness every day for businesses. Getting your business listed with directories and lead aggregators can be highly effective as well.

However, these tactics aren't the only ways to make Internet marketing work for you. Because using more than one marketing channel to drive business your way is always a good idea, consider using new advertising media based on old-school marketing tools, such as display ads, newsletters, sponsorships, and classified advertising. Each of these has its own online version, and they translate very effectively to the Web.

This chapter looks at these new media approaches. They aren't difficult to use and they all can be very productive ways to generate impressions, conversions, and better yet, sales.

Casting a Wider Net with Online Tools

One tried-and-true marketing principle is to never rely on one form of advertising to reach new customers. Effective campaigns — whether Web-based or not — have always relied on the advertiser's ability to adopt a sound media mix. Ideally, you want to cast a wide net to reach customers anywhere you can.

In addition to and as a counterpart of search, these tools help cast a wider net:

- **Banner ads:** A *banner ad* is a form of online advertising that most closely mirrors print or display advertising. It simply entails embedding an ad into a Web page. In the past, your business may have used outdoor advertising, newspaper ads, or magazine ads. Banner advertising essentially does the same thing, but on the Web with potentially more impact.

- **E-newsletters:** Surely you've received a printed newsletter and maybe you even subscribe to receive it. Marketers love newsletters because they're cheap to produce, give consumers a more complete feel for the company, and provide an in-depth look at the products and services offered. E-newsletters can easily accomplish the same thing — without killing trees and at a far lower cost (after all, killing trees and mailing them all around your area can be expensive). Plus, with no printing and mailing necessary, e-newsletters are far more customizable and far more measurable as a marketing channel.

- **E-newsletter sponsorships:** For example, ever sponsored a little league team? You put your company's name and logo on the kids' jerseys and may even place your company's name and logo on the outfield wall, depending on how much you're willing to spend. An online e-newsletter sponsorship is an idea that's cut from the same cloth in that it allows you to brand your local business (and possibly gain some good will) with an audience that may not otherwise receive exposure to your business. The only difference is that instead of little league fans, your business gets exposure from whoever the e-newsletter owner's subscriber base happens to be.

- **Online classified ads:** What business hasn't used classified ads? Even today, the Classifieds section of the local Sunday paper is big and heavy. The upside of print classifieds is that they're divided neatly into distinct categories; the downside is that they cost money to run. Online classifieds are also broken into categories, but they're almost always free.

Like their traditional counterparts, each of these online tools is *opportunistic* — the stream of traffic each generates isn't usually steady, but occasional. Because you never know where your next customer will come from or what marketing vehicle will rope a customer into your business's fold, each of these online tactics is worth some serious consideration. And don't forget that just like search marketing, you can always try them, test them, and then decide whether they're making a significant contribution to your return on investment (ROI).

Running Banner Ads

A lot of people respond to banner ads, which is why you see lots of them online. Banner ads can also do wonders for establishing a brand (which we discuss a bit further in the "Leveraging the power of banner ads" section, later in this chapter). In other words, banner advertising is popular because it works.

Banner ads appear on a Web page in a separate box containing graphics, bright colors, a little bit of copy, and sometimes even animation. Somewhere amidst all that is usually a link that goes to the sponsor's Web site to read more about whatever the ad touts.

Each time someone sees a banner ad, it counts as an impression. Each time someone clicks the link, it counts as a click-through. Advertising rates for banner ads are often based on impressions, click-throughs, or on some combination of the two. Many sites are hesitant to pay on a cost-per-click basis in that actual clicks depend on your banner ad's creative design (which they often have no control over).

Figure 12-1 shows an example of banner ads on a local portal site.

Figure 12-1: The local portal site Your Town with banners flying on the top and right.

Leveraging the power of banner ads

Banner ads can accomplish a lot of things for an advertiser, including

- **Generating more Web site traffic and ultimately, sales:** Banner ads put your message prominently in front of potential customers. Executed well, they can be sufficiently enticing to drive prospects to your Web site in significant numbers. Unless your Web site is seriously sub-par, that can markedly increase your sales.

- **Effectively advertising new products:** Banner ads are an excellent way to create consumer interest in the new offering because they give you the freedom (albeit in limited space) to make your key copy points as well as present photos and animation to drive home the points.

- **Building a brand:** Your brand name is perhaps your most important business asset. Your brand is what people first become familiar with, what they remember most, and what becomes the basis for putting their trust in you. Establishing a brand is tough if you — and/or your Web site — aren't widely known yet (in the case of a local business, in its specific locale). Banner ads can help fix this because, in essence, they find your potential customers rather than making you wait for them to find you. Your Web site and your logo appear while your potential customers are on someone else's site. Advertising people call this *interruptive,* but it's a great way to draw attention — and new business — to your company's door.

Choosing a type and size for your banner ad

Banner ads come in a variety of flavors. Sizes, for example, range from miniscule button ads to page-wide leaderboard ads. Banner ad formats are varied, too. Although the most popular banner ads remain the standard Web image formats — JPEG, GIF, and PNG — Flash ads are becoming the dominant format on many sites. Flash allows the use of animation and even game-style interaction to maximize the impact of banner ads.

As shown in Figure 12-2, the most common sizes (in width x length) for banner ads are

- **Standard banner:** 468 x 60 pixels
- **Half banner:** 234 x 60 pixels
- **Vertical banner:** 120 x 240 pixels

- ✔ **Leaderboard:** 728 x 90 pixels
- ✔ **Microbar:** 88 x 31 pixels
- ✔ **Square button:** 125 x 125 pixels
- ✔ **Skyscrapers:** 160 x 600 pixels or 120 x 600 (more typical)
- ✔ **Medium rectangle:** 300 x 250 pixels

Figure 12-2:
The standard sizes for banner ads and what they usually look like on the screen.

Picking the location, location, location

Where your banner ads appear depends on two questions:

- ✔ **On what sites should your ad appear?** This decision usually comes down to our old friend, relevance. Running a banner ad for your house-cleaning business on a local accountant's Web site doesn't make sense. On the other hand, running that ad on a local home-remodeling business's site is smart. Of course, some relevant connections are a lot more obvious (such as selling chiropractic services on a local gym's Web site).

- ✔ **What kind of consumers are you after?** Pay attention to *demographic* relevance — target the right people in terms of age, gender, interests, income, education, and so on. Probably the easiest place to find a demographically correct audience for your ad is to use a Web site operated by a popular magazine. The magazine's demographics are usually pretty obvious (*Adirondack Life* for upper New York summer residents and year-round outdoor types, *Memphis Sport* for sports and fitness buffs, *North Shore Living* for affluent Massachusetts folks, and so on).

  Local magazine sites aren't the only easy pickings available. You have lots of other Web sites to choose from, such as those that cater to a particular hobby, specialize in career-finding, or offer medical information. Are the people who visit one of those kinds of sites the same people you want to visit yours? If so, rock on.

Making contact with the site to place your banner ad

You may think that getting in touch with another site owner to find out about placing one of your banner ads is a difficult process; it isn't. The easiest way to get in touch with a site owner is to use the site's contact e-mail address or phone number and then ask about placing advertising. (Doing so is money in their pocket, so they'll get back to you pronto.) Some sites make it even easier by posting a For Advertisers link at the bottom of their home page. By all means, click that.

After you make contact, find out what rates the site charges for banner advertising. (We talk in some detail about prices later in this chapter in the sections "Pricing of banner ads" and "Paying to create a banner ad.") Assuming you're satisfied with the price involved — as well as with the visitor-volume numbers, demographic information, and average click-through rates the site-owner gives you — you're good to go.

In the online world, you discover quickly whether the ad gives you an uptick in your site's traffic numbers. Nice uptick? Hang in there. No uptick? Look for another site to place your ad on. In most cases, you can track what happens after people arrive at your site. For instance, do they stay, fill out a form, or just fall off? This is all highly useful stuff.

Sort of like in doubling down in blackjack, place banner ads on more than one site (budget permitting, of course). This almost always brings you higher visibility, a wider audience, and more potential sales.

Making your banner ad perform well

None of the tips that follow are difficult, but they can make a big difference in the amount of Web site traffic your banner ad draws:

- ✔ **Design your ad for specific sites:** One way to get more click-throughs is to design your banner ad to closely mirror the look and feel of the site that it appears on. Another way (oddly enough) is to produce an ad that's in stark contrast to the host site to be interruptive and grab attention.

- ✔ **Animate your banner:** Animated banner ads outperform static ads by a significant margin because movement nearly always attracts the reader's eye. You can make your visual element blink or actually have the object(s) in your ad do something. This probably requires the services of a Web designer and will cost $100–$300 (perhaps less).

- ✔ **Keep your copy brief and provocative:** Words like *Free, Act Now,* and *Discount* are proven attention-getters. You can also try different copy approaches to see which ones draw the most traffic to your site.

- ✔ **Control the graphic weight of your banner:** Most Web sites that take banner ads have *weight restrictions* — the graphics you use in your ad can't be so complex and bandwidth-hungry that the Web-page won't load efficiently. A good guideline is to keep your banner's file size less than 20KB.

- ✔ **Test versions of your banner ad:** Create more than one version of your banner ad and then test each version for, say, 72 hours to see which version generates the most click-throughs and conversions. You can then use this winner as a benchmark against which to test other versions. *Note:* If the versions differ in too many ways, you can't get a clean read as to which elements are working best, so limit your changing elements to one or two per version.

- ✔ **Track the banner ad's performance:** Regularly review the performance statistics for your banner ad. Most ad networks or publishers are well-equipped to provide these stats. The average click-through rate is between 0.5–2 percent. If after about three days, you aren't getting an acceptable return rate, swap out your current ad for a different version.

Just as with search engine advertising, make sure that the landing page that appears when people click your ad is consistent in subject matter with the message of the ad. Doing so almost always boosts your conversion rate, whereas not doing so can make you look like a con artist or a dolt.

Choosing the best place for a banner ad

People once believed that the most effective place to put a banner ad on a Web site was at the top of the page. This is simple common sense (or at least it was): People always see the top of a page, whereas they rarely see the bottom.

Today, however, a new school of thought says you should place your ad on the right side of the page, preferably in the lower-right corner adjacent to the scroll bar. Seems pretty obvious when you think about it, eh? This is also good placement for those businesses on a tight budget because this generally means using a smaller, less expensive ad.

Pricing of banner ads

Banner ad placement costs can be figured on a number of different bases, including

- ✔ **Flat fee:** You get unlimited impressions, clicks, leads, and sales over a specified period for a single fee. Sounds great, but be aware that this is usually offered only by relatively unsophisticated publishers, and the number of those is shrinking rapidly. If you do happen into such an arrangement, ask how many impressions and so on that you can expect. You may find the deal isn't actually so great.

- ✔ **Cost-per-thousand-impressions (CPM):** This is the most common arrangement. You pay a certain amount for every 1,000 times your ad is displayed. So a $5 CPM means you pay $5 for every 1,000 appearances. The publisher of the hosting Web site determines the CPM cost based on the traffic volume of each of the site's pages.

- ✔ **Cost-per-click (CPC):** This is the amount you're charged every time someone clicks your banner ad. A $5 CPC therefore costs $5 for each click.

- ✔ **Cost-per-lead (CPL):** Also known as cost-per-action (CPA), CPL is usually based on the number of Web addresses you've gathered from visitors to your site — and that you can prove you've collected. These are usually addresses people have given you to receive an e-newsletter or have furnished as part of filling out an online survey. (People who go further and actually buy from your site are also considered leads for CPL purposes.) This can be a great way to be billed because you're paying only for quality prospects, not just a mass of clicks. However:

    - • CPL rates can vary widely depending on the ad program you sign up for.

    - • A lot of publishers don't offer a CPL arrangement because it depends on the conversion power of your landing pages, which is something they have no control over.

Like so much else in life, banner ad rates are highly negotiable. Don't hesitate to regard a host site's initial rate or quote as simply a starting point and then to counter with a lower, realistic, and reasonable offer. True; some sites may treat their prices as ironclad. If that's the case, either sigh and accept the price, or harrumph and take a pass.

Paying to create a banner ad

You have basically three ways to create a banner ad, and of course, each entails a different level of effort and expense:

- ✔ **Do it yourself (DIY):** Several online tools are available to help you construct and place your banner ads, and many are free. These tools give you step-by-step instructions that can help you move pretty quickly from the Huh? stage to the Hey, Look, It's Done stage. Some of the most popular of these tool suppliers are

Tool	Web Site	Cost
BANNERSERVER.COM	www.bannerserver.com	$19.95+
FlashFreezer.com	www.flashfreezer.com	$4.99+
Banner Designer Pro	www.bannerdesigner pro.com	Free trial and then inexpensive software to buy

If you decide to go the DIY route, make your ad eye-catching, yet simple. Don't let your ad get so ornate that it won't load. Make sure the links work and that the corresponding landing page (see Chapter 5) continues the ad's story in a seamless way.

- ✔ **Use a professional graphic artist:** Searchable databases, such as MarketingScoop.com (www.marketingscoop.com) or Elance (www.elance.com), can help you find a designer to render your ad in the size you need. The cost obviously depends on the complexity of the project, and the particular designer, but as the saying goes, you get what you pay for.

- ✔ **Use an online advertising provider:** Services can provide small businesses with a complete solution. These folks handle banner ad creation and placement as well as reporting services. (Many also offer a sort of hybrid arrangement in which they provide an appropriate ad template that you use to design the ad, while they retain the responsibilities for placement and tracking.) The costs here can vary over a pretty wide range depending on what you ask the provider to do. If this kind of service sounds appealing to you, check out providers like BidPlace SB (www.bidplacesb.com) and AdReady (www.adready.com).

Using E-Newsletter Advertising and Sponsorships

In this section, we talk about advertising *in* e-newsletters, not *for* them. Although in terms of execution, these ads are a little different than banner ads, their aim is exactly the same: to reach a target audience of readers who are already highly engaged with the kind of products or services you offer.

According to Forrester Research, e-newsletter advertising creates a markedly higher level of trust among consumers than any other form of interactive advertising. Forrester reports that more than 22 percent of readers trust an e-newsletter or e-zine to which they're subscribed versus only 2 percent who trust unsolicited e-mail marketing. As a result, e-newsletter ads often produce some of the highest conversion rates for local online advertisers.

Like banner ads, e-newsletter advertising is highly targeted and is also usually very cost-effective. Plus, you can never be accused of spamming because e-newsletter recipients have already signed up to get them. Figure 12-3 shows an example of an e-newsletter with a sponsored ad spot.

Figure 12-3:
A sample e-newsletter with a banner sponsorship along the right.

Choosing an e-newsletter for your ad

So many e-newsletters float around, covering so many different topics of interest, that it won't take much effort on your part to find the right one(s) to advertise in. As with placing banner ads, look for those e-newsletters that are a natural fit for what your business sells. For example:

- ✔ A dog groomer advertises in an e-newsletter published by the local ASPCA and offers a free shampoo for any dog or cat that someone adopts.

- ✔ A hair salon advertises in an e-newsletter published by a regional weddings Web site and offers the bride-to-be a shampoo, cut, and style when all her bridesmaids get their hair done there, too.

Another hidden benefit of advertising in e-newsletters is that almost all are archived, and thousands of people actually scour these archives. So, potentially, your ad can be seen by a whole lot of extra people over time — exposures that you never had to pay for. Your ad becomes, in effect, a gift that keeps on giving.

Tips for e-newsletter advertisers

To get your e-newsletter advertising running on all cylinders — and produce a bunch of interested new leads or even increase the number of opt-ins you get for your own e-newsletter — do the following:

- ✔ **Target your audience:** Research the e-newsletter's demographic breakdown to make sure you want to reach at least some segments of its audience. (The e-newsletter publisher can usually provide you with this information, based on the information it gets when people sign up for the e-newsletter.) Many publishers let you buy selected segments of their audience, so you can target your best prospects without paying for exposure to the entire subscriber list. Although this may wind up costing you more per impression, the specificity you can achieve will result in actually paying less per acquisition.

- ✔ **Arrange a package deal:** Don't be surprised to discover that multi-ad exposures attract more potential customers than single-ad exposures. That being true, many e-newsletter publishers offer a package price to any business that advertises both in their e-newsletter and via a banner ad on their Web site. You may even be able to extend the package to include a print ad in the e-newsletter's companion magazine. This can be an extremely cost-effective way to get maximum impact and exposure for your business.

✔ **Buy with frequency:** Because of the multiple exposures principle, recurring ad placement in a given e-newsletter is obviously going to be more effective than a one-shot appearance — and these multiple placements can usually be had at a discount. If the e-newsletter publishes weekly, try buying six weeks in a row or buying at least an every-other-week placement. If the e-newsletter is monthly, buy three months in a row, and so on. You may well be surprised how much you end up saving per placement.

✔ **Be mindful of your metrics:** Publishers often pay close attention to how many e-newsletter subscribers they have, and more important, how many of those people actually open (and presumably read) the e-newsletters. A particular e-newsletter's once-hot subjects can start to cool off and vice versa. Just like the publisher, pay regular attention to the e-newsletter's delivery, readership, and bounce rates — and adjust your buy accordingly.

E-newsletter sponsorships

You might have the opportunity not just to advertise in an e-newsletter, but actually to sponsor one. In return for a fee, you get a certain degree of exclusivity, a preferred placement for your message, and a somewhat more extensive space to communicate your message. Obviously, you also can feature a link to your Web site.

Sponsorship ads are sort of like mini-editorials. They usually offer a good deal more room for content than any banner ad and consequently, they can be terrific relationship-builders between you and your target audience.

If you have the chance to buy a sponsorship, keep these pieces of advice in mind:

✔ **Research your target audience before you start writing your ad.** Figure out who you're talking to, what they're interested in, and what kind of voice you should use (that is, should you be blunt and businesslike, friendly and warm, concerned and expert, or something else?).

✔ **Write a short descriptive advertisement that states what your company is all about.** Include important and compelling information about your products or services and how your company can benefit the readers. (Obviously, also include your company's name, logo, phone number, and e-mail address.) Even if you're given more space than what you've written will actually require, go through the exercise — it will help you boil down your message to its essentials, and you can always expand a bit on this point or that one before the ad appears in finished form.

✔ **Don't forget to include a link to your Web site.** This whole exercise is kind of pointless if you don't.

You probably want to know how much e-newsletter and sponsorships ads cost. And — guess what? — prices vary. But even as they vary, they tend to mirror that publisher's rates for banner ads, which means that you can use the banner ad rates of different publishers to get a good idea where each of will fall on the e-newsletter and sponsorship price scales. Then again, you could just go completely wild and ask the publisher to send you a rate card.

Advertising with Online Classifieds

Like most forms of printed media, the lowly but effective classified ad has found its way to the Internet. Unlike its traditional newspaper counterparts, however, Internet classifieds aren't usually billed on a per-line basis. They're also easy for search engines to find and post, they can be localized to a fare-thee-well (right down to the zip code), and as a general rule, they're really inexpensive.

They're so inexpensive, in fact, that sites like Craigslist and Kijiji don't even bother to charge for them. What's more, the content on a classified ad site turns over so quickly (as the goods and services offered come and go) that they're never at a loss for an audience.

Don't get too giddy. Most classified ad sites do charge, at least a little. Still, the cost of classifieds is sufficiently low that many local businesses, such as the following, gravitate to them naturally as an effective marketing tool:

✔ Small (to a-little-bigger-than-small) businesses that offer individual services, such as piano teachers, pet sitters, photographers, and auto mechanics that specialize in a particular type of car (like, say, classic Jaguars), are prime examples of the kinds of folks who often run online classifieds.

✔ Somewhat larger local businesses, such as community dental practices, financial consultancies, and child- and elder-care providers, are discovering that classified ads offer a cost-effective way to build business and are taking advantage of that revelation.

Developing a classified advertising plan

To develop a classified advertising plan, follow these steps:

1. **Find good (preferably free) classified ad sites to post on.**

   You can find a number of these by simply using a search engine and entering a query for *free ads, online classifieds, free online classified advertising,* or some other variation of those terms.

2. **Compare these sites on Alexa (`www.alexa.com`).**

   Alexa can give you a lot of details about a given site, such as how it ranks among others of its kind, any other sites that link to it, and even other free classified ads sites you can check out. Here are the steps you could follow to utilize Alexa rankings:

   1. Log on to Alexa and enter the name of your domain (URL) in the Search text box at the top of the page.

   2. Click the Site Info tab.

      This is where you can find out more about the site's popularity, traffic rank, and other useful information.

   3. Click the See Complete Stats link at the top of the page.

      Here you can find how many pages are viewed in the Web site and the general trend of traffic.

   4. Click the Related Links tab at the top of the page to view the competition.

      From here you can also research competitive site information.

   5. Click the Sites Linked In icon to discover which major Web sites people are using to find the site.

You can always use the old standby technique: Visit any of these sites. See what kinds of businesses are represented and ask, "Is this a good place for me to be?" See Figures 12-4 and 12-5 for examples of classified ad sites.

Some of the leading classified ad sites today are

   ✔ **Craigslist:** `www.craigslist.org`

   ✔ **Oodle:** `www.oodle.com`

   ✔ **Kijiji:** `www.kijiji.com`

   ✔ **OLX:** `www.olx.com`

   ✔ **Backpage.com:** `www.backpage.com`

   ✔ **WebLeeg:** `www.webclassifieds.us`

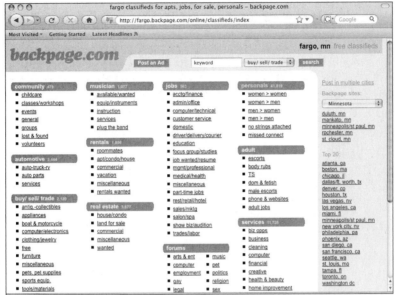

Figure 12-4:
The home
page of a
popular
online clas-
sified site.

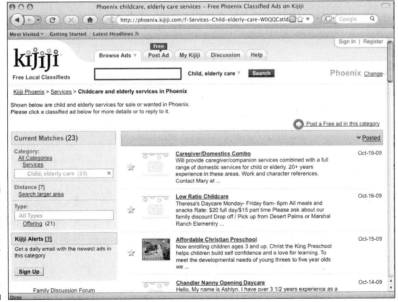

Figure 12-5:
Several
ads from
a popular
online clas-
sified site.

Creating a classified ad with clout

After you pinpoint the proper Web sites for your classified ad, follow these guidelines to create your classified ad:

- ✔ **Tweak your ad presentation:** Use an attention-grabbing headline, along with some arresting images. (Many classified ad sites allow graphics.) Eye-tracking studies show that text located near an image gathers 90 percent of the average reader's attention for the critical first few seconds. Your copy and image(s) need to work together and strike a nice visual balance. Also, capitalize only the first letter of each keyword in the headline, and keep it to ten words or less.

- ✔ **Include info in the body of your ad:** Include the most important — and only the most important — information about your product or service. Your objective here is to capture the reader and send him to your Web site where you can convert him into a lead, or better yet, a paying customer. Because of that, your goal is to create both interest and action. Make sure each sentence has a definite purpose and contains the keywords you think people would be likely to submit to a search engine.

- ✔ **Use your visual assets:** If you have a digital camera, use it. Take photos of your products or of your services in action. And speaking of action, a lot of classified Web sites allow you to include video clips as well. Be sure to use your ad title (usually the headline) as the filename for your photos and video clips. More and more people are becoming aware that they can now search for images and videos, so a descriptive image title makes yours easy for them to find.

- ✔ **Read the site's guidelines:** The classified Web site probably offers its own tips on creating an effective ad, and because they're in the business, those tips are likely to be highly useful. The site probably also has its own set of rules, which you need to follow in order have your ad accepted.

- ✔ **Choose the correct category:** Carefully figure out which of the available ad categories is the best fit for your particular classified and base that decision on where you think readers would be most likely to look for whatever it is you're offering. Some classified ad sites let you place your ad in more than one category, which is obviously beneficial for all the parties involved.

- ✔ **Be stingy with capitalization:** The general rule with capitals is that they're okay as initial caps in your headline, but shy away from using them in the body copy. Capitalizing whole sentences of text is a bad practice.

- ✔ **Stress the features and benefits of your product/service:** This classified may be your only chance to catch and interest the people you reach, so make sure your copy is about exactly what it is your product or service does, and how exactly it benefits them. Put yourself in their shoes, and ask the time-honored question: What's in it for me?

✔ **Prompt the reader:** Entice, nudge, or otherwise propel the reader into taking the next step, which in this case, means getting her to visit your Web site, where the real selling can begin. Try to create a sense of urgency, which can often be accomplished with language like Limited-Time Offer, Available Only until Midnight Tomorrow, or even just Visit Our Site Today!

✔ **Proofread your ad:** No doubt you can make up your own hypothetical horror story here. A good way to avoid embarrassing typos is to have someone else read your copy before you submit it. (Authors have a way of not spotting their own mistakes, especially if they've already read the text a few dozen times.) A fresh reader can also alert you to something in your copy that doesn't make sense or that just sounds weird. For this exercise at least, when someone else points out something wrong or odd, check your ego at the door.

When you've done all these fun things, you're ready to submit your classified ad. Some classified sites post your ad immediately. Others confirm the ad with you, and may consequently need a day or two after submission to post it on their sites.

Choosing the Right Venue for Your Ad

Deciding whether to use banners, an e-newsletter or sponsorship ad, or a classified ad is largely a matter of common sense:

✔ **Consider the nature of your industry and assess any credibility issues that might arise.** A cosmetic surgeon, for example, may conclude — rightly — that running classified ads will make her practice look tacky and cheap, whereas that same placement may be just perfect for a pet sitter or a piano teacher. Conversely, a pet sitter who runs a splashy banner ad may look a little too slick to be fully trusted. Ad placement is a sterling example of the classic axiom, "The medium is the message."

✔ **Consider what advertising opportunities are open realistically to you.** Running a banner ad of any appreciable size on a particular host site may be beyond your financial reach, but that doesn't mean running a considerably less expensive e-newsletter ad on the same site is out of the question. After all, you'll be reaching pretty much the same audience while saving some significant expense. Then again, a dental practice or some other big-ticket service provider may have both the resources and the desire to use a large banner ad to promote its capabilities and to establish its brand.

Testing Your Ads for Fun and Profit

Finding out how well your online advertising is actually performing in the real world is really pretty interesting — not to mention sound business practice. Happily, and like just about every other online marketing tactic we discuss in this book, your banner, e-newsletter, sponsorship, and classified ads can be tested easily. As with the others, you can easily and quickly dump the ones that aren't working and continue enhancing the ones that are.

But what do you need to test? That's simple: Everything — the formats, placements, headlines, copy, images, and offers. For instance:

- **If your banner ad isn't generating the kind or number of leads you'd hoped for, try running it on a different Web site (or two) with the same demographic.** If that proves disappointing as well, consider testing a new message, a new offer, or even a different format altogether.

- **Make the most of the testing opportunities that e-newsletter ads provide.** Test a message or offer one week and then test a different one the next. Pick the best performing of those (based on click-throughs and/or lead quality) to run for the balance of your scheduled buy.

- **Customize your message to the particular site or publication you're advertising on to see whether fine-tuning lifts your results.** If the answer is yes, chances are you're really engaging your audience, so stick with it.

As the great author C.S. Lewis once pointed out, progress isn't just a matter of moving forward in a given direction; it can also mean realizing you're headed down the wrong path and turning around.

Test, take stock, refine, and try again. Doing so doesn't really take much effort — only a genuine desire to succeed. (And we're guessing you already have that in spades.)

Chapter 13

Hanging Out on Social Networks

. . . .

. . . .

Social creatures that we are, human beings have been networking since the dawn of civilization. Now, we have Facebook, MySpace, LinkedIn, YouTube, and Flickr. *Social networks* are Web sites where users submit (and share publicly) content such as news, photos, videos, and audio clips as well as post their personal comments on everything imaginable. The only rules are that the contributions be personable, respectful, and constructive.

As the number of these networks grows, and their services and tools and capabilities expand, they're steadily revealing themselves to be viable marketing channels for local businesses. Keep in mind, however, that marketing that fits in social networks doesn't look or feel like the marketing most of us are used to. And because the whole social network phenomenon is so new, the rules are still being written as to how and when the networks are best used.

This chapter gives you a snapshot of where the social media stand at the moment and how to use them to boost your business. Just remember that things keep changing on a regular basis.

Joining In: The Social Networking Phenomenon

The goal of stepping into the world of social media is to place yourself right in the midst of people who are likely to become your customers. Unlike a lot of online marketing tactics — tactics where you're essentially speaking *at* your target audience — social networks put you into an ongoing conversation *with* your prospects. And, like any good conversation, this one involves people engaging with one another as individuals. You use the social networks to present yourself as a business owner with a name and a face and a personality.

In a sense, social networks replace the closely knit communities of yesteryear, when people in a town or neighborhood traded news or gossip or sad or funny stories. And when they did business, they did it with some*one* — not some*thing* — they knew personally. From friendship comes trust, and from trust comes business.

An excellent place for non-advertising advertising

It's long been a sort of unwritten rule of marketing that where there's a crowd, there's opportunity. And the social networks represent (if nothing else) a humongous crowd. So if there's so much opportunity here, how can a business (local or otherwise) capitalize on it?

Happily for us, the networks have been around just long enough for certain behavioral rules of the road to have been established where advertising is concerned. And the foremost of these seems to be: "I don't mind you selling to me as long as you don't appear to be selling to me." What it means is that folks who frequent the social networks are interested in dealing with people as people. They want to be on a first-name basis with one another, and they want to interact with people they like and people they trust.

In that type of environment, then, there's a kind of healthy mistrust of anyone who comes across too loud, too pushy, and particularly, too sell-y. So, yes, your local business can find a welcoming audience here as long as you're willing to relax, be personable, speak softly, and leave your big marketing stick at home.

Consumers use networking sites to get social proof from others that a move they're about to make is a good one. They ask for comments and advice from their fellow networkers, and they put great stock in any review that may touch on a product or service (or product or service provider).

What you get out of it

Social media can be useful for almost any kind of local business in any kind of category. It just takes a little imagination and a rounded teaspoon of restraint. For instance, a café owner who talks about some new recipe he just concocted after hours of trial and error sends the implicit message, "I take real care in preparing the food I offer." A local attorney who's relaxing a bit now that she's just helped a client successfully manage a complex tax matter says, "I prevail in tough cases." A local locksmith who shares an anecdote about being called out in the middle of the night to help someone get into his house is saying, "You can count on me for help, no matter what the hour."

Approaching your audience this way can carry a lot of benefits:

- ✔ By presenting yourself as a person first and a business person second, you help allay skepticism among your fellow networkers.

- ✔ You can sprinkle in a lot of relevant, good-quality links to your Web site that search engines will spot and reward you for. We talk about how to add links to your site on your social network profiles later in this chapter where we discuss setting up profiles for each of the various social networks.

- ✔ You forge relationships, not just with potential customers, but with those other people in the social network whose opinions matter to their peers (a tactic often referred to as *indirect sales*).

- ✔ You can build your business' reputation as an authority in your field: someone to whom people can confidently turn for guidance and advice.

- ✔ You can generate direct sales.

As if they're not a helpful-enough tool, social media are also free. All it takes to become a player in this online universe is the investment of a little time to learn the ropes. Your first step will take a couple of hours. Fire up your computer and sign up. (You can't get in without joining, although joining is usually as simple as entering your name and e-mail address.) Then look around; experience the site as a user and observe how others are using it. It shouldn't take you long to assess just how that particular site could help attract business. Obviously, some social sites are ripe with opportunity more than others, but keep looking. Eventually, you'll arrive at a manageable group of useful networks that will form the hub of your social media efforts.

Wooing the search engines

We mention earlier that social sites are great places for presenting links to your own Web site: links that search engines will spot. A smart business owner (such as yourself) optimizes social media content around the keywords that you already chose in your general search engine–optimization efforts.

This tactic will obviously help you get higher rankings in search engines' organic listings, but there's another benefit in that many social sites offer their own search functions. Someone who enters one or more of the your keywords is likely to find you ranked very high on the page that comes up — even higher, in most cases, than you'd appear on a generic search engine's pages. In other words, you're getting a two-fer.

Sharing Information about Your Business

In traditional advertising, you pay to run an ad. On social networks, though (except for the occasional pay-per-click ad), you don't. In traditional advertising, you focus on something that's good for the prospective customer. In social network marketing, you present something that's good for the community. In traditional advertising, self-serving is at the heart of your sales efforts. In social marketing, it's the kiss of death. See what we mean?

What it comes down to is engaging the community's members on a personal level and giving them a reason to listen to you. Your posts to the site can offer your occasional opinions on this or that. Share links to informative Web sites and blogs. Offer suggestions when someone has a problem that touches on your area of expertise. Expect to receive comments back, too. They might be reviews of your business. Keep in mind that even a negative review can be helpful because it can help you correct and improve your operation.

When you're on a social network hoping to market your local business, you should communicate, not sell. Here's a good way to think about it. When you get home from work and tell your spouse what went on that day, you're not trying to get your spouse's business. You're simply sharing interesting tidbits about the day's events, and maybe tossing in your own pithy comments about it all. That's the model for posting on a social network.

Deciding what to share

Trust us, you'll come up with something that will play well on Facebook, YouTube, or whichever of the social sites offers the best audience. For instance

- **Share news and information.** Social networks are hotbeds of word-of-mouth communication, and news travels fast. Have you made a new hire at your high-end salon, started offering a new service at your medical spa, opened a new location of your gym?

    Don't overdo it. Post regularly about a variety of things. That way, when you do get around to dropping in some business news, people won't think you're just a spammer or some other lowlife. They'll already know you as a regular person, one who today just happens to have a little news about his own business to impart.

- **Share your expertise.** Look for ongoing topics of conversation that you can comment on as a voice of authority. Don't push it and come on all high and mighty. Just pretend your neighbor or friend is asking you, and respond as a good neighbor would.

✔ **Create and share incentives.** Say you're a pet store owner and you're introducing a Red Cross–sponsored Dog Safety Course. You can publish the news to your Facebook or MySpace fan base and include a link to the page on your Web site where they can learn more and maybe download a coupon that gives them a discount when they register online for the safety course. It's really no different than the kind of incentive you'd offer in your regular online and offline marketing efforts. Just remember that because you're among friends, a light touch is key.

✔ **Make and share videos.** Short, how-to videos are always attention-getters, as are tour videos that walk the viewer through your restaurant, building projects, or showroom. You might already have some of these on your Web site. Great. You can repurpose them for the social media, and YouTube is an obvious place to start.

✔ **Take and share photos.** Flickr in particular has amazingly active photo groups, so pictures of your products, operation, and so on, are a natural fit. For example, Flickr is home to dozens of animal-related groups, each of which can be counted on to have hundreds, even thousands, of members. So if you're a pet store owner, put up a couple photos of your store, your tropical fish department, your grooming facilities. Similarly, a builder could post pictures of his finished homes in an appropriate city-related group, say the greater San Francisco Bay area.

Marketing tips and tricks for social networks

Here are a few hints on how to comfortably fit yourself on social networks:

✔ If you find all this social media stuff a little off-putting, the odds are excellent that someone you work or socialize with is already an avid member of one or more of the networks. Let that person be your guide and show you what a particular site is about and how it works.

✔ When you start wandering about a given social site, it shouldn't take you long to get a feel for what its population is all about. Are these folks in your local area? Are they a good target audience for you? A quick way to find out is to use the site's search tool. Most of the sites keep their members' profiles (including location) organized in some way or other, so zeroing in on the kind of members you're looking for is pretty easy.

✔ When you join a network, you're asked to create your own profile. Keep it short, concise, and interesting. It can be a personal bio or a brief bio of your company. Whatever it is, think before you write: Is the profile you're submitting likely to catch local people's attention? And remember that, online, first impressions are made very quickly.

✔ After you join a network, contribute. It's okay to lurk for a brief time just to absorb the ins and outs of the environment, but then dive into the conversation. After all, that's what you're there for.

✔ Test, measure, learn, and adjust your networking approaches. The brass ring here is to move online conversations offline. Is your social media persona accomplishing that? Is there some way it can do the job even better? You know the drill: Measure your results and fix whatever you think might be broken.

Putting Your Best Facebook Forward

Facebook started out as a way for college students to get to know each other, but wow! has it ever grown. Today it's a hugely populated place for people to network on both a personal and professional level. See Figure 13-1.

What on earth are all these people doing here? Well, colleagues update one another on business stuff. People you went to high school with (and have long since forgotten) contact you and ask what you're up to these days. Goofy questions are asked, and surveys are taken ("Who's your least favorite movie star?" "Was building the Panama Canal a good idea? Discuss.") People look for help with their dating problems, recipes for their company picnic, ideas for what they dress as for Halloween, advice on how to gently let a troublesome salesperson go. The fun, as they say, never stops.

Figure 13-1:
A typical member page on Facebook.

But is it right for your local business? Probably. Facebook currently has vast demographic appeal, particularly for people 25 and older, so it's a natural for almost any kind of business to be on as well.

If you're not really, really careful, you could find that being on Facebook is actually oodles of fun — so keep focused on what brought you there in the first place: to drum up customers for your local business. The key to that is building trust.

Creating your profile

To sign up for Facebook, go to www.facebook.com, fill in the First Name, Last Name, Your Email, and Password text boxes, select your gender and birthday from the drop-down lists, and click the Sign Up button. Then to build your profile, upload a photo, enter your education, business, and contact information, and join your local sub-network (Schenectady NY, Cincinnati OH, or whatever). The more complete your profile, the more easily — and more comprehensively — you can connect with people and start building your own growing network of friends.

If you're concerned about privacy, Facebook offers highly customizable privacy settings that let you control who can and can't see different elements of your profile. So, for example, you can share photos of your kids with friends and family but prevent the pictures from being seen by your employees or customers.

Next, you can upload your existing contact database to see which of your contacts are already on Facebook and ask whichever ones you want to become your friend. This can get you started right off the bat rather than leaving you to start cold in building your own little community.

Creating your company page

After you have a personal profile, you can create a Fan page for your local business. You can populate the page(s) with company information, news about upcoming events, photos, videos, discussion forums, and links to your business Web site. You can also add applications that increase the functionality of your page (such as an RSS feed to your blog or a link to the news page on your Web site), or embed videos from YouTube. Your page or pages are made publicly available, which means that search engines can find and index them — an added benefit. A sample business page is shown in Figure 13-2.

Figure 13-2:
A Facebook
business
page.

If you're wondering why you need a Facebook company page when you already have a business Web site, you want to be where your existing and prospective customers are. In other words, it's about location, location, location.

Joining and creating groups

Another great way to network on Facebook is through the use of groups. Unlike the site's fan pages, which can be viewed by the general public, groups are visible only to Facebook members, and can be formed around any subject from business type to political affiliations to love of a particular kind of plant or breed of dog.

It shouldn't take you long to find a group or groups that are likely to include good prospects for your local business, but if you can't, no problem: Simply start a new group yourself, and get the ball rolling by inviting some friends and fans to join it.

Or you can use the handy feature that lets you bulk-invite people who are already connected to you on the network to join your group. They can then bulk-invite their friends to join as well. With any luck, your membership rolls will fill up fast.

Building relationships

Say you meet someone at a cocktail party. One thing leads to another, and he says, "You know, I've got a gizmonometer that I can't get to work." You volunteer to help him out because you know those gizmonometers can be trouble. He says he'll call you next week. Sure enough, he calls — and you've got a new customer for your business.

It's the same with Facebook and the other networking sites. You engage users as individuals, and often before you know it, you find out they need something you can provide.

Of course, you can force the issue a little bit by posting a special offer to your fan base, something like, "It's a great time to show someone you care. This week, I'm offering a dozen roses for $8 to my Facebook friends. Let me know if you're interested." That still doesn't cross the line, we'd say. It's just friends being friendly. And the fact that you pick up some business along the way is just the happy and gratifying way it worked out.

Here's the nasty flipside. There's always someone who comes on waaaay too strong and tries to sell you something as soon as you tell him your name. Don't do that. People who are obviously jumping into social media just to make a quick buck are likely to get found out, called out, and shut out. And the only thing they wind up accomplishing is putting a dent in their reputation.

Facebook lets you welcome a whole bunch of friends aboard. The more friends you have — and the better your friends get to know you — the better your chances are of converting some into prospects, then into customers, without in any way diminishing the relationship.

Schmoozing your Facebook business fans

Facebook gives you a lot of ways to get your business noticed and, ultimately, patronized. Pre-built tools let you plug in an offer, a sign-up page for your newsletter, a path to the discussion board you host, and on and on. You can also add some neat, Facebook-supplied applications from outside developers to customize your business page. For instance

✔ A restaurant might add the Reservations application to let users book a table online.

✔ An independent movie theatre might add the Movie Times & Tickets application so users can preview what's currently showing, and even buy tickets in advance.

✔ A local business owner can add the Visa Business Network application to cast a wider social net.

And that just scratches the surface.

Facebook also offers an excellent ad targeting tool that lets you submit all sorts of search

(continued)

(continued)

criteria and narrow down its vast user base to the group of people you most want to reach and attract to your business page. This particular resource, however, isn't free; you pay for it on a pay-per-click basis.

When you accumulate 1,000 fans, you're entitled to a brand URL. This will be `www.facebook.com/yourbusinessname`, which is a very cool and easy way to enhance your marketing efforts.

Making MySpace Your Space

MySpace started life as an online place for teens and 20-somethings to hang out and socialize. MySpace was once the be-all and end-all of the social networking movement. Since then, though, Facebook, Twitter, and the other networks have stolen a good bit of its thunder, and its market share has shrunk accordingly.

However, as the network market in general continues to expand, even a diminished share can become a big and fast-growing one, and MySpace's share has been doing just that.

Taking advantage of MySpace strengths

Initially, MySpace's user base centered on people younger than 35: college students, younger career-types, and so on. In recent years, the MySpace crowd has been expanding to include plenty of people over 35.

One thing hasn't changed even as the demographics have, though: MySpace has always been mostly about pop culture. Bands, movies, food, fashion, celebrity comings and goings — they've long been and continue to be the primary grist for the MySpace mill. This makes MySpace a great place to be for local businesses that cater to just those sorts of interests: entertainment, dining, lifestyle, travel, music, and the rest.

In March 2009, MySpace announced a partnership with Citysearch, the local review site, to create MySpace Local. This means that Citysearch business listings from 1,000 U.S. cities will come under the MySpace umbrella. As this book is being written, the full details of the new entity haven't been announced, but it certainly bears watching by any local business contemplating a move into social network marketing.

Setting up your profile

Setting up a MySpace profile for yourself and your business is extremely easy. (Figure 13-3 shows the layout of a typical MySpace business page.)

Figure 13-3: A MySpace business page.

Go to `www.myspace.com` and click the Sign Up link. In the sign up process, you're asked to fill in the following information:

- ✔ **The Basic Info:** This part of the process is a little weird in that when you're setting up a business profile, MySpace asks for its gender, marital status, and astrological sign. See? Weird. Anyway, just fill in your own data, and leave it at that.

- ✔ **Your name and URL:** When choosing a name and URL (`www.myspace.com/yoursite`), you have two options. You can choose the name of your business (such as `www.myspace.com/barkingboutique`) or use keywords that describe what you offer (such as `www.myspace.com/petgrooming`). It's your choice, but a keyword-rich name will often be the better way to go.

- ✔ **Company Overview: The About Me section:** This is essentially the bread and butter of your MySpace page. It's where you provide a concise overview of your company and the ways it can benefit your target audience. And just because you have to keep it brief doesn't mean you can't be creative to grab your target's interest. Remember that ironclad rule of marketing: Tell your prospective customers what's in it for them.

✓ **Potential Clients: The Who I'd Like to Meet section:** Here's where you sharpen the definition of your target audience. It's helpful to ask yourself, if your product had a mind of its own, who would it like to meet? Water skis would want to meet water sports enthusiasts. High-end collars for dogs would want to shake hands with the owners of pampered pets. And so on. We know it sounds a little strange, but it can help you clarify exactly who your prime targets are.

✓ **Adding Pictures and Video sections:** If you don't provide an image for your profile, you get a default No Photo icon, which isn't the best way to win friends and influence people. If you're building a personal profile, it should obviously be a picture of you. If it's a business profile, you should probably insert your logo or some other unmistakable signal of what your business does (such as a mousetrap for an exterminator).

In the View My Pix section, you can put up additional images, which can be a good way to present pictures of your staff, your location(s), before-and-after photos, and so on. You can include videos in the Videos section that demonstrate your business' strengths and will, hopefully, generate some valuable word-of-mouth.

✓ **Your MySpace Blog:** As discussed in Chapter 14, blogs are as big in their own right as social networks are. Blogs offer you an informative, personal, and entertaining way to provide readers with information about your business. This can include company news, users' experience with your products or services, and so on. Perhaps best of all, the titles of your blog posts act as links, so making those titles keyword-rich will help you get noticed by search engines.

✓ **Making Friends: The Friend Space section:** While you can try a basic MySpace Search to find individuals who may be interested in your business, your best chance of finding the type of consumers you want is searching MySpace Groups. In either case, you then send that person a Friend Request. Most people check out your page before deciding whether to accept your invitation. Your odds of success will increase if you send a personalized message along with your Friend Request (on the order of "Hi Sheila. I saw that you're interested in masonry, and that's my profession. Maybe we should be friends?")

✓ **Posting Bulletins and Sending Messages:** A Bulletin Post is a terrific way to communicate (or message, in MySpace-speak) all your friends at once. Give them something they're likely to be interested in reading, such as new product offerings, news related to your products or business, special offers, and so on. Keep your message short. Of course, you can also message your friends individually, which you want to do as you sense someone is becoming increasingly interested in what you sell.

✓ **Posting Comments:** This can be another effective way to build your clientele. Seek out pages that touch on your type of business and that feature active discussion groups. Post a comment occasionally (but don't do it too often, or you'll look too aggressive). For example, say you own a local public golf course. You find a discussion board on a popular golf-oriented page. Your comment (in a relevant discussion) could be "Check out my blog for tips on choosing a good public course in the area." It's nothing more than what a real-world friend would do for another.

Getting LinkedIn

It was inevitable that business people would find a way to extend their networking efforts to the online world as well. And, sure enough, along came LinkedIn. LinkedIn gives small (and large) business owners a pretty painless way to increase their customer base and enhance their bottom line.

The site's mission is to help professionals and businesses make better use of a professional network, to connect professionals to make them more productive and successful.

User demographic data shows that LinkedIn caters to a slightly more affluent, more male-centric audience than Facebook and MySpace. Many users are decision makers for their businesses.

Many local businesses that offer professional services — doctors, attorneys, financial consultants, and the like — find LinkedIn a useful place to be. A lot of professionals also use LinkedIn to find new jobs, ask for advice from peers, scout out potential new hires, and so on. Even if you're not looking to the site to market your business, you may still find it a highly useful network to be part of.

Establishing a LinkedIn account

Assuming that your target audience fits the LinkedIn mold, setting up an account on the site for your business and yourself as a business person is easy. (We stress the business person part because this is not a socially oriented place for personal chitchat.) Go to www.linkedin.com, fill in the First Name, Last Name, Email, and Password text boxes, and then click the Join Now button.

Like with Facebook and MySpace, you can create a professional profile or business page that can be viewed by the membership. To keep all your opportunities open, you're best off creating both.

Unlike the social sites, however, LinkedIn does charge a nominal membership fee (on the order of $25–$50 per month for premium services) although you can use the basic level for free. About 95 percent of LinkedIn's membership find that's really all they need.

Using LinkedIn tools and features

Among the more widely used tools and features of LinkedIn are

- **Recommendations:** Part of your profile can — and, over time, should — include recommendations of your business made by other members. If you haven't accumulated any of these, LinkedIn users might well conclude that your business has some kind of competitive or credibility problem, so acquiring recommendations should definitely be one of your goals. The best way to get them is to give them. Choose people in your network with whom you've worked, and write an honest statement that recommends them. (If, on the other hand, your experience with some of these folks has been lousy, don't fudge a positive statement. It's best in that case to just stay mum.) After you submit some recommendations, don't be surprised to find yourself receiving some in return.

- **Question & Answer function:** Jump into a discussion and answer other users' questions in a thoughtful and professional manner, demonstrating your expertise and potentially generating contacts who are impressed by your knowledge. It bears repeating, however: Your comments/answers need to be thoughtful and definitely not oversell-y. Remember that these are business people, so don't go overboard in bragging about yourself. LinkedIn rewards good answers (and good questions) through a rating system; the better your rating, the better the chances that LinkedIn will give you some added exposure.

- **Group Discussion:** Any member can launch a group on LinkedIn and lead discussions on a specific topic of interest. Just make sure that the topic under discussion is one that you really know cold. Putting some effort into starting and leading a one of these niche groups can gain you added influence within your network. Groups are also open to the LinkedIn universe as a whole, which can only help you expand your network.

- **Informational Content:** Members of the larger LinkedIn community, and even of your own network, may only come in contact with you and your business on the LinkedIn platform, so it's important to enhance your profile with educational information that already resides on your Web site. LinkedIn has collected some third-party applications that can help you out in this regard:

  - *Box.net:* Allows you to create links to files on your site, such as resumés and sales/marketing kits

  - *SlideShare:* Embeds slideshow presentations and demos

  - *Blog Link:* Displays the latest blog posts from your Web site on your LinkedIn profile

  - *Company Buzz:* Searches Twitter (discussed later in this chapter) for mentions of your brand or of other topics you select

Exploring Some Other Networking Sites

Facebook, MySpace, and LinkedIn are the leaders in today's social media space, but they're not the only players. Some other social networking sites are more narrowly focused and are quite successful in their own right. These include Twitter (for news sharing), Flickr (photo sharing), and YouTube (video sharing). And they can definitely play a part in building your business.

Tweeting with Twitter

Seemingly growing in popularity every day, Twitter connects businesses with consumers. (It also connects a lot of regular folks with each other.) Go to www.twitter.com to create your username and password. An example of a business Twitter account is shown in Figure 13-4.

Figure 13-4:
All sorts of business use Twitter.

Twitter connections occur in real-time via the Web, a desktop application, or mobile devices. The messages themselves — *tweets* — are limited to a maximum of 140 characters, including spaces. That limitation doesn't allow much space for news, but a lot of local businesses make it work.

The most important thing about Twitter is its immediacy. You type in your message, and off it flies. Businesses can communicate with their consumers at light speed, and this kind of quick response can create loyal, lifelong customers. You can think of Twitter as your own personal press room, with news bulletins flashed instantly to interested parties.

For example

- A nail salon tweets a special, today-only deal on nail polish.

- An Italian restaurant tweets info about its Tuesday night off-menu pasta dishes.

- A store tweets that it's closed because of weather, thus sparing customers a wasted trip.

- A local company tweets news of its grand opening of a new location for several days leading up to the event.

Any tweet can also provide a link to your Web site, but be advised that your URL counts against the 140-character limit. A great workaround for this limit is to use a URL shortener service, such as `bit.ly` or `ow.ly`.

Twitter supports a variety of functions to help local businesses, including letting you send out product update previews, deliver customer service, announce contests, present market research, offer promotional and other special discounts, and more. It's definitely worth taking a look at.

Sharing photos on Flickr

Photo-sharing sites have been popping up at a mind-boggling rate. Some of the biggest ones are Google's Picasa, Smugmug, Zooomr, Photobucket, and Flickr, which seems to have the greatest similarity to other social media.

Flickr was also one of the very first social photo-sharing sites, having started in 2004. It lets you upload your photos, tag them with descriptive titles, sort them by groups, and add them to public pools, where they're showcased for viewers interested in a certain subject, style, or genre. There's no cost for a basic account, which allows you to upload two videos and up to 100MB of photos per month.

To create an account, go to `www.flickr.com`, and click the Create Your Account button. If you already have a Yahoo! username and password, enter them in the Yahoo! ID and Password text boxes. (If you don't, you'll need to sign up.)

Flickr and similar sites can be used in any number of ways to promote your business. The owner of a catering business can use Flickr to showcase her services by posting photos of her clients' weddings, banquets, and other fancy events. Real estate agents can post shots of their current house listings. Jewelry makers and other craftspeople can use photo-sharing to create an online portfolio, document their creation process, even get consumer feedback on new designs. (Of course, you can use Flickr to upload and organize personal pictures to share them with close friends and family members.)

However you use it, Flickr is an extremely friendly place to begin your social media experience. The people in the Flickr community are generally very supportive and collegial, plus there are lots of FAQs that come in handy for newbies and oldbies alike. There's even a site tour available to help you get started.

Sharing videos on YouTube

So there was little ol' YouTube just sitting around, a fairly modest little place where people (many of them college kids) could watch entertaining video clips of this and that submitted by other people just like them. Better yet, the clips could be blasted out worldwide in no time flat. The simple interface made YouTube easy to use. There had never been anything quite like it before. It was a whole lot of fun. And, not long after its launch in 2005, it had become a prominent part of Internet culture. All of which swiftly brought it to the attention of Google, who then snapped it up (for a lot of cash) and quickly turned it into a household name. Today, YouTube might just as well be called HugeTube.

Like with any good Internet-oriented idea, YouTube now has its competitors, notably DropShots, Panjea, Viddler, Vimeo, and VideoEgg. They are all similar to photo-sharing sites in that they let you upload, tag, and categorize your videos.

Some of these sites also allow you to edit your videos after you upload them, which means you can shorten the piece and add music and titles if you want. Oddly, YouTube doesn't give you this capability. Rather, YouTube seems to want to host videos in all their un-slick glory, apparently on the theory that it's exactly the homeliness of some clips that makes them viewer favorites and turns them into viral videos.

Going *viral* (when a message or image spreads quickly around the Internet) is all the rage in Web marketing these days. And why not? It's virtually effortless. People just love calling up video-sharing sites to see what the current most-viewed ones are or to use the site's search utilities to find specific videos. YouTube videos also show up in the results pages of the major search engines, which can do wonders for your business' online visibility.

So how can all of this help your local business? Well, the most obvious way to put YouTube and its brethren to work for you is to upload videos that clearly demonstrate the product or service you offer. Product demos, how-to videos, customer testimonials: They're all fair game and excellent subjects for these sites.

The goal is to present something about your business that engages viewers and separates you from your competitors. Your video doesn't have to be funny or dramatic. It doesn't have to feature dancing camels. As long as you make it interesting to at least some segment of the video-sharing population, your submission will get noticed, then likely passed along from one user to another with a "take a look at this!" message attached.

Finally, the video-sharing sites are as easy to join as Flickr and Twitter. You simply go to www.youtube.com and select a username and password. That's it.

To get the absolute most out of video sharing in the way of additional search engine optimization benefit (so that people in your area will find your videos on the search engines), make sure that the descriptions and titles you give your videos include your chosen keywords. This will allow them to be properly indexed by search engines and will target the right audience. You can also help search engines by tagging your location on your YouTube profile and uploading transcripts of your videos so that search engines know what they're about (unlike kids these days, search engines can read but don't watch videos).

Using Social Media Specific to Your Business Segment

It probably won't surprise you to find out that social media are becoming devoted to particular market niches. (It's similar to cable TV, where 600 channels means there's bound to be something of interest to everyone.) This segmentation is good news for businesses because the more sharply targeted the audience, the better the return on investment is likely to be.

For example, if a company wants to market custom orthotics to people with back problems, would it make more sense to advertise to legions of people on Facebook or MySpace, or to aim at a smaller group of people on a site like DailyStrength (www.dailystrength.org), with its 500+ groups dealing with health and medical issues?

Your challenge, then, is to search for those niche social media that best sync up with your product or service offering. And, as usual, the best way to do that is by using Google (or Yahoo! or Bing), as well as by going to Ning (www. ning.com), a social media platform provider, to find the networking sites frequented by just exactly the kind of prospects you're after.

To give you a feel for all this, here's a small sampling of some prominent niche sites:

- ✔ **BeGreen:** A community that aims to generate environmental awareness among Web users. (www.begreen.org)

- ✔ **beRecruited.com:** A dedicated online community for athletes, coaches, and hardcore high school sports fans. (www.berecruited.com)

- ✔ **CarGurus:** An automotive-based community Web site that lets users post car reviews and photos, and share opinions. (www.cargurus.com)

- ✔ **Center'd:** A fun, interactive way for people to connect with others from the same neighborhood. (www.centerd.com)

- ✔ **Going.com:** Also a fun place where users can interact with folks in their communities. (www.going.com)

- ✔ **GirlSense:** A community for girls to promote their fashion designs. (www.girlsense.com)

- ✔ **IYOMU.COM:** A social networking Web site for adults that allows users to search for site members who share the same interests or business needs. (www.iyomu.com)

Chapter 14

Generating PR Buzz

In This Chapter

▶ Managing your online reputation

▶ Building your business credibility

▶ Using message boards to enhance your reputation

▶ Joining blogs to present your business on a personal level

▶ Putting online press releases to work for you

*H*ere's an unlovely fact of life: It's almost impossible for any business to succeed, online or off, if its reputation stinks. And that's why a genius invented public relations (PR). If your PR is handled correctly, people won't only know you, they'll think you're a solid citizen — someone to trust, listen to, and buy from.

A lot of businesses that advertise online get tripped up by simple, old conversation. People who use the Internet talk incessantly. They use blogs and social networks to compare notes on everything from politics to pudding recipes, and the plusses and minuses of this business or product are bandied about all the time.

People gossip. They take part in impromptu surveys (who's the best local cleaning service?). And more and more these days, they write reviews. In fact, reviews have probably become the single biggest determinant of a company's online reputation. (According to a survey by the Opinion Research Corporation, 84 percent of Internet users say that online reviews influence their purchasing decisions.)

Some businesses recognize this and become downright paranoid. They convince themselves that their critics far outnumber their fans, and consequently try to keep a low online profile — or even pull themselves off the Web entirely — to stay out of the line of fire. But that's just self-defeating.

Figure out how to monitor and manage your reputation and how to leverage the inevitable conversation that goes on to keep your reputation nice and shiny and drive new business your way.

In other words, find out how to handle online PR, which by no coincidence, is what this chapter is all about.

Managing Your Reputation Online

The three aspects to managing your online reputation are monitoring, managing, and promoting. The following sections look briefly at each.

Monitoring

Right now, somewhere on the Internet, people are probably talking about you. The first step in any PR effort is to find out what they're saying.

Start by running a search of your business name and see what appears. Are you easy to find — does your listing come up at least somewhat prominently in the search results? Looking through your customers eyes, what sort of first impression does that listing make? Assuming you have a Web site and maybe even a blog, are they up-to-date and looking good? Would someone clicking through your listing be impressed by your professionalism?

Even more important, is your business reviewed in any online forums or blogs? These almost always appear on a search results page. Look at local directory sites, such as Yelp (www.yelp.com), Citysearch (www.citysearch.com), and Yahoo! Local (http://local.yahoo.com). With forums for customer feedback springing up all over the place, don't be surprised to find at least one that mentions your business. Check the social networking sites, such as Facebook and MySpace, as well as any local ones you're aware of.

Don't forget that Angie's List (www.angieslist.com), TripAdvisor (www.tripadvisor.com), OpenTable (www.opentable.com), and even Google Maps (http://maps.google.com) largely focus on publishing reviews. Don't think that any reviews you find today won't be added to tomorrow. Ideally, you want to have a system in place that lets you stay on top of the online buzz. You can sign up for Google Alerts, for example, which automatically informs you whenever your business is mentioned in a review, on a blog, or in an online publication (see Figure 14-1). Some of the larger review sites also alert you via e-mail when your name appears.

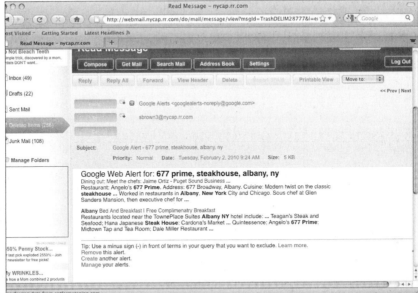

Figure 14-1:
A Google
alert.

Other sites that take a pulse of your business

Some other sites can help you keep tabs on the state of your online reputation and promote your business:

- **Trackur** scours blogs, news sites, images, and videos for mentions of their clients' businesses. You can even restrict the scouring to mentions that include your keywords. (www.trackur.com)

- **Technorati** is a blog search engine. Its free service indexes posts as they're published. When you search on the site, you can use the RSS button to subscribe to the blog you're mentioned on. (http://tech norati.com)

- **MonitorThis** is a simple online tool that lets you subscribe to the results of searches

from 22 search engine feeds at the same time. (Maybe it should change its name to ThisCanKeepYouReallyBusy.) (http://alp-uckan.net/free/monitor this)

- **Naymz** is a Web profile aggregator and reputation metrics service. Its primary goal is to make sure that you're in control of your name on the Internet. The service lets you configure your Naymz profile to include links to other online profiles, as well as recent endorsements you've received and recent Web activity that includes your name. Naymz doesn't charge for its basic services, but makes Premium features available for $14.95 a month. (www.naymz.com)

Managing

After you tune in to the online conversation that's taking place about your business, your next move is to manage it. That usually means responding to the reviews you're getting, particularly the negative ones, which is an extremely delicate process.

A negative review — especially one that you think is groundless or unfair — can really get your blood boiling. Most people's first reaction upon reading public criticism of their company is to come out with guns blazing. If that's your first reaction, *stop*. Cool off before you compose your response.

Fight the urge to respond to every negative review or comment you might receive. If your reviews are positive overall, it may be best to just let the bad one pass without commenting. Readers who frequent review sites are smart enough to know that in any string of comments, one or two malcontents inevitably appear and just rant for ranting's sake. Usually, the more rabid someone is in panning something, the more likely readers are to just write them off as cranks.

However, you will get some negative reviews that deserve to be taken seriously and responded to in a reasoned, rational manner. The basic rule here is, when in doubt, apologize. You can make the apology public by posting it on the Web site where the negative review appears, or you can privately message the reviewer.

Note: Apologizing doesn't mean groveling. Acknowledge that a mistake might have been made in the critic's specific case and that you've taken steps to ensure that it doesn't occur again. Ask critics for one more try and assure that you'll go out of your way to make sure they're satisfied the next time. Remember that the complainer's review isn't the end of the conversation. Engage people in a receptive and responsible way, and you may well win them over. You might even get brownie points for your prompt response to their problems. In the best case, the critics may ultimately revise their earlier reviews or at least take down the negative ones.

If your give-and-take with a dissatisfied customer takes place in a public forum, that customer isn't the only one who sees — and can appreciate — your calm and sympathetic response. You could impress a lot of onlookers who'll make positive mental notes about your responsiveness and professionalism.

We aren't kidding about taking corrective steps — and you shouldn't be either. The complaint posted is likely to have at least a grain of truth. Take the complaint to heart, and really see whether some part of your operation needs fixed. Then fix it. Remember that these are your customers talking and that although they may not always be completely right, they may also be on to something that can make your business better.

Online review do's and don'ts

Don't: Some local business owners take the bull by the horns and try to counter bad reviews by making up and submitting their own positive ones. Some even go so far as to use their phony submissions to trash a competitor. Don't. More than likely you'll be found out, and the reputation you were trying to save will go up in flames.

Do: Nothing is wrong with gently asking your satisfied customers to submit a positive review online. You could say something along the order of, "You know, probably the best advertising we get is by word of mouth. If you get a minute sometime and wouldn't mind, we'd sure appreciate a review from you online." Subtlety is the key here. The friendlier and more offhand you make your request, the better the chances are that you'll get that nice review.

Promoting

Using review sites and social media to help protect and solidify your good name has other benefits, such as serving as tools for marketing and analytics. After diving politely into online conversation, use your presence to get involved, answer questions, and keep prospects and customers informed of your latest business goings-on.

Position yourself as an authority in your field. Over time, people may come to view you that way and recommend you to friends (or better yet, to the media), and in the case of social networks, to post a link to your Web site.

You can also invite bloggers — particularly those who seem to be the most influential — to review your business and what you have to offer. Sure, you're taking a chance here. However, if your company runs smoothly and takes care of customers properly, you have little to fear and potentially, a lot of positive visibility to gain.

Also consider becoming an advertiser on the site(s) that features your reviews. The benefits of this tactic vary by site, but advertisers generally get a prominent display position and other helpful tools. Yelp, for example, lets advertisers highlight one of their favorite reviews at the top of their page (as long as the review is sufficiently current to still be relevant — see Figure 14-2). Citysearch even helps advertisers with copywriting or video segments, and pushes out the content to partner sites like MapQuest (www.mapquest.com), AOL CityGuide (http://cityguide.aol.com), and MySpace (www.myspace.com).

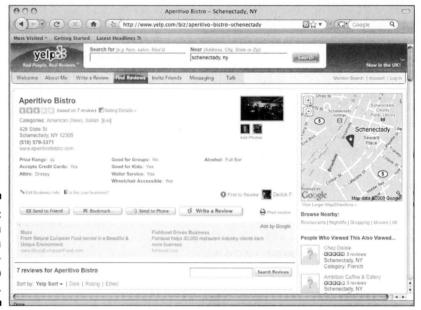

Being active on review, social, and blog sites can also help businesses mine customer data. For instance, Yelp has a dashboard that allows business owners to keep track of page views and responses to promotions — information that the business can then use to fine-tune its marketing tactics. A lot of the data you gather here can be combined with the other Web analytics you're already using to give you an even more complete picture of where you stand in the marketplace.

Building Credibility: Associations, Certifications, and More

Endorsements result from receiving certifications of one kind or another from professional associations in your industry that you can join. Not surprisingly, these certifications can be used in self-promotion.

The easiest way to do this is to display the seal or logo of the endorsing organization along with your own. Do this sparingly, however, and only on the right materials (such your Web site, directory listings, and social media profiles). Otherwise, the organization may contact you and tell you knock it off.

The two ways to establish credibility are

✔ **Assigned credibility:** This is the traditional, old-school way to burnish your reputation, and it can still be remarkably powerful if you put in the work necessary to attain it. Assigned credibility grows out of everything from your formal education and credentials earned to industry certifications you've acquired and the breadth of your career experience. The common thread in all these is that the credibility you get comes from an outside source, usually an institution. To earn credibility, behave, play the game, and do what's necessary to deserve the honors you get. People inside your industry know that this kind of credibility isn't necessarily all it's cracked up to be, though it does show that you've jumped through the requisite hoops. People outside your business, however, will usually be impressed by the credentials you've piled up.

✔ **Borrowed credibility:** This is a shortcut to gaining recognition as an authority or expert in your field — and it's often surprisingly easy to get. Here are some typical ways to borrow credibility:

   • *Memberships in professional organizations:* Most professional organizations have a sort of halo effect around them. They sound important, and in many cases, they are. Become a member and bask in the rays of credibility that the organizations have generated for themselves. These types of organization could range anywhere from industry-specific groups like the Plumbing Heating and Cooling Contractors Association (if you are plumber) to the Better Business Bureau in your area, to your local chamber of commerce. Figure 14-3 shows a local business site that prominently displays its professional affiliations.

   • *Partnerships:* Is someone in your area in the same kind of business you are, but for whatever reason, currently enjoys more credibility in the field? If so, see whether you can occasionally join forces with that individual. Perhaps your two businesses could jointly sponsor an industry event, or host some sort of seminar or presentation via the local chamber of commerce. Just by being paired with this other person, your own credibility is likely to be inferred.

   • *Articles in recognized publications:* Could you write articles in industry publications whose readers you could help and impress? Approach the publications and ask. Just make sure that these publications are intended for your target audience and that they have their own credibility. Having something printed in a third-rate magazine or newsletter won't advance your case at all and may even hurt it. Stick to the solid, respected ones.

   • *Client list:* Keep track of who your most prominent existing customers are and then use their names to borrow credibility. Restaurants do this all the time by plastering pictures of their famous customers on a wall near the entrance. Doing so is effective (even if just subconsciously).

- *Expert endorsement:* Asking for endorsements by experts in your field generally yields a lot of turn downs, but even the occasional okay can be well worth the effort. Here again, you're hitching a ride, so to speak, on someone else's credibility. If you feel a little squeamish about that, keep in mind that the expert you're courting probably did the same kind of credibility-borrowing earlier in her career. This is just how business gets done.

Figure 14-3:
A local business site displaying its professional affiliations.

Affiliation logos

Using Message Boards, Forums, and Other Places to Strut Your Stuff

A *message board* or *forum* is an online discussion area modeled after a traditional bulletin board (without the risk of incurring pushpin wounds). Like-minded users gather here to talk about issues and interests they have in common. A lot of expertise — or in some cases, what masquerades as expertise — gets thrown around on message boards, and that can provide a good opportunity for local businesses, particularly service businesses, to showcase their knowledge and build credibility with potential customers/clients.

Put another way, message boards are micro-communities. They're always much smaller than the Facebook-type networks we talk about in Chapter 13, though they may approximate the size of some of the specialized subgroups found on those networks. Message boards tend to be composed of members who are intensely interested in one subject. Many users gravitate to a particular board because they feel a strong connection to the forum's host or simply because they feel they'll come away from the board with more solid, useful knowledge than they came in with.

Similar to message boards and forums are *user groups* — sets of people who, again, have similar interests, goals, or concerns and who regularly share their ideas online.

Marketing on message boards takes patience

Marketing a business to people within message boards is an extremely delicate process. Regular users can become suspicious of newcomers who start tooting their own professional horns when they first arrive. Before you make any attempt at marketing via a message board, make a concerted effort to become a contributing community member.

Be forewarned that this can take patience, and if you're the naturally sales-oriented sort, a heaping helping of restraint. At first, join an ongoing discussion rather than start a *thread* (that is, triggering an ongoing discussion by posting a topic and/or question). After you have a feel for how the board's users interact with each other, you can initiate a thread. By then, you'll be known as something of a regular.

Having a goal for posting on message boards

Before you execute a message board marketing strategy, identify your goals. Then determine whether the long-term commitment you have to make will ultimately be worth your time and effort. Getting comfortable on a board — and having others become comfortable with you — takes a while, so don't think that you can contribute a few posts and then start hawking your wares. It just doesn't work that way.

That being said, however, joining a message board(s) and engaging with the other members can be an effective marketing tactic if what you hope to accomplish is one or more of the following:

- **Gaining key information about your target demographic:** Message boards are a great place to collect information about your potential consumers and their habits. All you really have to do is observe, but you can pose a question or otherwise introduce a topic and see what the responses are. Board users like this kind of two-way communication; in large part, that's why they're there.

- **Gathering information about your competitors:** Chances are a discussion centered on your line of business in your area will eventually (maybe even regularly) produce mentions of your competition. Here again, all this takes from you is observation. Finding out how a competitor is perceived — its strengths and weaknesses — gives you an invaluable window into what's really going on in your marketplace and therefore, where your own place in that market is or should be.

- **Building respect for and confidence in your business:** Hang out on a relevant message board long enough, and you'll probably answer questions raised about products or services like yours, helping other members troubleshoot a particular problem they're having and giving your expert opinion on this, that, and the other thing. Keep up this sort of helpful dialogue, and people will increasingly come to rely on you as a trusted authority and to view your business as a particularly credible one to deal with.

Finding the right message board

So how do you find the right message board, the kind of place where your expertise will be valued and your reputation polished? The best way is to go to one of the sites in the following list and search the keywords and geographic modifiers that are most likely to narrow down things for you:

- **BoardReader:** http://boardreader.com
- **ForumFind:** www.forumfind.com
- **Big Boards:** www.big-boards.com

✔ **BoardTracker:** www.boardtracker.com

✔ **iVillage:** www.ivillage.com

✔ **Yahoo! Message Boards:** http://messages.yahoo.com

✔ **Yahoo! Groups:** http://groups.yahoo.com

✔ **AOL People Connection:** http://peopleconnection.aol.com

✔ **Google Groups:** http://groups.google.com

For example, if you own the Vegan Café in Seattle, Washington, and you search ForumFind for *vegetarian message boards,* you discover www.veggieboards. com (and no, we aren't making this up). When you get on VeggieBoards, search *Seattle,* and you'll discover several discussions going on about which veggie restaurants in the city are absolute must-eats. See? Your table's waiting.

Don't be surprised if your search for message boards produces more than one contender. In that case, concentrate on the one or two with the highest search results page rankings. After all, you don't want to be regularly imparting your pearls of wisdom on some board that few people actually read.

Getting started on message boards in five easy steps

Although it does require an ongoing commitment, participating in message boards is relatively easy. Just follow these simple steps:

1. **Search for large message boards, user groups, and forums dedicated to your industry.**

   Look at the number of registered users on the forum at any given time (most boards show the users somewhere on their page) and decide whether the board is active enough to warrant your attention.

2. **Create an account on the message boards that discusses local companies in your field.**

   Use the same name on every board you join and choose a name that shows you're affiliated with the company (for example, *BobofAkronVentilation*). Add your work e-mail address and your Web site address to the signature of your account.

3. **Use the forum's search function to find *threads* (specific discussions) that are related to your area of interest.**

Obviously, this saves you a whole lot of time. Subscribe to any threads that you want to watch, and you'll receive an e-mail whenever a new post appears.

4. **Politely respond to posts, even if you disagree with what's said.**

   Being respectful and handling criticism calmly is an excellent way to manage your online reputation. If a thread contains comments that praise your products and services, post a nice, humble thank you.

5. **Add your e-mail address to the user groups that pertain to your area of business.**

   Although some of these groups communicate solely on the Internet, others hold regular face-to-face meetings or events. Your e-mail address helps ensure that you get on the guest list — and when you show up, your own personal magic can take over.

Making the most of message boards

These tips get you started on crafting efficient and effective message board comments:

- ✔ **Every word counts:** Make sure that the content you post — whether as comments on message boards, on your blog, or on your Web site — includes the keywords that you know are the most heavily searched by people looking for your kind of business. That way when consumers search for something related to your business, they're likely to see your comment and hopefully move on to your Web site. For obvious reasons, your message board content needs to also — subtly — include your URL.

- ✔ **Your time is money, so don't go nuts:** Set aside a modest amount of time (say, two hours a week) to look through your favorite message boards, find relevant discussions, and enter your posts. Try to remember that although appearing regularly on a relevant board is important, quality trumps quantity. More effective is to contribute a few well-thought-out, well-expressed comments to a discussion than to launch as many message missiles as you possibly can.

- ✔ **Aim every comment at potential customers:** Any message board worth its salt has a lively mix of people on it. Somewhere in there, amidst your competitors, current customers, and folks who just won't ever be in need of your particular products or services, are potential new customers. Concentrate on talking to them. Create content that will appeal to them, answer their questions, and maybe even allay any concerns they have. Focus on their needs, not yours.

Hitting the Blogs

Blog — or *Web log* — describes Web sites that maintain an ongoing chronicle of information. Each blog is a frequently updated, personal site featuring diary-type commentary and links to articles on other Web sites.

Many professional blogs focus on a particular topic, such as Web design, home improvement, politics, sports, or mobile technology. Others are more eclectic, presenting links to all types of other sites. Still others are personal journals.

Although there are exceptions, blogs generally have a few consistent elements:

- ✔ A main content area consisting of posts listed chronologically, with the newest on top. The entries are often organized into categories.

- ✔ An archive of older articles.

- ✔ A way for readers to leave comments about the articles.

- ✔ A list of links to other related sites (or a *blogroll*).

Some business owners find that blogging is a great way to get noticed by prospective customers and search engines, and to drive Internet traffic to their Web pages. But maintaining a blog is immensely time-consuming and demands an ongoing commitment that most local business owners just don't have. In the upcoming sections, we talk about how participating in someone else's blog can have an almost equally positive impact on your business.

Using blogs for your business

You'll find that making use of blogging for your business really isn't all that difficult. Do the following:

- ✔ **Read blogs:** Blogging has its own unique language that's different from other forms of writing. To understand how to speak that language, follow a few blogs that interest you. To find some, simply search for your area of interest on Technorati (`http://technorati.com`) or Google Blogs (`http://blogsearch.google.com`).

- ✔ **Keep blogs short and sweet:** If people wanted to read a novel, they'd read a novel. When blogging, use short, breezy, conversational posts. Also try to maintain a regular presence on the blog you contribute to. Not only does this keep you firmly in the community, but many blogs give their most frequent contributors special privileges, such as initiating surveys and opinion polls.

- ✔ **Don't use adspeak:** Okay, you're blogging to promote your business, but that shouldn't seem like your primary goal. Most bloggers hate that. Give readers what they want — useful, specialized information that comes from your own experience. (Posting something like "The Top Ten Ways to Do *XYZ*" often gets a lot of folks' attention, and your hard-earned expertise in your field should make compiling posts like that a piece of cake.)

- ✔ **Tell a story:** Many blogs have a personal, diary-like feel to them. The author keeps a daily record of what's going on in his life. If you're authoring your own business-oriented blog, adding the occasional personal touch to your entries can help humanize you to your readers and encourage their interest in your business.

- ✔ **Think search engine optimization:** You can choose from a lot of ways to make your blog posts friendly for search engines. Probably the most effective tactic is to use the keywords and phrases that people searching for a business like yours can be expected to use. For example, if you're blogging about plumbing and your company's in Buffalo, you're wasting an opportunity if you just blog about drain clogs. Better to write about drain clogs you've fixed in Buffalo. Another good approach is to insert links to other pages in your posts; that improves the chances that search engines will find you.

If you really want your own blog

If you want to spend the time and effort necessary to start and run your own blog, a variety of resources enable you to do so easily and, even better, for free:

- ✔ **Blogger:** www.blogger.com
- ✔ **LiveJournal:** www.livejournal.com
- ✔ **WordPress:** http://wordpress.com

The person-to-person nature of blogs helps a lot of business owners establish and maintain a close relationship with their potential customers. Importantly, this personal relationship can be exactly what separates the owner's company from those of his faceless competitors.

Using blogs the right way

Say you're a consultant of some sort (such as a lawyer, event planner, or local investment advisor). As it happens, consultants are frequent blog users because they give them a terrific way to show their expertise. (A co-blogger might post, "Hey, Denise. I'm inviting 100 guests to my wedding. How big a cake do I need?") This also lets consultants network with other people in their field and can even save them the time and expense of traveling to distant conferences and trade association meetings.

Or maybe you're a landscaper. Posting to a blog about how the change of seasons can affect different kinds of shrubs is of great interest to local homeowners who take particular pride in their outdoor plantings. ("If you own hydrangeas, the first frost is going to tear them up. You can cover them with burlap though, and that should minimize the damage. Here's a picture of how the burlap covering works.")

Or here's an example from real life. A friend of ours owns a successful roofing business. He employs a big crew of workers, big enough that his company is frequently working on several jobs at once. One day he was out and about and decided to check in on one of his crews to see how they were progressing. He was horrified to find them tearing the old roof off the wrong house. Boy, did that spark days of conversation on the blog he frequented. Rather than making him look like an idiot, his posts about the incredible lengths he went to (and the thousands of dollars he spent) to make things right with the wrong homeowner wound up earning him a lot of praise and respect — and amazingly enough, a number of new jobs. People saw him as a good person who was only human, but also as someone who wouldn't rest until a job was done to everyone's satisfaction.

Making the Most of Online Press Releases

One of the best things about local online PR is that it doesn't have to cost much. A perfect example is an online press release (or Web news release) to provide educational, informative, valuable online news content to prospective customers. This tactic can really improve search engine rankings, drive people to a company's Web site, and generate new business. Online press releases are being used more and more by business owners looking for affordable local PR and by local media who are always looking for content.

You can use an online press release to break all sorts of news items, from scheduled events and personal promotions to recent awards and new products or services. This is a great way to trumpet your latest record sales figures and your most significant new accomplishments. More than a few of your recipients will be impressed, and the local paper or TV channel can extend your reach exponentially if they decide to pick up the story. Figure 14-4 shows an example of an online press release for a local business.

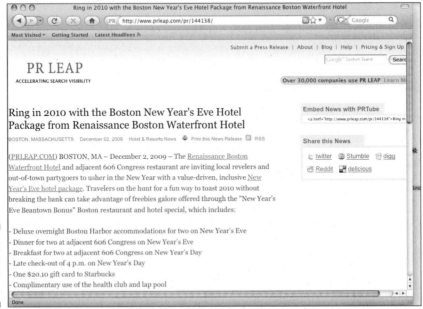

Figure 14-4:
An online press release.

Comparing traditional and online press releases

Traditional and online press releases are the same, only different. This section explains the differences between the two.

A traditional, paper press release really had no reason for being unless it was received and run by local media. Whoever handled a business's PR usually had a long list of phone and fax numbers for dozens of press outlets, both local and statewide. Getting the releases placed was often a case of sending them out, and then following up with phone calls or e-mails prodding the recipient editors or producers to run with what was sent. This whole process could devour a lot of work hours.

With online press releases, getting media attention is still a primary goal, but it's hardly the whole ball of wax. Online releases can be posted at multiple, non media-specific locations on the Web and will usually (as in, should always) include the originator's Web site address. This in turn gets the attention of search engines, which can then help move the releases to the online public at large. This process isn't so much a case of cutting out the middle man (the *media*) as it is of viewing that middle man as just one channel of distribution.

Another difference is that unlike their traditional counterparts, online press releases can be optimized for the benefit of search engine crawlers (which we talk about in Chapter 7). All this requires you to do is pepper the content of a release with your chosen keywords, which is easy. Start out by writing a traditional press release and then follow these steps:

1. Research the keywords your target audience is likely to use to get information about your subject matter.

   You've probably already done this research.

2. Include your most competitive keywords in the headline of the release.

3. Repeat those keywords at least three times in a 300-word release.

   This is the longest any optimized online press release should run.

4. Use a geographic modifier, such as your state or city, in your copy (and if possible, your headline) and mention it frequently.

5. Add keywords in the link(s) you provide back to your Web site.

If you sponsor local events or you offer several promotions each month, issuing a calendar-based press release can be a great way to go. Unlike traditional releases, a digitally produced calendar can easily be changed or added to without issuing a new press release. Check out the Web sites of your local newspaper, radio, and TV stations, as well as chamber of commerce and community college. If they feature calendars somewhere on their site, make sure they receive your calendar.

Distributing online press releases

In the preceding section, we discuss the role of media outlets in making sure your online press releases are seen by large numbers of people in your area. Here are several additional ways to disseminate your online releases by using distribution services, including:

✔ **1888PressRelease.com:** Despite a name that suggests it's a good place to find press releases from the 19th century, 1888PressRelease.com offers both free and paid ways of accessing distribution outlets and increasing your visibility. This site can also furnish you with tracking data. (`www.1888pressrelease.com`)

✔ **I-Newswire.com:** A service that allows you to distribute one online press release per week to a global audience. Features both free and paid options. (`www.i-newswire.com`)

✔ **MediaSyndicate.com:** A free service that specializes in distributing press releases for small- and medium-sized businesses. (`http://mediasyndicate.com`)

✔ **SBWire:** A paid service that enables you to distribute press releases to specific, targeted industries and geographic areas. This service also distributes your releases via RSS (Really Simple Syndication) to numerous third-party-sites. (`www.sbwire.com`)

Point to your Web site

All the things we mention in this chapter are excellent ways to promote your business and maintain your reputation among customers and prospects. But none of them is ultimately worth much unless you keep in mind that cardinal rule of online marketing: Everything you do has to be linked back to your Web site or landing page.

After all, this is where the real business gets done — providing information, wooing and converting prospects, and transforming them into paying customers. Whether you're hitting the message boards or blogs, or distributing optimized press releases to here, there, and everywhere, never forget to provide a link that enables consumers to come visit you. This is the payoff that everything else points to and facilitates. This is where you make the sale.

Chapter 15

Using Offline Channels to Drive Online Traffic

. . . .

In This Chapter

▶ Making your URL an always-and-everywhere marketing tool

▶ Using tracking codes, vanity URLs, and cross-pollination

▶ Maintaining consistency between your online and offline efforts

. . . .

*T*hroughout this book, we discuss a host of online tactics you can use to build your business, but chances are you use offline marketing channels as well. The goal is to get the online and offline marketing to work together in a way that makes them mutually supportive — and mutually productive.

Here are some fairly obvious ways to do this: Include your URL on every piece of promotional material you send out. Make sure your URL is on newspaper ads, in radio commercials, on letterhead, on business cards, in *Yellow Pages* ads, on the signage on service vehicles, and in the front window of your retail space. To put this simply, everyplace you are, your URL should be, too.

Getting your online and offline tactics to work together also means that if you say, send out postcards advertising a special promotion of some sort, your Web site spotlights the same promotion. Not doing so can make for some very confused and unhappy customers.

Another approach is to offer coupons via your offline marketing that promise special, Web-only deals. Trust us — folks will be primed to visit your site and collect their goodies while being exposed to all the wonderfulness of your Web site.

Good things can result from all this integration. Done right, integration will make both your marketing methods work harder by creating a whole that's bigger than the sum of its parts. And the activity on your Web site can help you gather useful feedback about how well your offline advertising is working.

Putting Your URL in All the Right Places

Despite the obviousness, many business owners forget to put their URL on their offline marketing materials. Your direct mail, print advertising, and radio and TV commercials are all indispensable places to include your Web address. These days, people almost think it's suspect if you don't include a URL.

Plus, remember this good stuff:

- A lot of consumers simply don't want to call a local business. Maybe they don't want to get a hard sell by a pushy salesperson, or they're just shy. Whatever the case, these folks are more likely to reach out to you online.

- Phone numbers are easily forgotten, especially when they're in a broadcast message. (The exception is when you have a really snazzy number like 1-800-Got-Junk.) A URL, on the other hand, is usually easy to remember because it's often the company-name-dot-com or something very close.

- Including a URL on all your offline materials is just one more way to get in front of potential customers, cement your name in the public's mind, and help build your brand.

Tracking with landing pages

You can also use a few online, Web site-based tricks to help you get a handle on which of your offline channels are bringing new customers to your business. Say you're a fencing contractor in Phoenix, Arizona, your Web address is www.thefenceguyaz.com, and you use offline channels, such as direct mail and newspaper ads, in addition to your online efforts.

Being smart, you include your URL on all your offline materials and prospects come to your Web site. But doing this alone isn't really enough because of the following questions:

- **Where exactly are your customers coming from?** People are winding up on your home page, but how did they get there? Did they see your URL in your newspaper ads, on your billboards, or in your mailers? Because you don't know that, you can't know which of your offline materials work and which are just dead weight. Granted, if you're using Web analytics on your site, you probably can differentiate between Web site visitors who found you on a search engine versus those who directly navigated to you by typing your URL into their browsers. But that still doesn't answer the question of which offline channel brought 'em.

✔ **Which promotion brought the customers?** Additionally, say one of your offline marketing initiatives is running a special promotion. You've included links on your home page that are keyed to the specific promotions that you've included in offline materials. That is, your current newspaper ad promotes a certain kind of fencing, while your direct mail offers a 30-percent discount on installation, and your home page provides corresponding links (no pun intended) for each promotion.

The problem is that Web site visitors are notorious for their short attention spans, and they won't like clicking through links on your home page to get what they came for.

Given the two preceding problems, what do you do? The answer is a landing page (or pages). By creating a specific landing page for each of your various offline campaigns and by creating unique URLs for each, you can easily track the sources of your site's visitors.

In adopting this strategy, don't include paths to these landing pages on your home page or site map because for your tracking to be accurate and actionable, the unique landing pages you create have to be completely isolated from any access points other than the unique URLs you use. If you let people navigate to landing pages from your home page and/or site map, you completely muddy the waters and will still wonder who came from where for what.

Suppose you're sending direct mail offering savings on a product or service. Instead of including your primary URL (www.thefenceguyaz.com), the mailer could point recipients to a directory listing, such as www.thefenceguyaz.com/savings or to a sub-domain, such as www.savings.thefenceguyaz.com. Doing this lets you

✔ **Tailor the landing page's message specifically toward what first got the prospect to that page.** If your direct mail advertised a special 30-percent discount offer, the corresponding landing page can prominently display the same deal.

✔ **Tailor the page's look to make it consistent with the direct mail's look.** Use the same color schemes and fonts, copy style, and call to action. Any images you used in the mailer need to also be on the landing page. You want the potential customer to get to the landing page and think, "Good, I'm in the right place." This helps move customers seamlessly along in the conversion and sales process.

✔ **Measure precisely how well your offline advertising efforts are working.** If you've created a landing page that matches a particular piece of direct mail — and that matches only with that mailing — you know for sure that it got the customer onto your site. Put another way, the mailer, with its distinct URL to a page that isn't otherwise navigable to via your home page, is the only way the customer could have arrived on that particular landing page. Measure that and you get a clean read.

Using vanity URLs

Another way to send people to a specific landing page (and whose visits you can then track) is through the use of a vanity URL. A *vanity URL* is an easy-to-remember URL that promotes a particular product or service. For example, maybe your company URL is www.company.com and your vanity URL for your A, B, and C product or service is www.abc.com. The vanity address can then be made to redirect to the corresponding product/service landing page you've set up already (which has an actual URL of www.company.com/abc.html). You then track the redirects to the landing page.

URL redirection (or *URL forwarding*) is a simple coding function that automatically changes the URL a user types into a different URL when she hits Enter. Think of this as giving out different business phone numbers; when any of those numbers are dialed, they immediately reroute to the main office number.

Using vanity URLs can be beneficial in several ways:

- ✔ **As with sub-domains and directory-based URLs, your vanity URL sends prospects to the most appropriate landing page.** This is far better than just dumping visitors onto your home page and expecting them to find the information they want.

- ✔ **Vanity URLs allow you to have a much more memorable URL.** Pick something that's easy to say and spell. This is especially important if you're using radio or television, which has an audio component. (Using a relatively detailed Web address in broadcast advertising is clumsy because the person in the commercial has to say things like *slash, dot,* and *html.* Not only is this cumbersome, it chews up valuable seconds.)

- ✔ **You can easily tie a special promotion, product, or service into the vanity URL.** A company whose primary address is www.stephensshoestore.com and is offering a new and uncommonly comfortable line of footwear could use www.comfyfeet.com.

- ✔ **Vanity URLs can also be used to measure the effectiveness of one media buy versus another.** Say you're airing the same radio commercial on three different stations in your market. The commercial's content is the same no matter which station it's heard on, but at the end when your URL is given, you use a different vanity URL on each station. All three vanity URLs then redirect prospects to the same landing page. You measure each redirect to find out which of the three radio stations performs best.

And here's some additional good news about using vanity URLs: They probably won't cost you anything in extra hosting fees because a redirect isn't usually considered a separate site or landing page. A few hosting services may want to drag a few extra bucks out of you for using the vanity-redirect approach. But even these guys won't charge you more than a little extra.

Some Web marketers don't put much stock in using vanity URLs because they believe that branding one's business Web site is so vitally important that any mention of any URL different than the home page's dilutes the brand and therefore, wastes money that could otherwise be spent on brand-building. We admit this argument has a certain logic, but it's also fair to say that most local businesses aren't nearly as brand-obsessed as the critics. Where does that leave you? Ultimately, the question of whether to use vanity URLs is one that each business has to answer based on its own needs and marketing philosophy.

Promo codes

Ever hear something like this? You're listening to the *Biff's Cavalcade of Twisted Gothic Chants* radio show, and Biff reads a commercial on air, gives the sponsor's URL, and then says, "And don't forget to use the promo code *Biff*." Using promotional (or promo) codes are a pretty big thing because they let a business track the visits to its home page without using separate landing page URLs.

A *promo code* is simply a brief string of characters that allows advertisers to differentiate how a potential customer heard about them. Did the visitor come via radio? Direct mail? Newspaper? A home page that encourages the prospect to enter a promo code? Each of which is keyed to the advertisement/medium from which it came and lets the advertiser identify the source of the visit.

Using promo codes has a couple downsides though, such as many people flat out won't use

them. Maybe people are just uncooperative, or maybe it's that in addition to having brief attention spans, a lot of people have short memories. Whatever the cause, typically less than 50 percent of those consumers given a promo code will use it. Consequently, a particular advertisement might actually have brought the prospect to the site, but the advertiser will never know it. (This is further complicated because a few Web sites do nothing but provide promo codes for free for dozens of companies, meaning that the people who use these particular codes are coming to sites without necessarily seeing any advertising.)

As a general rule, promo codes are best used by businesses that want or need only a very general sense of which of their advertisements are driving traffic.

Using Cross-Pollination for Search

URLs are effective devices, no matter where they're used, but they aren't the be-all, end-all of online advertising. A lot of consumers will read an ad or a direct mail or be attracted by a TV or radio commercial, yet not use the URL that the sponsor provided.

This isn't particularly odd; think about it. An advertisement probably mentions the business's name far more often than it does the company's URL, so that's what most likely sticks in a consumer's mind. Even if that person remember the URL, it generally takes more keystrokes to type that address into a browser than it does just to query the company's name on a search engine.

How often does search versus direct URL navigation happen? According to a ClickZ (www.clickz.com) survey of consumers who searched for a company, product, or slogan, 37 percent were motivated to do so by a television commercial, 20 percent were drawn by a print ad, and 17 percent were sent by a radio spot. These numbers are significant.

This phenomenon has a couple important implications:

✔ **Keywords are (still) key:** Having your organic listing appear in one of the top spots on a search engine results page is terrific. Your branded keywords (which, for many businesses, include the company's name) have obviously done a lot of good. But knowing that a hefty percentage of your prospects may have come through search rather than by using your URL, you have to make sure you've covered all the bases as far as your business name is concerned. Seriously consider buying your company's name for a pay-per-click (PPC) campaign. (Studies show that a PPC ad for a branded keyword will usually provide incremental sales for a business, even if that business already holds the top organic-listing spot.)

So, back to PPC you go — and back to your chosen keywords. In this case, we're talking specifically about buying your company name as a keyword. That way no matter which advertisement or marketing channel brought your name to a consumer's mind, that consumer will find you through a search engine. Even if your business's name is the only keyword you buy, you'll be spending your money wisely.

✔ **Be consistent:** Consumers who see and/or hear the name of your business through an offline advertisement and then find you via a search engine, will rightly expect your Web page to look and feel wholly consistent with whatever ad it was that motivated them to find you. This kind of consistency includes color scheme, copy style, imagery, and so on. In much the same way as you make sure that your Web site and search engine efforts are all operating around the same keywords, so should your site offer consumers a smooth, easy, coherent transition from their offline stimulation to their online experience.

Leveraging the Insights You Gain Online

When you run a PPC campaign, you quickly find out which of your keywords are best at driving prospects to your Web site (and one hopes, converting them into customers). You then make an effort to focus most of your attention — and dollars — on keeping your business at or near the top of the results page that appears when those keywords are used.

You can do something very similar with your combined online-offline marketing efforts: Let one of them guide you in maximizing the effectiveness of the other. Although consumers tend to behave somewhat differently in an offline environment than in an online world (obviously, they can't explore any links in offline media), there's plenty of similar behavior, too.

Applying online lessons to offline marketing

Here are couple examples of how this kind of leveraging can work:

✔ For example, your company does gutter cleaning. You notice from using Google AdWords that as fall approaches, more people are searching for *gutter cleaning*. Wisely, you then launch a special promotion for your gutter-cleaning services in the local newspaper.

✔ For example, you own a house painting company, and your Web site metrics indicate that most of your site visitors spend considerable time on your Gallery page, where you display several before-and-after photos. You decide to promote your gallery in your print ads and direct mail pieces because you infer that that's a great way to drive people to your Web site.

Because online marketing easily lends itself to detailed analysis of your prospects' behavior, it can tell you a host of things that you could never find out from offline efforts alone. Promptly put that analysis to work across the board.

Applying offline lessons to online marketing

Online-offline leveraging works in the opposite direction as well. For example, you own a local fitness center, and you're currently running a radio campaign that offers a 30-day free trial membership, and the campaign is creating an increase in your Web site traffic. Consequently, you decide to use the same promotion in the ad copy for your PPC campaign and throughout the appropriate landing pages on your site.

This kind of leveraging can even work both ways almost simultaneously, especially when a fortunate outside event pops up. For instance, maybe one of the services you provide at your beauty salon is a new and super-effective kind of electrolysis. In your newspaper ad, you've included that new technique in the long list of services you offer, and that mention has generated a small increase in new business. Then a local news show runs a two-minute piece on this electrolysis breakthrough, and suddenly your phone starts ringing and ringing.

Being nobody's fool, you make sure you have a special landing page on your site that goes into extensive detail about the new process, complete with before-and-after pictures, testimonials, and so on. At the same time, you go back and revise your newspaper campaign to focus on the new technique, and you include a vanity URL that sends consumers directly to that dedicated landing page. Within days, your salon is absolutely packed with soon-to-be-less-hairy people.

Using Integration as Your Key to Success

We talk earlier about integrating your online and offline advertising, but it's a lesson that needs emphasis. Your online and offline marketing efforts must work together, both pulling in the same direction to the same end, and doing so as seamlessly as possible.

You may start thinking of them as two distinct marketing channels, but in truth, they aren't. They're simply two prongs of exactly the same strategy. This strategy is *integration,* and it's key because consumers don't behave in neat and tidy ways. In gathering information about products and services and about the local businesses that provide them, people will ricochet constantly among what they see in the media, come upon in the course of an online search, read or hear in offline advertising, talk about with their friends, and so on. In short, they're bouncing all over the place — and your single-minded sales message needs to be all over the place, too.

The transitions a consumer makes from offline sources to your online marketing messages needs to feel completely natural and effortless — which is to say, consistent in content, look, and feel so that the different venues come across to that consumer as just slightly different windows that all share the same view.

An offer you make in one medium needs to be echoed in all others. If you run a promotion in print, broadcast, outdoor, and/or direct mail, consumers will rightly expect that same promotion to be emphasized online (and vice versa). If that sort of tight integration isn't there, prospects will likely get confused and take their interest — and their business — elsewhere.

A conceit exists among Internet marketing companies and consultants that online marketing will soon make offline advertising obsolete. Of course they'd say that given the nature of their business. But, in any case, that prediction is just silly.

People don't live online — they just visit. What they see and hear in the offline, non-Internet world will always influence their buying decisions. You have to market your business both offline and online. The surest path to success is to make those two channels of communication work as one.

Further, success means making all your efforts work together. Cherry-picking just this one and that one and leaving the rest undone won't get you much of anywhere. (It's like saying, "My airplane now has a tail and one wing. That oughta do it.") We're talking integration here.

Think big picture. Think teamwork. Thing synergy. Just don't think that the online tactics you use can be fully effective in a vacuum. Align them closely with your offline efforts and with any skill and luck at all, you can be doing more and better business in no time flat.

Part IV
Keeping Your Customers Coming Back

The 5th Wave   By Rich Tennant

"Oh, we're doing just great. Philip and I are selling decorative jelly jars on the Web. I run the Web site and Philip sort of controls the inventory."

In this part . . .

Y ou're poised on the threshold of designing and executing a first-rate online marketing campaign, so it won't be long before prospective customers start beating a path to your door. And that's terrific. But then the question inevitably arises: How do you keep those customers coming back for more? How do you keep them interested in the things you have to say and to sell? How do you keep your business's front door swinging open, day after profitable day?

Chapters 16 and 17 tell you how. The first discusses the finer points of building and nurturing customer *relationships* — those fragile, fertile things that any business relies on to stay in business. And the latter talks about the importance of mining your customer database to keep the proverbial ball rolling — and keep sales rolling in.

Building customer relationships are all very, very doable, which you can see by reading on.

Chapter 16

Staying at the Top
of Customers' Minds

*Y*ou've been busy. You've been planning your online campaign, executing it, measuring it, refining it — and, thanks to all your efforts, you've generated a goodly number of actual sales. Excellent, bravo, and way to go.

Now what? Well, now comes the critical business of making sure that these hard-earned, first-time customers return to you the next time they're in the market for what you sell. Presumably, you treated them right the first time around, and it would be a downright pity, shame, crime, you name it, if next time, they unthinkingly drifted off to one of your competitors. So how do you keep that from happening?

First off, don't count on automatic loyalty. Customers — even established ones — are fickle. Not unlike packrats, they're attracted to new, shiny things, and if your competition comes calling with something that twinkles, they're liable to forget you and go for it.

The truly important step is to keep you and your company top-of-mind for your customers so that your business is the first — and maybe even the only — place they think of when they're again ready to buy. The good news is that your business can keep its top-of-mind position without expending much in the way of money, effort, or time. In this chapter, we show you how to make the most of your best new business opportunities — your existing customers — using proven online tactics that include everything from e-newsletters and customer surveys, to rewards and referral programs, to contests and giveaways.

Standing Out in the Crowd

No matter how smart a business owner you are, at least one of your competitors will think he's smarter. He figures he'll undercut your prices, spend more on new-customer advertising, or open a flashier store.

But what this competitor may not (and, we certainly hope, doesn't) quite grasp is the importance of building relationships with existing customers to the point where they'll think of him first when they think of the kinds of goods that you both sell.

Always make sure that your company is at the top of customers' minds — that they think of your company first and foremost. So, whether you're surprising your customers with freebies, regularly providing them with useful information, asking them for feedback in a way that flatters them, giving them a chance to win big, or using some other technique that keeps you front and center in their minds, you're instantly putting yourself at a true competitive advantage.

Your existing customer base is the easiest to reach, the easiest to sell to, and the most cost-effective to influence overall. Nurture and retain those folks, and in effect, you'll be drilling a veritable well from which you can keep drawing business for years to come.

Making Nurturing Second Nature

Sure, it's Basic Business 101, but we want to say it anyway: The best source of new customers is existing customers. And here's another truism: Customers just want to feel wanted.

Put together those two thoughts and you have an airtight case for taking care of the customers you already have. Show them attention and appreciation, and they'll come back to you again and again. They'll also recommend you to others who may then become new customers, and the business chain just gets longer and longer.

We make this quick trip to Planet Obvious because a lot of local business owners manage to forget these simple principles. Somehow they convince themselves that a bird in the hand will stay there without any further care and feeding. Then they wonder why the person they sold X to last year hasn't since come back for Y.

What makes this especially problematic is that it isn't all that easy to create a new customer from scratch. The American Association of Advertising Agencies reports that although consumers receive literally thousands of marketing messages each day, the human brain can process only a tiny fraction of them. The odds of that tiny fraction of messages inspiring an actual sale are a whole lot tinier still.

Your existing customer base, on the other hand, is already in your corral . . . at least for the moment.

Knowing why customers run away

The reasons most commonly cited by business customers for buying from a given company just once are

- ✔ They felt, in retrospect, that the business's pricing was too high.

- ✔ They had a complaint that went unresolved.

- ✔ They found a competitor's offer more attractive.

- ✔ They left because the business didn't care.

The last two reasons in the list are the ones that customers give most often, which means that they fly the proverbial coop because a particular company made them feel unwanted or unvalued — and made them easy prey for some dastardly competitor.

Building relationships = Building profits

Here are some statistics (compiled by www.customersfirst.com/ps_ cust_serv_research.html) regarding your existing customer base:

- ✔ Repeat customers spend 33 percent more than new customers.

- ✔ Referrals from repeat customers occur 107 percent more often than referrals from non-customers.

- ✔ Selling something to a prospect costs six times as much as selling the same thing to an existing customer.

Considering the importance of a business's existing customer base, why do many businesses spend 80 percent of their marketing dollars chasing after new customers? Why is such little effort made to nurture and retain the customers they already have?

You don't have to be an MBA to conclude that your marketing dollars go a lot further toward producing profits if you use them to build, nurture, and develop your current customer relationships.

Retaining long-term customer loyalty is a long-term challenge. Doing so takes effort every day in response to every sale — no matter how big or small — but it's eminently doable and at very little cost.

Finding Cost-Effective Ways to Keep in Contact

The most powerful incentive for a customer to give you repeat business is (not to go all Hallmark on you, but . . .) emotional. Sure, bang for the buck, stand-out service, and quality products are all big factors. But a customer who feels personally connected to a particular business will keep coming back even if, in objective terms, you aren't really all that different from your competition.

Developing one-to-one connections with your customers is pivotal in your efforts to build long-term loyalty. Establishing and maintaining two-way communication with your customers is the key to creating these kinds of relationships.

Where did I put all those old customers?

Before you can foster an ongoing relationship with your existing customers, you have to remember who they are, which shouldn't be particularly hard if your business has been computerized to some extent for a few years.

Dive into your sales database and arrange the customers into three piles: recent ones, not-so-recent ones, and old ones. If you were wise, you captured their e-mail addresses along the way. If you weren't and didn't, you can always call them and ask whether you can put them on your e-mail list to, you know, let them know about special deals and the like. *Note:* Simply making the phone call can be the start of building a bridge to the customers you contact.

Okay, now that you have your three piles, which ones do you contact first? We suggest the following order:

1. **The new ones:** They have the most recent experience with you and will think it's pretty natural that you're contacting them.

2. **The old ones:** It's high time you jogged the old customers' memories and put yourself back on their radar screens. "Hello, Mr. Backus. It's been awhile since we've done business with you, and we wanted to let you know about our exciting, new [fill in the blank]."

3. **The middle ones:** They'll probably have at least some memory of you, but they'll need a bit more coaxing than your recent customers. Time for them to enjoy all your considerable charms.

Of course, if you have the wherewithal to contact all your existing customers at once, go right ahead. But if your time is limited, prioritizing them into a logical working order is the best way to proceed.

Sending thank you messages

The one kind of business e-mail that nearly always gets read and almost never gets treated like spam is the confirmation e-mail that a business sends to a customer immediately after a sale. In earlier times, this was known as a thank you note, like the kind your mom insisted you write to Aunt Lydia, thanking her for that hideous Christmas scarf she knitted for you.

Sending a business thank you is much simpler — and more sincere. You may already have some sort of e-mail system set up to confirm your online appointments, orders, or reservations (and if you don't, create one).

The e-mail you send should not only confirm the activity and, if possible, specify a delivery or service date, but it should also emphatically thank the customers for their business and invite them to call or e-mail you with any questions. The following example shows a sample of a no-frills thank you message.

> Dear Stephanie,
>
> I just wanted to thank you for your first visit to Hand & Stone Massage Spa. Here's hoping it was every bit as rejuvenating as you'd expected!
>
> In the future, if you're feeling stressed, don't hesitate to call or visit us online to make an appointment — a half-hour treatment for only $30 might be just what the doctor ordered.
>
> Wishing you good health,
>
> Jackie A. Smith
>
> Hand & Stone Massage Spa

A well-designed thank you message can also assist with other business goals:

- **To make more sales:** Of course you want to sell more, so use your thank you message to (politely and tactfully) suggest other products or services that may interest the customer. You can instead (or in addition) include a coupon for a discount on her next purchase from you.

- **To solicit e-newsletter subscribers:** Include a bit of copy promoting the benefits of a subscription to your e-newsletter and a link to the sign-up page on your Web site. Because you're inducing a sign-up from an existing customer, you could offer an incentive (like a free sample or a significant discount) for him to subscribe.

- **To acquire testimonials for your Web site:** In the course of thanking the customer for her purchase, ask whether she'd be kind enough to provide you with a quotation (and the permission to use it) about what she thinks of your business. If you think that sounds just a teensy bit too pushy, you can always offer the customer a small incentive to furnish the quotation. That can do wonders for your response rate.

✔ **To get more fans on Facebook:** This goal would've sounded strange a couple years ago, but with the explosion of the social media, it's an always-on connection with your customers. So in your thank you message, include an invitation to become one of your company's fans on Facebook, a friend on MySpace, or a Twitter follower. And provide a link to the site you want the customer to visit.

You can probably think of other ways in which your customers can support your business outreach. So ask them. You may be surprised at the positive response you get. Start with your most wanted actions or goals, and give one or more of them a shot. If the response helps your business, great. If not, try something else. Over time, you'll figure out what types of requests are the most likely to get results.

Exploiting e-newsletters

E-newsletters are regularly scheduled communications from your company that invite a two-way conversation with your customers. Although your e-newsletter can certainly contain some calls to action designed to give your business some short-term bumps in the sales department, the e-newsletter format is suited uniquely to accomplish the long-term goals of customer retention and loyalty. Plus, e-newsletters cost almost nothing to produce and send.

In Chapter 10, we discuss the nuts and bolts of how to produce and send marketing e-mails. Those techniques apply directly to e-newsletters, too, so checking out that chapter might be a good idea.

What makes e-newsletters so effective? In a word: Trust. A well-written e-newsletter is a subtle and extremely effective way to build your credibility and your customers' confidence in your company. After all, the e-newsletter is free to the recipients, non-threatening and non-intrusive (because they've signed up already to get it), and contains information that's relevant to their interests. E-newsletters also

✔ **Build your brand.** E-newsletters position your business as a valuable asset.

✔ **Are cost-effective.** You can send thousands of them for virtually nothing (as opposed to printed mailings with all that pesky paper and postage).

✔ **Stay current and fresh.** The topics of e-newsletters can constantly change; thereby a) not boring your customers to death, and b) making them feel they're in the loop on important information.

✔ **Keep your name in front of past and prospective clients.** This makes them far more likely to remember you when they're ready to buy something from a company like yours.

✔ **Keep your customer list working.** This is a list that might otherwise just be sitting there collecting dust mites.

Figure 16-1 shows a sample e-newsletter.

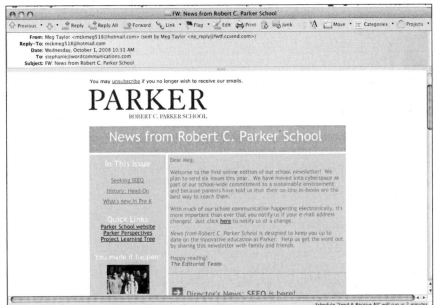

Figure 16-1:
A sample
e-newsletter.

Local business owners generally have two questions about the whole e-newsletter thing:

- ✔ How should they start?
- ✔ How should they keep going?

As soon as someone signs up for your e-newsletter, the process begins. Grab the e-newsletter recipient's attention with a proper welcome and hold his interest with compelling, relevant information. Follow these steps:

1. **E-mail a welcome letter to all signees a welcome letter that gives them a good idea of what they can expect from the mailings that will follow.**

   You can provide a preview of topics you plan to address, hint at news that you'll be announcing in the weeks or months ahead, and give access to your archive of previous issues. Make sure that your welcome letter also does the following:

   - *Thanks recipients for subscribing.* Tells them how to unsubscribe if they choose to and give them a way to change their contact information if necessary.

- *States your privacy policy.* The privacy policy tells visitors to your site what information is being collected, how that information is being protected, and whether or not you will share that information with third parties. This simply helps them feel more secure about doing business with you.

- *Promotes brand recognition.* Include your company's logo and your distinctive color palette and fonts. Remember, you're building your brand here.

2. **Identify and develop e-newsletter content that demonstrates what you know.**

You didn't get where you are, running your own successful business, without learning a lot of things that remain complete mysteries to your customers. Keep track of the questions that customers and friends typically ask you. Make note of what's going on in your industry that you know is important, but that outsiders aren't likely to appreciate. Dedicate a single e-newsletter to just one or two of the questions or industry developments on your list.

You're likely to be surprised at how many subjects you can easily come up with by relying on what you know. For a monthly e-newsletter, you need only 12 a year (or only 6 for a bimonthly e-newsletter).

Conducting satisfaction surveys

Sure, a lot of local businesses talk about satisfying their customers, but too few make the effort to find out whether they're actually doing it. Such lack of initiative is pretty goofy when you consider that finding out is simply a matter of asking, and asking your customers whether they're satisfied is well worth the effort. If you conduct your customer satisfaction surveys thoughtfully and with appropriate follow-up, they can be your single most effective tool for growing your sales and turning one-time buyers into loyal repeat customers.

Catching customers before they wander off

In most cases, dissatisfied customers won't stick around long enough to complain. They just vote with their feet and disappear. But if you offer customers a voice through a satisfaction survey, you may proactively discover that something is wrong with your products or services. If you do and can correct the problem quickly, you may keep your current customers from becoming unhappy ex-customers.

Satisfaction surveys have other benefits, too. They

- ✔ Give your customers the opportunity to think and express themselves about what you do for them, which can help underscore your value in their minds.

- ✔ Can nip small annoyances in the bud before those small problems snowball into big rock-and-ice-encrusted ones that crush your customer relationships.

- ✔ Give you a good way to identify your competitive differences, your strengths and your weaknesses in the marketplace — all of which you really need to know.

- ✔ Offer an extremely efficient, cost-effective way to market yourself in a positive light because you're explicitly demonstrating your concern for your customers' satisfaction and well-being.

Making them feel important

The less tangible, but still highly important virtue of satisfaction surveys is the message they tacitly send to your customers:

> *You value their business. You want them to be completely happy with the relationship. You're anxious to fix any problems that may arise. You really do care.*

Yes, we know it sounds kind of sappy when you say it out loud, but implicitly, it's powerful stuff.

The mere fact that you're soliciting your customers' honest opinions about your business tells them a lot about what kind of company you run. This also flatters them to know that their thoughts and feelings count. In short, these kinds of surveys are worth their weight in relationship gold.

Creating effective customer surveys

Here are the three steps to get a productive satisfaction survey up and running:

1. **Choose the right timing for your surveys based on how often your customers use your products or services.**

   Restaurants, for example, often have comment cards placed at each table or included with each customer's bill in one of those snappy little faux-leather folders. An event-planning business, on the other hand, may be hired by a given customer only once or twice a year — or maybe only once every few years — so sending that customer a monthly survey wouldn't make any sense. In that case, a survey given to the customer right after an event with another one sent out six months later would be the best approach.

2. **Include questions in your survey that are specific enough to address the survey goals but open-ended enough to encourage customers to answer fully.**

   Take the time to think through exactly what the goals of your survey are and then word your questions accordingly. If you're a contractor who's just finished building a house for someone, inquiring, "So how'd we do?" is just asking for a stream-of-consciousness answer that's unlikely to give you the specific guidance you're after. Better to ask: "Was our roofing work up to your expectations? If not, please tell us why."

3. **Plan and execute a follow-up to the survey that acknowledges customers' concerns and thanks them for their participation.**

   Whether you conduct your survey by e-mail or phone, personally thank each customer who responded. Tell them how much you appreciate their time and effort in participating, and tell them that you've clearly heard the concerns they expressed and are making the necessary changes to fix things. And then, of course, make the necessary changes to fix things.

Many business owners avoid conducting surveys out of fear that they'll just get a lot of bad news — and then have to actually do something about it. But if you're one of those owners, figure out whether you'd rather know what's going on while there's still time to solve any problems or whether you want to just gradually lose your customers altogether.

Doing surveys on the Web

Consider including a satisfaction survey form on your Web site or providing a special e-mail address on your e-newsletters that customers can use to give you feedback. In either case, the goal is to make it as easy as possible for customers to praise or critique your business. The fact that using the Web can also make it a lot easier for you to conduct your surveys is just icing on the cake.

Here are some great online resources, each geared to the needs of small businesses, which can help you create and distribute your online surveys:

✔ **SurveyMonkey.com:** For the Pro subscription rate of $19.95 a month, you can send an unlimited number of surveys and receive up to 1,000 responses per month. This is obviously a terrific choice for companies with a large mailing list or companies that want to mount several different surveys over the course of a year, for instance. (www. surveymonkey.com)

✔ **SurveyGizmo:** Similar to SurveyMonkey. com, these folks offer options ranging from free surveys to paid plans. The latter plans gives you not just survey capabilities, but also the ability to send e-mail invitations to events, as well as providing integration with Facebook and other social media (pretty much all of the features a local business might need are available for $49). You can use SurveyGizmo for just one month at a time if you want, with no obligation to sign up for longer periods. The figure in this sidebar shows a sample survey from SurveyGizmo. (www.surveygizmo.com)

✔ **Zoomerang:** This company features free and paid packages. A Pro version lets you send surveys in several languages, with no limit at all on the number of responses you can receive. (www.zoomerang.com)

✔ **SNAPPOLL.com:** This outfit offers you an easy (and free) way to put a one-question survey on your Web site. Respondents aren't required to sign up to participate, you can customize the colors on your survey form, and the service can block multiple votes from the same person. (www.snappoll.com)

✔ **Advanced Survey:** This company offers both free and paid services that provide Web-page and e-mail surveys. In the latter case, you invite participants to take part in the survey via e-mail. You can ask multiple questions in a single survey, as well as yes/no questions and open-ended text questions. You can also use customized numeric-scale questions (Rate X on a scale of 1 to 10, and so on) and multiple-choice answer formats. (www.advancedsurvey.com)

Rewarding Customers for Their Business

Customers want to feel valued by the local businesses they deal with. If you don't offer them positive reinforcement and instead treat them as disposable commodities, don't be surprised if those customers start shopping only on the basis of price. After all, you've given them no deeper reason to be loyal to your company.

A far more productive and profitable way to do business is to reward your customers on a regular basis. Do that, and price alone will stop being their only decision factor.

Luring new customers to your business is expensive, and the money you spend to do so won't necessarily produce any incremental business.

Programs that reward existing customers, on the other hand, can deliver a strong return on investment (ROI). Here are two reasons why:

✔ *Incentives,* or rewards, not only inspire customers to return to you, but also encourage them to tell other people about your business. That word of mouth can generate a new wave of potential buyers. In effect, you're acquiring new customers, even though your expenditure is targeted only at current ones.

✔ Incentives reinforce your relationship in a way that can prevent customers from taking their business to your competitors, even if those competitors make lower price offers.

Promotions that perform online

Several kinds of promotional strategies can reward your customers through cost-effective online (and offline) tactics:

✔ **Pre-purchase discounts:** Get a 10 Percent Discount When You Pre-Purchase a Series of Exercise Classes is a good example of this technique. Pre-purchase discounts are generally both affordable and cash-flow positive. You can put money in the bank now, the benefit of the discount is immediately (and attractively) apparent to the customer, and if she fails to use all the products or services she's signed up for . . . well, your profit margins get that much better.

✔ **Cash reward after reaching a purchase level:** You offer an $X credit when the customer has purchased a certain amount of your product or service. This can both increase your sales and keep your customers just the way you want them: loyal.

✔ **One free after reaching a purchase or service level:** Offering free products or services is a bit less motivating to customers than a cash reward, but it can still be quite effective. An example is Get a Free Fall Cleanup When You Buy a Summer Lawn Service Contract.

✔ **Discounts for planning ahead:** Book a Room at Our B&B for a Winter Weekend Getaway and Save 15 Percent on Your Stay. This sort of thing works well for businesses whose sales are seasonal or otherwise follow a predictable up-and-down cycle. Provide discounts that encourage purchases during those otherwise quiet times of year, and you may wind up boosting your future in-season sales as well.

✔ **Other gifts, upgrades, and special treatment:** Giving extras to your most loyal customers may cost you relatively little, but it can have a big impact. For a restaurant, this may involve offering a free dessert with every entrée (though not served at the same time because that would be gross). For a boutique, this might mean giving free alterations with any dress purchase. The byword here is *bonuses* — and customers love them.

Promoting the program

Simply put, the key to promoting customer rewards is integration. Make sure you promote your incentive program at every customer touch point. Get the word out via direct mail (such as a postcard), via your Web site, via e-mail, and/or via social media. Some businesses make a point of including incentive information with every sales receipt they hand to a customer. And of course, your regular advertisements and online PR efforts should hit the incentives as well. One other thing: Make sure your staff and everyone else who interacts with customers actively promotes the program.

Measuring your results

As for practically everything else in your marketing arsenal, measuring the results of your reward programs is indispensable. First, of course, you need to set realistic goals for your program. Then on a regular basis (no shirking allowed), measure increases in your sales to existing customers and in your revenue. Modify or abandon incentives that are underperforming, and stick with those that are working well. You know the drill.

Some businesses just flat refuse to believe that rewards work. "We're not in the business of giving away things" is a too-common sentiment. If your competitors feel the same way, you're golden. But if you're one of those reluctant business owners, simply remember the airlines. Their frequent flyer programs are so effective at generating repeat business that you'd be hard-pressed to find one that doesn't offer this incentive. Granted, your business is probably a good deal smaller than one with a fleet of planes, but the principle is exactly the same — what's different is the scale.

Reveling in referral e-mail programs

Referral e-mail programs — also known as viral e-mail, pass-along e-mail, or e-mail that includes a Tell a Friend feature — are another easy way to reward existing customers while also acquiring new ones. Best of all, this kind of e-mail message can propagate quickly as it's forwarded from person to person. Figure 16-2 shows a sample of a Tell a Friend referral e-mail form.

Seeing how (and why) they work

Referral programs generally involve nothing more than the offer of some kind of reward or other enticement to a loyal customer in return for that customer's recommending your business to a potential new customer. In effect, referral programs are another cost-effective way of drawing new customers to your company — and far more cost-effective than marketing cold to a pool of unknown prospects.

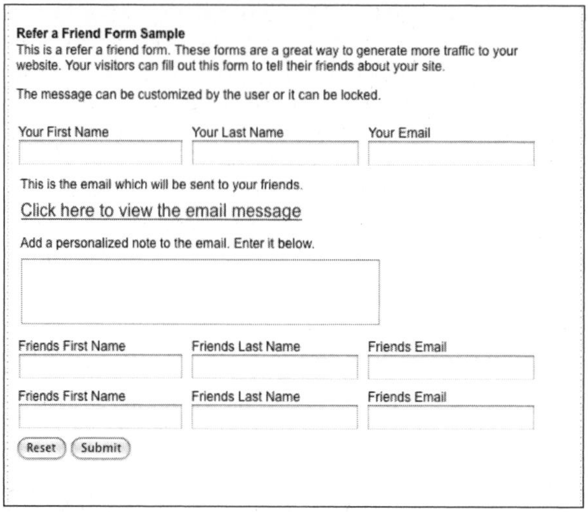

Refer a Friend Form Sample
This is a refer a friend form. These forms are a great way to generate more traffic to your website. Your visitors can fill out this form to tell their friends about your site.

The message can be customized by the user or it can be locked.

Your First Name   Your Last Name   Your Email

This is the email which will be sent to your friends.

Click here to view the email message

Add a personalized note to the email. Enter it below.

Friends First Name   Friends Last Name   Friends Email

Friends First Name   Friends Last Name   Friends Email

Reset   Submit

Figure 16-2:
A mocked-up referral e-mail form.

Referral marketing is so effective because people listen to their friends, respect their advice, and then act on it. When someone you've never seen before walks into your store and says, "My friend was in here recently and bought one of your professional-strength doodads, and she loves it; I'd like one, too," you're about to make a very easy sale.

And here's another wrinkle (as though anyone needs more of those): When you send a referral e-mail that rewards customers for passing the message along to their friends, that message needs to include a link that lets the passee sign up to be on your mailing list, which is a great way to grow that list without doing much of anything.

Producing referral e-mails

Putting together a referral e-mail program isn't difficult, particularly if you're already working with an e-mail service provider of the sort we discuss in Chapter 10. These providers typically offer all the features and functionality you need to implement your referral campaign, including the following:

- ✔ **A Forward link** that appears on all your outgoing e-mail messages.
- ✔ **A Forward to a Friend feature** that links directly to your Web site.
- ✔ **A Subscribe Me link** that appears in all forwarded messages so the recipient can opt-in to your mailing list.

As for the content of your referral e-mail messages, that's pretty easy, too. Something like, Get Five Friends to Sign Up for a Swedish Massage, and Receive a 20 Percent Discount on Your Next Visit should do nicely.

Good ol' human nature is at least partly responsible for the success of simple referral programs. Humans have a primordial desire to know more than the next guy, an earnest desire to do nice things for their friends, and a natural hunger to acquire new knowledge. At the intersection of these three desires lies the potential for profit. The customer who refers feels like a bit of an expert and gets a nice reward. The customer who gets referred discovers something useful, helpful, self-improving, and so on. And you — you lucky fellow human and business owner — have managed to both promote customer loyalty and pick up new business.

Capitalizing on contests and giveaways

Come on, who doesn't like the prospect of getting something for nothing? Nobody, that's who. And although most would probably prefer to win an enormous pile of cash, you're also pleased to win smaller prizes, too. That's why online contests and giveaways are great ways to increase your marketing visibility, drive traffic to your Web site, and build sales leads.

First, we want to distinguish the two techniques (contests and giveaways). A *contest* rewards someone for doing something of merit. They've written the best essay, taken the most beautiful photograph, submitted the tastiest recipe, or made the best guess as to the average height of a North American beaver dam. A *giveaway,* or *sweepstakes,* on the other hand, picks winners purely by luck of the draw.

Prize-wise (which, incidentally, is kind of fun to say out loud), you can award winners with something as simple as a sticker or a T-shirt, on up to something of appreciable value, like free merchandise or free services.

Knowing why you need to use them

You'll find lots of excellent reasons for using contests and giveaways to reward your customers, and maybe attract some new ones, too. Contests and giveaways

- ✔ **Create buzz about your product or service.** They get people talking about your business and what you sell.
- ✔ **Promote Web site visits.** Your related hope is that the person who visits and enters the contest or giveaway also sticks around to investigate all the products and/or services you offer.
- ✔ **Help build up your e-mail list.** While you're asking a prospect for permission to send him e-mails, you can quite naturally strike up a conversation that can plant the seeds of a good customer relationship.

✓ **Strengthen existing customer relationships.** By creating a sense of fun and a small adventure, you can implicitly inform customers about your products while you're entertaining them.

✓ **Generate great advertising content.** This is especially true for contests. When customers submit photos, recipes, or essays that involve your products or services, you can use the submissions later (with the customer's permission, of course) in your advertising campaign. For example:

- A dentist might create a contest whereby her patients send in photos in hopes of winning the Best Smile prize. The winner might get a year's worth of free teeth cleanings (which is nothing to spit at), while the dentist uses the Best Smile photograph for self-promotion on her Web site or in her online ads.

- A café's contest might offer a free meal to the person who writes the most glowing (and honest) review of the restaurant on say, Yelp. This can only help boost the café's search engine marketing efforts, besides impressing would-be diners who come across the review.

Pondering before plunging in

If you're considering launching a contest or giveaway, take a moment to consider the following:

✓ **What your goal is:** Are you hoping to involve your customers and prospects in the naming of your new product or service offering or in deciding on the best place to open a new location? Are you looking to generate customer video testimonials for your Web site? Or will you be happy just to build your e-mail list? Structure your promotion accordingly.

✓ **What the prize should be:** The prize you offer needs to be somehow related to your business. (A shoe store offering a free meal at the burger-joint down the street is, by definition, one clueless shoe store.)

The whole point of the promotion is to increase your sales, so it only makes sense to choose a prize that will attract people who already have some degree of interest in your products or services. The bottom line: Choose a prize that your average customers would just love to buy. Even if he doesn't win, you've probably whet his appetite, and he may well come back and actually buy whatever it is later.

✓ **How you can advertise your promotion online:** Online promotions are a terrific way to generate sales leads. Whether you're promoting the promotion via e-mail, newsgroups, social media, and/or directly on your Web site, you're giving people a reason to visit your site — and you can use these hits to harvest new names for your leads list. Ask the participants to opt-in to your future e-mails, updates, postal mailings, or whatever it is that best suits you. Then, set about converting these leads into customers.

✔ **How to set up the contest rules on your Web site:** Contests and give-aways absolutely must have their rules stated clearly. This is the law, and the applicable statutes vary by state. You can usually find the legal requirements for the type of promotion you're planning online but when in doubt, find an attorney who can advise you.

Even though you've included all the impenetrable legal jargon that you're required to use, also put the rules in understandable layman's terms. This information includes things like what people need to do to enter, any restrictions that apply, when the prize(s) will be rewarded, and even, in some states, what the actual odds of winning are. Don't skip this step unless you think it's really, really fun to be really, really fined.

✔ **How to notify the winners:** This isn't much of a hurdle. Send the contest or giveaway winners an e-mail, send a letter, phone them, or do all three. Just don't forget to notify them. (People running promotions occasionally do forget to do this, and it's unforgiveable.) Be sure to ask the winners whether it's okay for you to post their names and photos on your Web site. Not only is this exposure a giggle for them, but it also proves to your contest participants that you were completely on the up-and-up with the promotion.

Some prize suggestions (in both senses of the phrase)

Need a little help in coming up with the perfect prize? Well, we can't promise perfection, but here are some good thought-starters:

✔ A month's worth of your product or service free of charge

✔ A free consultation and/or evaluation

✔ For pet stores, a year's worth of dog food

✔ For health clubs, a free 6-week membership

✔ For a chiropractor, a free massage with a (paid) new-patient exam

✔ For a dentist, a free teeth-whitening kit with a new-patient exam

✔ For a florist, 12 months of free roses

✔ For an electronics store, a free flat-screen TV

✔ For a travel agency, a free weekend's stay at the casino down the road (and there always seems to be a casino down the road)

✔ A donation of $1,000 to the charity of the winner's choice (yes, this is generic, but it's also a great way to present your company as a caring, sharing kind of hero — plus it's just a darned nice thing to do)

And so on . . .

Chapter 17

Leveraging Customer Data: Reach Out and Touch 'Em

Many times throughout this book, we stress the importance of capturing customer information. You get that information from the contact form on your Web site, the sign-up (or opt-in) form on your landing page, or even from the virtual phone service that logs inbound phone numbers when you aren't around to retrieve them. When you put together all that customer data, chances are you'll discover you've accumulated piles of it. So then what do you do? Leverage that data; use it to build stronger customer relationships and thereby increase your sales . . . which, after all, is the name of the game. This concept is *database marketing;* whatever you call it, adopt this extremely important tactic.

This chapter tells you how to do just that. And though you can certainly contact your customers through many channels (including offline ones), we concentrate on e-mail marketing — with good reason. E-mail is one of the most cost-effective ways to communicate with customers. E-mail's effectiveness goes beyond cost because it allows you to *personalize* the messages you send to your customers. You won't find a better method of maintaining and strengthening your customer relationships than e-mail.

Years ago — when e-mail marketing was in its squalling infancy — a generic e-mail message sent to all customers was more than enough to get a healthy response rate. The whole idea of e-mail was new and exotic then, and people wanted to fool around with it.

With today's consumers, the novelty of receiving e-mail has worn off. Many people get hundreds of e-mails every day and read only the best-conceived and best-presented ones. As with other facets of online advertising (for example, landing pages), relevance is the key to having your business' e-mails opened, read, and acted on.

Mining the Gold in Your Data

Marketing types have lots of little sayings, one of which is: "The money is in the list." That sounds (and is) kind of trite, but it's also 100 percent true.

Having an active and up-to-date customer database is simply and undeniably one of the most important assets a successful business can have. The market niche you serve or how big (or small) your company is doesn't matter; the fact remains that your data is a potential goldmine.

Your customer database doesn't have to be anything fancy. In many cases, depending on the specifics of your business, a simple Excel spreadsheet suffices (see Figure 17-1).

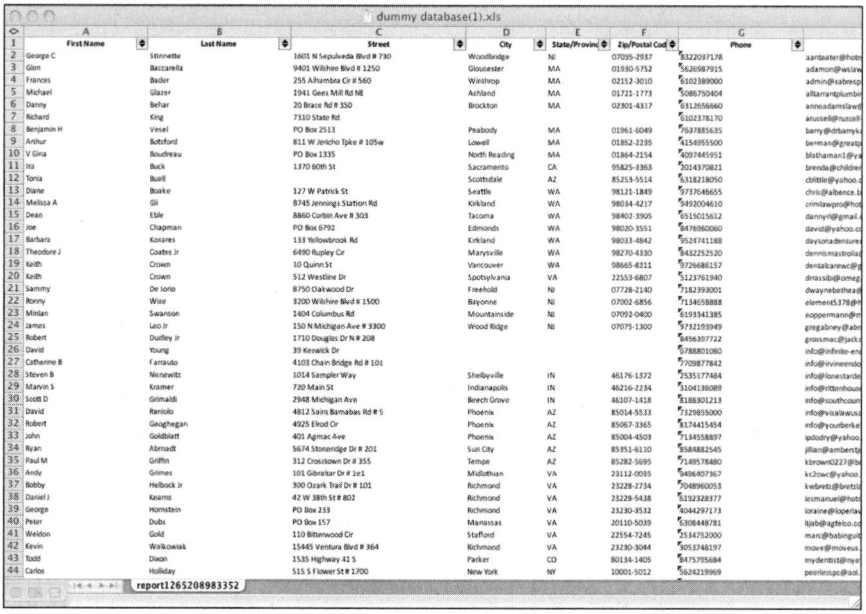
dummy database(1).xls

	A	B	C	D	E	F	G	
1	First Name	Last Name	Street	City	State/Provinc	Zip/Postal Cod	Phone	
2	George C	Stinnette	1601 N Sepulveda Blvd # 730	Woodbridge	NJ	07095-2937	8322037178	aanteater@hotr
3	Glen	Baccarella	9401 Wilshire Blvd # 1250	Gloucester	MA	01930-5752	5626987915	adamon@wslaw
4	Frances	Bader	255 Alhambra Cir # 560	Winthrop	MA	02152-3010	6102389000	admin@sabresp
5	Michael	Glazer	1941 Gees Mill Rd NE	Ashland	MA	01721-1773	5086750404	alltarrantplumbir
6	Danny	Behar	20 Brace Rd # 350	Brockton	MA	02301-4317	6312656660	anneadamslaw
7	Richard	King	7310 State Rd				6102378170	arussell@russell-
8	Benjamin H	Vesel	PO Box 2513	Peabody	MA	01961-6049	7637885635	barry@drbarryk
9	Arthur	Botsford	811 W Jericho Tpke # 105w	Lowell	MA	01852-2235	4154955500	berman@greatp
10	V Gina	Boudreau	PO Box 1335	North Reading	MA	01864-2154	4097445951	blathaman1@ya
11	Ira	Buck	1370 60th St	Sacramento	CA	95825-3363	2014370821	brenda@childre
12	Tonia	Buell		Scottsdale	AZ	85253-5514	6318218050	cblittle@yahoo.c
13	Diane	Boake	127 W Patrick St	Seattle	WA	98121-1849	9737646655	chris@albence.b
14	Melissa A	Gil	8745 Jennings Station Rd	Kirkland	WA	98034-4217	9492004610	crimlawpro@hot
15	Dean	Eble	8860 Corbin Ave # 303	Tacoma	WA	98402-3905	6515015612	dannyrl@gmail.
16	Joe	Chapman	PO Box 6792	Edmonds	WA	98020-3551	8476960060	david@yahoo.co
17	Barbara	Kosares	133 Yellowbrook Rd	Kirkland	WA	98033-4842	9524741188	daytonadenture
18	Theodore J	Coates Jr	6490 Rupley Cir	Marysville	WA	98270-4330	8432252520	dennismastrolia
19	Keith	Crown	10 Quinn St	Vancouver	WA	98665-8311	9726686157	dentalcarewc@g
20	Keith	Crown	512 Westline Dr	Spotsylvania	VA	22553-6807	5123761940	drrassibi@omeg
21	Sammy	De Iorio	8750 Oakwood Dr	Freehold	NJ	07728-2140	7182393001	dwaynebethea@
22	Ronny	Wise	3200 Wilshire Blvd # 1500	Bayonne	NJ	07002-6856	7134658888	element5378@h
23	Minlan	Swanson	1404 Columbus Rd	Mountainside	NJ	07092-0400	6193341385	eoppermann@m
24	James	Leo Jr	150 N Michigan Ave # 3300	Wood Ridge	NJ	07075-1300	9732193949	gregabney@abr
25	Robert	Dudley Jr	1710 Douglas Dr N # 208				8456397722	grossmac@jacks
26	David	Young	39 Keswick Dr				5788801080	info@infinite-en
27	Catherine B	Farrauto	4103 Chain Bridge Rd # 101				7709877842	info@irvineendo
28	Steven B	Nisnewitz	1014 Sampler Way	Shelbyville	IN	46176-1372	2535177484	info@lonestarde
29	Marvin S	Kramer	720 Main St	Indianapolis	IN	46216-2234	3104136089	info@rittenhouse
30	Scott D	Grimaldi	2948 Michigan Ave	Beech Grove	IN	46107-1418	8188301213	info@southcoun
31	David	Raricolo	4812 Saint Barnabas Rd # 5	Phoenix	AZ	85014-5533	7329855000	info@visalawus
32	Robert	Geoghegan	4925 Elrod Cir	Phoenix	AZ	85067-3365	8174415454	info@yourberke
33	John	Goldblatt	401 Agmac Ave	Phoenix	AZ	85004-4503	7134558897	ipdodry@yahoo.
34	Ryan	Abrnadt	5674 Stoneridge Dr # 201	Sun City	AZ	85351-6110	8584882545	jillian@amberstj
35	Paul M	Griffin	312 Crosstown Dr # 355	Tempe	AZ	85282-5695	7149578480	kbrown0227@be
36	Andy	Grimes	101 Gibraltar Dr # 1e1	Midlothian	VA	23112-0035	9496407367	kc2cwc@yahoo.
37	Bobby	Helbock Jr	300 Ozark Trail Dr # 101	Richmond	VA	23228-2734	7048960053	kwbretz@bretzla
38	Daniel J	Kearns	42 W 38th St # 802	Richmond	VA	23228-5438	6192328377	lesmanuel@hotr
39	George	Hornstein	PO Box 233	Richmond	VA	23230-3532	4044297173	loraine@loperlaw
40	Peter	Dubs	PO Box 157	Manassas	VA	20110-5039	6308448781	ltjab@agtelco.co
41	Weldon	Gold	110 Bitterwood Cir	Stafford	VA	22554-7245	2534752000	marc@babinguit
42	Kevin	Walkowiak	15445 Ventura Blvd # 364	Richmond	VA	23230-3044	3053748197	move@moveus.
43	Todd	Dixon	1535 Highway 41 S	Parker	CO	80134-1405	8475795684	mydentist@nya
44	Carlos	Holliday	515 S Flower St # 1700	New York	NY	10001-5012	5624219969	peerlesspc@aol.

report1265208983352

Figure 17-1: A simple customer database in Microsoft Excel.

Happily, you can work wonders with even the most basic customer data, with items as mundane as

- ✔ First and last names
- ✔ E-mail addresses
- ✔ Phone numbers
- ✔ City, state, and zip codes
- ✔ The dates when customers *became* customers
- ✔ The offer(s) customers responded to
- ✔ Customers' purchasing history

A solid customer database (including a well-maintained e-mail list) can work for you in both good and bad times. When business is clicking along nicely, your data gives you an already-compiled, no-brainer, go-to stockpile of likely customers for your newest product, service, offer, or other promotion. But your database also proves invaluable in times of crisis or other radical change. When the economy goes blooey, for instance, people look not so much for what's new as for what's truly valuable for solving one or more of their real-world problems or frustrations. That value comes from a business that customers already know and trust. In the not-so-good times, your customer database gives you a powerful way to ride to the rescue.

Giving Customers More of What They Want

The database of customer information you collect doesn't do much good just sitting there. You need to exploit the living daylights out of it by using the information to put you in front of your customer's digital face with the most relevant possible message at the best possible moment. Although this strategy sounds logical and straightforward, applying it requires some solid thought, planning, and execution. Understanding particular online marketing practices helps you through this process. To be specific:

- ✔ **Database segmentation**, whether by age, income, address, or whatever other criteria you think are most important, helps you target your recipients efficiently.

- ✔ **Personalization** helps you create messages that are directly relevant to your customers' needs, wants or interests.

✔ **Attention to timeliness** gives your message a fighting chance at actually being read because you've timed it to show up when (or just before) your customer is ready to make a buying decision.

Targeting with segmentation

Not everyone in your database is a proper target for a particular kind of e-mail message. Some of your customers are young, and some aren't; some are affluent, and some not so much; some are regular buyers, and some buy only occasionally; and so on. Accounting for this diversity is why you need to use *segmentation,* which separates customers into target groups defined by specific, shared characteristics.

The segmentation criteria are almost infinitely flexible, so you can reformulate them whenever you find it necessary. For example, a country club might segment its list when it wants to send a scramble offer to golfers in one week, and re-segment that same list to send a meetings and events message to its business customers.

You need to have a couple prerequisites in place before you start the segmentation process:

✔ **Your e-mail marketing strategy:** For example, you know whether you plan to send periodic e-mails, e-newsletters, special events mailings, or some combination of the three. (See Chapter 10 for more about e-mail strategies and campaigns.)

Always keep in mind that whatever kind of e-mail you decide to send must be relevant to the segment you're addressing. Failure to make sure of that will leave you sending a lot of e-mails that never get opened.

✔ **Data about your customers' interests:** Start with the kinds of products and services they've bought already from you. Your sales and ordering processes help you collect this information. (Check out Chapter 5 for information on capturing customer information through your Web site.)

Outlining your segmentation criteria

Each customer is a unique individual, but can still be identified as a distinctive type of purchaser. Every business can segment its customer base into broad categories. For example, you probably have customers who deal with you all the time, some who do so occasionally, and others who buy from you rarely. By using this criterion to group your customers, you're segmenting based on *sales frequency,* which is a good place to start.

Sales frequency is one way to break down your customer list. Another (and coincidentally, rhyming) criterion that savvy e-mail marketers use for segmentation is *recency* — how recently a given customer bought from you. Targeting these folks falls squarely in the Striking While the Iron's Hot category because your business is definitely top-of-mind for them. Also consider adding the monetary value of each customer's purchase(s) as a segmentation criterion. Those people who are frequent, recent, and high-ticket buyers become your VIPs, or *preferred customers,* who deserve extra courting, stroking, and sustaining with interesting and valuable-offer e-mails.

Some other simple segmentations apply to most businesses. You can segment by

- ✔ **Customer zip codes:** This segmentation is useful if you're trying to boost sales specifically at one of your business's locations, or if you're interested in segmenting on the basis of income or property size.

- ✔ **Customers' birth months:** You can micro-segment your mailing list this way and offer special gifts or discounts during each individual's special month.

- ✔ **Known customer preferences:** You can segment based on what items customers have clicked in your previous e-newsletters.

- ✔ **Obvious customer attributes:** Characteristics, such as age or gender, can help you target a specific group of customers.

Having made these simple distinctions, think about what other segments make sense for your particular business and then target your communications to those segments. Some examples to illustrate include

- ✔ A garden nursery can e-mail its residential customers about new spring plantings and its commercial customers about the availability of bulk mulch.

- ✔ A cosmetics boutique can e-mail one discount coupon to customers who buy makeup and another to those who buy skin-care products.

- ✔ A financial services firm might e-mail its tax-preparation clients a timely IRS filing reminder, while its financial planning clients get e-mails about rebalancing their portfolios.

- ✔ A sporting goods store may send one kind of mailing to ski bums, while tailoring a different one to tennis buffs.

After you delineate patterns of interest, demographics, frequency, recency, expenditure levels, and other criteria among your customers, you can tailor your e-mails' subject lines and content to each segment. Creating unique e-mail messages for different groups takes some work, but a good template-based e-mail marketing tool can make that a lot easier to pull off. The e-mail service providers (ESPs) we talk about in Chapter 10 can often provide you with excellent templates.

Doing it (kind of) backward

Some businesses flip around the segmentation process and let e-mail do the segmenting for them. Suppose you have customers who don't specify their particular interests when they sign up to be on your mailing list (many times, they don't). Send them an e-newsletter or two that covers a wide variety of different (presumably relevant) subjects and then using your reporting data, take a look at which customers bite on what subjects.

Evaluating e-mail response results identifies customer groups who have, in effect, *self*-segmented — a process that can save you a good deal of educated guesswork.

In addition to segmenting, e-mail marketing can produce some very useful metrics. An often-used metric is your *open rates,* which tells you how many of your recipients almost always open your e-mails, how many do so only rarely, and how many never take a look. Here's what these numbers direct you to do:

- ✔ **Take the last group of folks (those who never look) off your radar screen and out of your e-mail list.**

- ✔ **Send your hardly-ever-open customers a polite e-mail that identifies whether (or how) they want to be contacted.** Such a message helps you find out whether they'd prefer to be taken off your list, have contact through a different channel (such as direct mail), or whatever other scenario makes sense in your business. The point is to get this group off the fence. If they bail on you, so be it. That doesn't mean the bailers aren't still customers, just that they aren't your *el primo* customers, and you can curtail your efforts to inspire them with e-mail.

- ✔ **Start treating the almost-always-open people like royalty.** Concentrate your efforts on your liveliest of live wires now, so be creative in your approaches and generous in your offers. Make sure that *every* e-mail you send to this group is really, really good at informing, benefiting, and even just plain old flattering them.

Personalizing your targeted message

Personalization, the process of tailoring specific elements of a given targeted message to individuals within a segment, enters the picture right after segmentation. First, formulate customer criteria to create segments and then get even more specific to sub-segment your segments.

Basic psychology reveals that people react differently when they're being treated as unique and special individuals than when they're being treated simply as part of a group. Needless to say (but we're going to say it anyway), taking the unique-and-special approach to your customers is the hands-down winner when it comes to the fine art of persuasion.

Consequently, *personalize* your messages as much and as often as you can and proper segmentation goes a long way in making that possible. We recommend venturing beyond segmentation alone, into the realm of highly individualized messaging. The goal is to strengthen and reinforce the bond that exists (or should) between you and each of your customers.

Following are a few ways to personalize your messages:

✔ **Salutations:** Your initial greeting to a customer has a huge impact on whether that person goes on to read the rest of your communication. For a business-to-consumer e-mail, "Hi, Rosie" is just fine. For a business-to-business message, however, stick with business-letter-type usage: "Dear, Rosie," or "Dear, Rosie Sherman," or "Dear, Ms. Sherman" (in descending order of familiarity) are the right ways to go.

✔ **Product and service references:** Include a reference to a specific product or service that the recipient has purchased already from you or about which that person has asked you a question. For example:

- How are you enjoying your new lawn mower?

- Thanks for letting us shampoo your rugs last Thursday

- I looked further into the capacity figures for that washing machine we discussed and . . .

Including concrete product references is a great way, not only to sell, but also to *cross-sell* or *upsell* (selling a complimentary or additional set of products and services to someone who has already made a purchase). Follow up your question about the mower with a statement about a related product: "We also sell an extra-large grass-catcher for that mower." Or follow up your thank you by expressing interest in providing other services: "We noticed a couple spots on your rugs that would probably benefit from steam-cleaning the next time." Don't be shy about trying this. Businesses do so all the time — and wisely include a link to the applicable landing page on their Web site — and it frequently works.

✔ **Location:** Alluding to your customer's location is a proven way to give that person a sense of belonging. So, a limo company might observe, "Probably no one knows better than you just how crazy L.A.'s traffic can get." An Italian restaurant could say, "Because you live in Chicago, you really know great pizza when you taste it. That's why we're offering . . ." Just be sure that your recipient does in fact live in the location you're referencing. Duh.

✔ **Affiliation:** Another good bridge builder is a reference to a known group or organization your customer belongs to. "We're currently offering a 25 percent discount to Chamber of Commerce members, such as yourself." When you use this kind of personalization, take care that the relevance between your message and the person's membership is super-obvious. Offering a good deal on pesticides to members of, say, the local Symphony Society just completely misses the connection and therefore the point.

✔ **Images and multimedia:** Images or multimedia pieces that tie into any other form of personalization can be devastatingly (in a good way) effective. This happens, for example, when your e-mail message uses images of the exact product the customer has recently bought from you. When you're making an affiliation pitch, you could use the logo or seal of the organization the customer belongs to. This can even be as simple as incorporating an image of the skyline of Grand Rapids (and yes, it has one) in the e-mails you send to Grand Rapidians. In each case, you're making a subtle but powerful connection between yourself and your customer as a flesh-and-blood person. And here again, as simple and obvious as the technique might sound, it works.

Instilling relevance and timeliness

For an e-mail to be compelling and actionable, it has to be about something — and probably to *offer* something — that the customer cares about. For example, if you own a pet store, e-mailing a special discount on a grooming appointment doesn't mean much to a customer who only owns tropical fish. Fish are fun to look at, but they don't need much in the way of brushing.

A sort of sub-facet of relevance is *timeliness*. Dog owners are likely to be most interested in grooming their pets in the spring, when Trixie's winter coat starts coming out in handfuls. The grooming discount e-mail then will be far more effective if it's timed accordingly.

Put together those two ideas together, and you get this mantra: *Delivering an e-mail to the right person, with the right message, at the right time is critical to e-mail marketing success.* Forrester Research reports that the combination of relevance and good timing is nearly as effective as discounting for driving conversions. On the other hand, the majority of consumers' complaints about e-mail marketing overall stem from their receiving way too many irrelevant communications.

Timeliness in online marketing depends on the sort of message you're sending. A friendly confirmation sent immediately upon receiving an order is always good. Or try timing your reminder e-mail to arrive 30 days before the expiration date of a customer's yearly service contract. Then you have the whole seasonal thing we allude to at the beginning of this section, or any number of other factors that can make the difference between your e-mail's being well-received or immediately tossed. But don't sweat it. You're a successful business person, and if anyone knows the best time to promote your products or services, you do. Just rely on your own experience.

Optimizing Your Outreach Tools and Techniques

Whether you know it yet, you probably already have a fair-sized mountain of customer information. Keeping all that info organized — and doing regular follow-up on it — has the potential to be an overwhelming job. You certainly can use Microsoft Office products, such as Excel and Access, to help you deal with all the data, but you may still find it hard to keep pace.

Fortunately, a number of tools and techniques exist that can take a big load off your shoulders. These can help you capture and organize your data, and generate the right e-mails at the right time without pulling you away from your day-to-day business tasks and obligations. Here are the main types of tools we're talking about:

- **ESP-designed databases:** You can get these simple software applications (for not much money) from most ESPs, such as those we discuss in Chapter 10. The simplest of these ESP-designed database products typically handle segmentation and personalization duties.

- **Full-featured customer databases:** You can license contact and customer management software for a few hundred dollars from companies, such as Act! (www.act.com). Considering how much work this kind of customer relationship management (CRM) solution can save you, that's hardly a steep investment.

- **Professional ESP programs:** Then again, if you're *really* reluctant to step into the wonderful world of database marketing, you can hire an ESP to handle pretty much the whole process for you, although going this route isn't likely to be cheap.

If you decide to outsource your database work to an ESP, be sure to keep a copy of all your customer data in your own possession. It's very unlikely that the company you're using will — how to put this tactfully? — mess up or lose your data, but stay on the safe side and hang onto a backup list.

Staying dynamic

To deliver a relevant, timely message, get comfortable with using *dynamic* (database-driven) content that's driven by your customer database in order to make segmentation and personalization work for you. After you get your database and marketing tools in place, you'll be positioned to markedly improve your sales.

So how do you learn from your customers and incorporate what you learn into your dynamic marketing efforts? You can

✔ **Uncover customer patterns and trends:** Use an e-mail marketing database to develop a picture of your customers' characteristics, including which are most loyal and which are most likely to defect. Here's a good indicator: People who regularly open your monthly e-newsletter probably fall into the faithful-and-true category; while those who don't, well, don't.

After you identify a potential defector, you can do something special to keep him in the fold. You can, for example, reach out to him with a particularly well-crafted e-mail that offers something above and beyond one of your normal deals — an extra-big discount comes to mind. And remember that you're only offering it to a very small fraction of your customer base, so it's really not likely to screw up your cash flow.

✔ **Improve the impact of your communications:** Data-driven e-mail messages that speak directly to a customer *as an individual* won't only be more welcomed by your recipient, but will also help build loyalty and grease the skids for future sales. A good first step is to personalize your greeting: *Dear, Larry* carries much more weight than *Dear, Valued Customer.* Another smart move is to ask your customers how they want to hear from you in the future. Find out whether they prefer e-mail, phone, or regular mail, and whether they want to receive your monthly newsletter. Then make sure you store these answers in your database to drive your next communication.

✔ **Refine your prospecting:** Create a *prospect database* to segment out those customers who, for whatever reason, are consistently unresponsive. Then give it one more good, old college try. Offer them something attractive (maybe a free copy of a report on a timely topic that you know should interest them) and ask them to respond. If you *still* don't register a heartbeat, it's probably safe to move them into your Yeah-well-maybe-someday pile, which you'll get around to revisiting . . . that's right — maybe someday.

Uncovering patterns and trends

Listen carefully at a business's door — especially during tough economic times — and you can hear the sound of numbers being crunched as the owners obsess over targeting their best potential customers with every possible efficiency of cost, time, and effort. Carefully ferreting out trends and patterns is an excellent way to identify those customers and determine what they want.

Some of the most valuable statistics you can gather are the response numbers that roll in after you send an e-mail blast. Pore over them carefully and look for the following:

- ✔ **Offers that are particularly effective in generating responses:** Say you own a golf course and club that hosts a lot of destination weddings. You may notice that your prospecting e-mails are getting a measurably better-than-usual response rate just after Christmas when many engagements take place. So tailor your messages accordingly — and shower (pun intended) brides-to-be with relevant information right after New Year's because that's when they'll be thinking about setting the date and finding a great place for their reception.

- ✔ **Clues that help you pick out precisely the customers (or at least, the *kind* of customers) who will respond most eagerly to a follow-up mailing:** Maybe you do in-home catering, and you find that women respond to your e-mails more frequently than men. This may tell you something important about your audience — as in, who your primary purchasers really are and to whom you should then target your next round of e-mails.

- ✔ **Specific content that seems to be driving more and better responses than other content:** For example, maybe you're a landscaper who discovers that sending quarterly e-newsletters containing lawn-care information about the upcoming season draw 20 percent more responses than those that discuss say, the care and feeding of African Violets or Coast Rhododendrons. This statistic tells you that you need to make a disciplined effort to always stay ahead of the next season in the information you e-mail, even if those lovely rhododendrons have to take something of a back seat.

Doing this kind of simple but careful analysis helps you better understand who your customers are and what pushes their buttons. Then, armed with that information, you can sharpen your efforts to an ever-finer point — and pull in ever-greater amounts of business.

Keeping a clean e-mail list

In the online marketing world, where just about everything comes with its own slightly over-the-top terminology, there actually is a list *hygiene* concept. All this really means is keeping your e-mail list up-to-date, accurate, and well-organized. Some of the basic principles are

- ✔ **Take any removal requests off your list immediately.** E-mailing someone after they've already told you not to is a good way, in some states at least, to get into legal trouble. And even if the authorities don't come gunning for you, the customer in question gets royally ticked off — so you lose either way. Better to just deep-six anyone who wants off your list.

- ✔ **Make sure you have each recipient's correct name as well as the right name of the recipient's company (if any).** You can easily stumble over this if you've collected business cards at a trade show or networking event and then manually entered the information from those cards into your database. Typos have a nasty way of rearing their ulgy heads (see?). The situation can get even worse if you're pulling names off a trade show or event list where people quickly wrote their names, and you can't make out their handwriting.

Whatever the cause of the mistake, there's no bigger, immediate turnoff to e-mail recipients than having their names misspelled in the address line. You might as well address the message to *Dear, I Don't Really Give a Rat's Tooter about You.* Be almost maniacally careful about entering customer names into your database.

- ✔ **Always remove duplicate entries, especially when you're sending to more than one of your lists at the same time.** People hate getting multiple, identical e-mails. Of course, if a customer has for some reason given you more than one e-mail address when signing up for your list, that's her problem.

- ✔ **Don't just automatically pull a name off your list after you've received a Delivery Failure message.** At least, don't do so after only getting *one* such bounce. Recipients' inboxes get full, servers go down, and other gremlins can sneak into the picture, so the address you used may still be perfectly valid, just used at an inopportune moment. If you get three or four of these bounces on the same address, however, take the name off your list.

Engaging in all these hygienic practices is extremely important because you'll want to have an accurate number of good addresses before you start tracking the performance metrics of your e-mail effort. Including a bunch of dead ends in your database will only undermine the usefulness of the statistics you ultimately get.

Part V
The Part of Tens

The 5th Wave   By Rich Tennant

"Jim and I do a lot of business together on Facebook. By the way, Jim, did you get the sales spreadsheet and little blue pony I sent you?"

In this part . . .

This book covers a whole lot of information. In the interests of wrapping it all up in a neat and tidy way, this last part quickly, briefly, and painlessly describes key online marketing campaign issues in handy top-ten lists.

Chapter 18 describes some pesky marketing mistakes that are easy to make, but thankfully, also easy to avoid. Chapter 19 covers the basics that go into coming up with a solid and effective online advertising plan. Chapter 20 concludes with a discussion of things to keep in mind if you decide to enlist the assistance of an online marketing partner.

Chapter 18

Ten Local Online Marketing Mistakes (And How to Avoid Them)

. . . .

*T*his foray into the world of online advertising is kind of a grand adventure. Although there is clearly a beaten path that you need to follow to maximize your chances for success, at times, you'll see your efforts come up short and wonder: What the heck am I doing wrong?

In a lot of cases, the fault isn't so much with the execution, but with the thinking or preconceptions. Because these things are part and parcel of your inner self, they can be really hard to recognize as the actual culprits when your efforts aren't having the results you want.

In our experience, many people make certain mental errors when launching themselves into the online arena — and in this chapter, we list the ten most common.

Assuming Your Customers Behave Like You

Maybe you're a 25-year-old running online marketing for a retirement community. Just because you go to the blogosphere before you buy any products or services doesn't mean that your target audience does. Conversely, you might be a 70-year-old dentist, and you think the Internet is just a fad. You need to think the way customers think and figure how they find businesses. No matter what your mom told you, in this case, don't be yourself.

Not Knowing Your Limits

You can create your own Web site, do search engine optimization (SEO), and run your own pay-per-click (PPC) campaigns. That's one of the reasons books like this exist. However, to do these things right, you need to spend an appropriate amount of time on them. That means that the five minutes you spend monthly on your PPC campaign may not be enough, and consequently, you're wasting money that could just as well go to pay someone to take care of your local online advertising for you. Think hard about whether you'll make an ongoing commitment to optimizing your advertising campaigns. If not, maybe the best thing to do is go with the pros.

Assuming Web Site Aesthetics Equals Web Site Success

You may think all the frames, flash, and images you've put on your Web site look great. Unfortunately, that great stuff is all but invisible to the search engines. Like Joe Friday, search engines want only the facts. The subjective stuff on your site can be a lot of fun to create, but if content on your Web site can't even be read by the search engines, you aren't even in the game. Think like a search engine does. Make sure you have

- A search engine–friendly URL
- A site map (or site index)
- Contact information on *every* page
- Keyword-rich copy
- Footers
- Reciprocal links

In other words, position yourself to be found before you worry about being impressive. And when in doubt, test and learn.

Creating a Web Site That No One Visits

If you build it, they will come, right? Wrong. Just because you have a Web site doesn't mean anyone will go there. To get people to your site, you need to drive traffic — whether that means using SEO, PPC, e-mails, banners, or some of the other tools we talk about in this book. The moral of the story: Give people a road; then they will come.

Making It Difficult for Potential Customers to Contact You

You'd be surprised how many local business Web sites we see that don't even show the phone number. Or the contact information is buried deep down the Contact Us page. Your phone number (or however you want your potential customers to contact you) needs to be large and in charge on your Web site. Throw an easy-to-fill-out form on your page, too. That way potential customers who don't want to call still have a way to contact you.

Caring Too Much about How Many People Visit Your Site

This may at first seem contrary to the mistake of creating a Web site that no one visits, but it isn't. True, you need people to go to your site to get sales, but not all site visitors are equal. You can waste a lot of money paying vendors or directories for meaningless clicks that don't convert into new customers. This is especially important to remember when you use something like PPC. Sometimes you're better off to pay a premium for expensive keyword search terms instead of driving a lot traffic that represents only traffic — and no sales.

Having Google Tunnel Vision

Yes, Google is the most important search engine by a long shot. We know this, you know this, and so do all your competitors. Although the most traffic is on Google, it isn't unusual for other search engines and directories to have more cost-efficient ways to drive traffic. When possible, the best strategy is to test a variety of sites (including Google) and see which one ultimately works best for your business.

Not Knowing whether Your Marketing Is Really Working

One of the greatest things about online advertising is that it's so measurable. The rub, of course, is that measuring takes work. But the payoff will be well worth it because you can focus your ad dollars on those channels and methods that work while cutting the fat out of your budget.

Arguably, the best five things for you to measure are

- ✔ Traffic numbers (the number of visitors you get)
- ✔ Conversion rates
- ✔ Your cost per lead
- ✔ Your cost per acquisition
- ✔ Your return on investment

You can keep track of other things as well, such as how long visitors from particular channels stay on your site, but the five items here tell you what you most need to know.

Not Getting Sales from Calls

Your phone rings off the hook, but you still aren't getting any new customers. What could be wrong? For starters, answer your phone! According to a survey by FastCall411 of 5,000 local businesses, approximately two-thirds of incoming calls to local businesses go unanswered. What's more, a study by market research firm Synovate found that four out of five Americans regard immediate availability by phone as an important — or the most important — factor when selecting a local service provider. In the end, not picking up your phone is akin to taking that cash that you paid for your advertising and throwing it into a bonfire. Additionally, make sure that you or your staff handles those calls with the utmost care. After all, those people on the other end of the line have your future in their hands.

Not Doing Any Loyalty/Retention Marketing

Getting new customers is far more expensive than keeping existing ones. Make sure you're doing everything you can to take care of the ones you have. Keep in touch via an e-mail newsletter or offer them occasional special deals. Today's online tools make that sort of thing easy to do. So do it!

Chapter 19

Ten Steps to an Effective Local Online Advertising Plan

● ●

*L*ocal online advertising can take many different forms. But one thing it absolutely can't be is a headless horseman. Similarly, the old idea of throwing a bunch of stuff up against the wall to see what sticks will wind up giving you nothing but a really dirty wall. No, your online advertising has to have a purpose, a mission . . . in other words, a plan.

This chapter takes you through the steps to make sure that what you're doing has all those things — the better to give you something to measure your success against and to help you plan the next steps your online advertising campaign should take.

Committing to the Planning Process

The old saying, "If you fail to plan, you plan to fail," is kind of tacky and trite, but it's also tried and true. You can't afford to forget it when you prepare to design and launch your local online advertising campaign because

- ✔ Your online efforts are too important to leave to ad-libbing. After all, the continued health and growth of your business are at stake here.

- ✔ A successful online campaign will usually have a lot of moving parts — parts that act separately and in concert to make the whole thing work to your benefit. Try to fix one particular element on the fly, and another element is likely to go haywire. Keep a close eye on the big picture and refrain from adjusting things as though they were wholly independent pieces. They're not.

- ✔ You're dealing with the Internet world where things happen really, really fast. And here again, reacting reflexively to every change in wind direction can make you nuts, and leave your once-promising ad program in shambles.

So, whether you're going to DIY the operation or entrust it to an outside online advertising company or consultant, think ahead. What can you realistically expect your efforts to produce? How many new customers? How much in new sales? Are you prepared to respond quickly — and on all fronts — if a big nasty competitor suddenly comes on the scene? Do you have enough staff to answer the phones on the first or second ring and respond to e-mails within 15 minutes, or are you better off using a virtual phone service from the start?

All this has to be part of the plan. Fortunately, you have this book — especially Chapters 2 and 3 — to help you get your plan thought out, filled in, and ready for prime time.

Having Clear Goals in Mind

Before you build a Web site, start worrying about keywords, or figuring out what your budget should be for a pay-per-click (PPC) campaign, stop. Take a deep breath and ask: What are your actual, real-world, short-term and long-term business goals?

- ✔ To drive new customers to your door?
- ✔ To expand into new geographical markets?
- ✔ To announce a new product or service?
- ✔ To support existing customers more effectively?
- ✔ To become your area's preferred provider of whatever it is you provide?
- ✔ To do all or some of these? Or something else?

You have to figure that out — and make it the foundation of your online plan — before you do anything else.

The point is to make sure that your business needs are driving your advertising, not the other way around. Because as weird as it may sound, that tail-wagging-the-dog thing happens to unsuspecting businesses a lot more often than you'd think.

Knowing Your Audience

You can't implement an effective online advertising plan unless you know who you're targeting. Identify your target audience by age, gender, average income, and education level. Try to determine what kind of things they buy, what they read, where they spend their time online, and what content intrigues them. Granted, you have to trudge around the Web a lot to see who's selling what to whom and how, but the effort's more than worth it.

When you've fixed on the unique characteristics of your target audience, let those characteristics be your guide. Put yourself in your audience's shoes and — at every stage of your planning — stay there. Your targets won't lead you astray. They'll tell you what motivates them, what interests them, what they like to buy, and how they like to be sold to — everything, in short, that you need to know to start constructing a solid advertising plan.

Understanding How Users Behave Online

Knowing how people browse the Internet, what they use it for, and what kind of tools they use in the process is important for the development of any workable online advertising plan. For example:

- ✔ People tend to use organic search engine listings when they're researching a particular kind of purchase and then look to sponsored listings when they're ready to buy.

- ✔ People turn to online classifieds for the same reasons and in the same way as the classifieds in the newspaper.

- ✔ People who frequent social networks expect and reward extremely soft and highly personal selling techniques and will punish marketers who come on too strong.

When you've grasped dynamics like these — and this book provides plenty more of them — you can choose your advertising tactics wisely and execute those tactics in an effective and profitable way.

Considering Your Investment of Time and Money

Planning your online advertising campaign takes some time, and putting it into action requires both time and money. How much of each of those you're willing to spend is something you need to determine upfront.

Say you want to have a first-class Web site. You can design and build it, which doesn't cost much money but eats up a lot of time. On the other hand, you can outsource the site's creation, hosting, and monitoring to a professional online company or consultant. Go that route, and your time investment shrinks to almost nothing, but the expense can be steep. At the other extreme is online classifieds. They're often free to place and don't require much in the way of time or effort to create. But they aren't likely to be nearly as effective as a PPC campaign, which can claim a significant chunk of both time and money.

So what to do? Follow these steps:

1. **Be completely honest and determine just how much time and expense you want to — and actually can — dedicate to your online campaign.**

   A lot of local business owners make the mistake of overestimating on both counts. Then reality comes calling, and they're too busy to dedicate as much time to the effort as they thought they could, and/or their budget is tighter than they'd anticipated. This can be a recipe for disaster down the road.

2. **Be realistic. Really realistic.**

   a. *Come up with a budget of both time and money that makes sense today and will still make sense tomorrow, next month, or even next year.*

   b. *Operate on the basis of what's actually possible, not on what could be possible if you never slept and had all the money in the world.*

Building a Web Site Designed for Conversion

Your Web site is the linchpin of your online advertising campaign. Your site is what captures the online traffic your advertising generates. If the site is designed properly — which is to say, with the customer in mind — it's also where traffic is converted into qualified leads.

So your site better be good. Make sure your site quickly tells people who you are, what you do, what you sell, and what qualifies you to be their vendor of choice. And for heaven's sake, provide ways for them to convert themselves — to call, click, accept an offer, and/or visit your physical location.

Prominently display your contact information (telephone number, e-mail, and physical addresses) so people know how to reach you. Use techniques that are as time-tested as coupons and as high-tech as virtual phone services and proactive chat.

In short, make your site a place that people want to come to and then want to stay when they're there.

Taking Advantage of Local Search

The latest, hottest trend in online marketing is *local search* — searching for local businesses and destinations. If you do most of your business locally, get educated pronto about this new and potentially very lucrative tool.

Here are several options for capitalizing on local search:

✔ The big three search engines (www.google.com, www.yahoo.com, and www.bing.com) offer free local search listings that integrate search results with local maps.

✔ Several new search engines focus exclusively on local search (such as www.local.com, www.truelocal.com, and www.yelp.com), and their appeal to both users and advertisers is growing fast.

✔ Internet Yellow Pages, local directories, and community sites are expanding their local search capabilities to appeal to users looking for area-specific businesses.

Best of all from your standpoint, local search isn't only hot, it's eminently affordable. This makes it one of those things you literally can't afford not to know about and put to instant use for your business.

Choosing Your Tactics Wisely

The Internet, bless its little digital heart, offers an enormous array of tactics to help you target your audience and build your business. From search engine optimization, to PPC, to listings with directories and lead aggregators, to e-mail marketing, to banner advertising, to social media, and more, you have a virtual sea of options to pick from. So which ones work best for you?

One excellent way to find out is by putting yourself in your customers' shoes. Try to think like they think. Hang out on the sites where they hang out. Get to know their habits. See if you can determine what attracts them, what impresses them, and what moves them. (And no, this isn't stalking, it's research.)

Are they searching Google? Good. That means they're using keywords. Which keywords do you think they're using to find businesses like yours? Try entering those words, and see where they lead you.

Spend some time on at least one social network (such as Twitter or Facebook) and don't be surprised if you find throngs of great prospects gathered there.

You're only crippling yourself if you let quick, arbitrary decisions or personal preconceptions steer you toward or away from a given online tactic. They're all fair game if they're where your customers are. Your choice of tactics is ultimately dictated by how and where your target audience spends its time on the Web.

Tracking and Measuring Results

Tracking and measuring are fundamental to online advertising. Test what you think might work, find out what actually works, test it again and again, and your success is all but guaranteed.

If your PPC advertising brings strong results, go ahead and increase your spending. On the other hand, if the advertising is underperforming, tune up your ads and test again. Measure the effectiveness of one offer against another. Try two different pieces of ad copy and see which one yields better results. And so on. If you're going to play the game — and win it — you have to track and measure.

Everything comes back to your old friend, the conversion rate. Maybe most of the offers you try underperform, whereas one other offer absolutely shoots the lights out when it comes to bringing consumers to your Web site and inducing them to fill out a form, call your business, or opt-in to your e-newsletter. If so, bingo. That's your winner.

Optimizing Your Ads and Web Site

Optimization is the process of making something better. You can make your Web site or your online advertising campaign better in any number of simple, quick, and affordable ways. Test the various elements of your site or your campaign to find out which work and which need some improvement. Your optimization might be as simple as moving the contact information from the right side of a Web page to the left side so it's easier to see; it might mean trying out a big, red Download button to make it more obvious what you want visitors to do. Or you can try out different phrasings in your e-mail blasts, or make one part of your banner ad bigger and another part smaller.

Sure, you might make yourself a little nuts — but you'll make some big, profitable improvements, too. And you'll celebrate and then, you'll test the improvements. Just don't forget that while you're optimizing and optimizing again, what you're really optimizing is your return on investment (ROI).

Chapter 20

Ten Considerations When Choosing a Local Online Advertising Partner

· ·

*W*hile enlightening you on the intricacies of local online advertising, this book might have convinced you that, depending on the time and money you're willing to invest, you may be better off hiring a partner to help you with local online advertising. Here are ten key questions you need to ask before going with any particular vendor or consultant.

How Measurable Will Your Advertising Efforts Be?

One of the beauties of online advertising is that things are so eminently measurable. Oddly, though, many local online advertising consultants and vendors don't really give their clients a way of tracking their sites' performance. This is especially true with many search engine optimization (SEO) vendors who sell themselves primarily on their ability to place a keyword. Although placement generally leads to more clicks and traffic, if you get clicks and traffic from keywords that don't perform well for you in a business sense (for example, they don't result in actual conversions), those keywords aren't doing you any favors, good placement or not, and should be jettisoned. The best local online advertising partners offer excellent reporting interfaces that give you a realistic view of how your ad dollars are actually performing, particularly with respect to

✔ Keyword performance

✔ Ad performance

✔ Click-throughs

  ✔ Conversions

  ✔ Cost-per-click (CPC), where applicable

  ✔ Return on investment (ROI)

If the provider you're considering doesn't offer this kind of detailed reporting, keep looking.

Do You Care about the Metrics the Vendor Promises to Provide?

Even the most expert and overall splendiferous online ad partner can only bring customers to you. Whether you can close those customers, retain them, upsell them, and so on is ultimately up to you. That doesn't mean you should go with a partner who talks about clicks, CPCs, and traffic alone. Important as those metrics are, they don't necessarily equate to dollars in your pocket. Better to find an ad partner who can give you assurances (or at least estimates based on real-world experience) regarding the volume of phone calls you get, the cost per lead (CPL) they can deliver, the number of appointments that are set up, and so on. Those are the metrics that impact your revenue, and someone who refuses to acknowledge that fact is likely to be an unworthy partner.

How Big Is Your Commitment to the Vendor?

Rome wasn't built in a day (it actually took a whole weekend), and no, you won't see big results from your online advertising efforts as soon as they hit the Internet. However, that doesn't mean you should get tied into a vendor contract that extends for, say, 12 or 18 months. So how long is just long enough? Well, a good rule is that your pay-per-click (PPC) results should be credible after three to six months. SEO results take a while longer, so figure on six to nine months for those. If a prospective ad partner insists that you sign a contract for much longer than those periods (and isn't offering you some too-good-to-refuse incentive to do so), it's Red Flag City — and you might want to look elsewhere.

What Industry Expertise Does the Vendor Have?

Unsurprisingly, vendors who have worked with other businesses in your industry are more likely to have the experience and expertise to get you strong results right away than vendors who are new to your field. These veterans will know what keywords and ad copy strategies have the ability to perform, and that will translate into loads of time saved. Sure, good local online advertising companies can get results for any kind of local business through persistent research and optimization. But do you really want them to learn your business on your dime? Didn't think so. In short, don't be afraid to ask how many other clients a prospective partner has (or had) in your industry. And don't hesitate to ask for references, which you then need to follow up on.

Is the Partner Interested in Your Web Site?

This is critical because one of the most acidic of acid tests is whether a given online advertising vendor demonstrates that they actually care about your Web site. If you're looking for someone to help you increase traffic for your current site, a reputable vendor will take a good deal of time examining and assessing the site as is, before taking you on as a customer. They need to be able to quantify how well your site's performing at present, if for no other reason than to have a benchmark against which you can measure the effects of the improvements they make going forward. At minimum, they need to give you an educated appraisal of your site's

- ✔ Layout and design
- ✔ Keyword content
- ✔ Landing pages
- ✔ Forms and phone-number presentation
- ✔ Calls to action
- ✔ Offers and promotions

Of course, if you don't currently have a site and are looking for someone to help you build one, you won't yet have anything to assess. But whether you're doing renovation or new construction, a prospective partner should commit to conducting some sort of review process on a regular basis. This gives you a periodic update as to how well your site is performing and in what respects it needs to be kicked up a notch or two. If, on the other hand, a would-be partner shrugs off the notion of checking in on your Web site, it's probably safe to assume that that company isn't really too concerned about your real, bottom-line performance. And the proper response in that case is no thanks.

How Wide Is the Vendor's Distribution?

Although hordes of companies can and will place you on Google, Yahoo!, Bing, and maybe one or two other major sites . . . so what? A reasonably bright sixth grader can do that (if that kid has this book, of course). The best local online ad vendors are those who have wide distribution networks, meaning they also take advantage of the significant incremental traffic that can be generated from lesser-known search engines — particularly local ones — and from online directories and other potential traffic sources. These other channels may not have quite the pizzazz of the big three, but they're often not nearly as expensive either and taken together, a combination of big and not-so-big resources can really help you cover the marketing map. Ideally, you're looking for a partner that can get you distribution on

- Google, Yahoo!, and Bing
- Ask.com
- Vertical-specific search sites
- Directories, such as Citysearch or Yelp
- IYP (Internet Yellow Pages)

Who Handles Your Account?

Operating on the model of many traditional media companies, many local online ad companies have a system in which accounts are essentially run and managed by your salesperson. Although this may work with some traditional print media when managing an account meant writing down how big you wanted your ad to be, it's a rare salesperson indeed who can be trusted to do say, keyword optimization for your PPC campaign. The better local online advertising partners will offer you a dedicated account manager (or two) to work with you in both developing your ad program and optimizing it on a regular basis.

Are There Any Hidden Fees?

What?! Hidden fees? Always check the small print because therein can lurk some interesting conditions. A common type of small print stipulates that if you decide to change the focus of your business from, say, selling tankless water heaters to handling only backflow jobs, you're obligated to pay a change fee for the necessary site adjustments that will have to be made. You may not object to that, but even if you're the go-along-to-get-along type, at least get clarification of how big a change counts as big enough to trigger the fee. In any case, make sure you read the small print and understand it — and you'll at least know what you're getting into.

Are There Keyword Limitations?

Although keyword limits may make sense for SEO (because it takes additional work to optimize your site for each set of keywords), putting limits on PPC keywords makes no sense at all. Time to be blunt: Any vendor or prospective partner who's trying to sell you a specific number of keywords for PPC is trying to prey on your supposed lack of local online advertising savvy. But lucky you, you have this book. And you can, politely but firmly, tell him to take a hike.

What Credentials Does the Partner Have?

Most of the major search engines offer certifications for PPC advertising companies who pass certain exams or otherwise prove their qualifications. Google, for instance, has several levels of certification, the highest being a Google AdWords Authorized Reseller. Although these credentials certainly aren't a guarantee that a certified vendor is honest, going to provide you with a 1,000-percent ROI, and can see through buildings, they do at least impart a certain level of credibility to a vendor who's vying for your business. And they're a whole heck of lot better than no credentials.

Index

Get $100 free
advertising credit
when you sign up with Yodle.

Yodle is a full-service local online advertising company that provides local service oriented businesses with a simple way to get more customers using online advertising.

More than just setting up your advertising campaigns across major sites like Google , Yahoo!, Bing, and its network of over 75 other popular properties, Yodle uses its patent-pending technology to constantly refine your campaigns so that they drive the maximum number of qualified phone calls directly to your business.

Yodle also provides a user-friendly yet powerful reporting interface that tracks every dollar spent, click made, and call placed so that you can make sure that your advertising dollars are driving a positive return for your business.